KU-524-286

A BOOK OF
AIR JOURNEYS

By the same author:

Naval
Sub-Lieutenant: A Personal Record of the War at Sea
Nelson's Captains
Pursuit: The Chase and Sinking of the *Bismarck*
Menace: The Life and Death of the *Tirpitz*

Crime and the Law
10 Rillington Place
The Trial of Stephen Ward
A Presumption of Innocence
The Portland Spy Case
Wicked Beyond Belief

Travel and Diaries
One Man's Meat
Very Lovely People

Play
Murder Story

Anthologies
A Book of Railway Journeys
A Book of Sea Journeys

A BOOK OF
AIR
JOURNEYS

Compiled by
LUDOVIC KENNEDY

COLLINS
St James's Place, London
1982

William Collins Sons & Co Ltd
London · Glasgow · Sydney · Auckland
Toronto · Johannesburg

HERTFORDSHIRE
LIBRARY SERVICE

387·742

1367006 1/83

Bishops Stortford Library
The Causeway, Bishops Stortford
Herts. CM23 2EJ
Telephone: 54946

British Library Cataloguing in Publication Data

A Book of air journeys.

1. Air travel
I. Kennedy, Ludovic
387.7'42   HE9786

ISBN 0—00—216377—2

First published 1982
© in the compilation and introduction Ludovic Kennedy 1982
Photo set in Old Style

Made and printed in Great Britain by
William Collins Sons & Co Ltd, Glasgow

For Rachel

ACKNOWLEDGEMENTS

Air Travel by Kenneth Hudson, by permission of the author and *Punch* Magazine; *Diamonds in the Sky* by Kenneth Hudson and Julian Pettifer, reprinted by permission of The Bodley Head; *Prisoners of Peace* by Rudolph Hess, by permission of Mr. T. Tindale-Robertson (Britons Publishing Co.); *Carrying The Fire* by Michael Collins, by permission of W. H. Allen & Co. Ltd; *Australia and Back* by Alan Cobham, by permission of A. C. Black Ltd; *The Right Stuff* by Tom Wolfe, reprinted by permission of A. D. Peters & Co. Ltd; *Catch 22* by Joseph Heller, by permission of Jonathan Cape Ltd; *The Second World War* by Winston S. Churchill, by permission of Messrs. Cassell Ltd; *747 London-Chicago* from *Forays* by Robert Conquest, by permission of Chatto & Windus Ltd; *Amy Johnson* by Constance Babington-Smith, reprinted by permission of A. D. Peters & Co. Ltd; *Time and Chance* by Peter Townsend, by permission of Collins Publishers; *Portrait of a Soldier* by Bernard Fergusson © Bernard Fergusson 1961, by permission of Curtis Brown Ltd; *Sagittarius Rising* by Cecil Lewis, by permission of Peter Davies Ltd; *Night Flight Over Ocean* by John Updike, reprinted by permission of André Deutsch Ltd; from *Tossing and Turning* 1977; *Labels* by Evelyn Waugh, reprinted by permission of A. D. Peters & Co. Ltd; *To Beachey, 1912* by Carl Sandburg, from *Chicago Poems*, by permission of Harcourt Brace Jovanovich Inc; *The Hot Gates* by William Golding, reprinted by permission of Faber & Faber Ltd; *Musée des Beaux Arts* by W. H. Auden, from *Collected Poems*, reprinted by permission of Faber & Faber Ltd; *Losses* by Randall Jarrell from *The Complete Poems*, reprinted by permission of Faber & Faber Ltd; *Miracle at Kittyhawk* by Fred C. Kelly, by permission of Farrar Straus & Giroux; *Men in the Clouds* by Leslie Gardiner, by permission of the author; *Flight to Arras* by Antoine de Saint-Exupéry, translated by Lewis Galantiere, reprinted by permission of William Heinemann Ltd; *The Life of a Genius* by Gerard Fairlie and Elizabeth Cayley, reprinted by permission of Hodder & Stoughton; *Fate is the Hunter* by Ernest Gann, by permission of Hodder & Stoughton; *The Eye of the Wind* by Peter Scott, by permission of Hodder & Stoughton; *The Flying Circus* by Ernest Gann, reprinted by permission of John Farquharson Ltd; *With the Guards to Mexico* by Peter Fleming, reprinted by permission of John Johnson; *The Death of a President* by William Manchester, reprinted by permission of A. D. Peters & Co. Ltd; *The Spirit of St Louis* by Charles Lindbergh, reprinted by permission of John Murray (Publishers) Ltd; *Travellers Prelude* by Freya Stark, reprinted by permission of John Murray (Publishers) Ltd; *Back from Australia* by John Betjeman from *Collected Poems*, reprinted by permission of John Murray (Publishers) Ltd; *Graf Zeppelin* by J. Gordon Vaeth, reprinted by permission of Frederick Muller Ltd; *Whatever Next* by Clive James from an article in *The Observer* of 10th January 1982, by permission of *The Observer*; *Love at a Great Height* by Kenneth Tynan from an article in *Punch*, and reprinted by permission of *Punch*; *The Astronaut* by James Kirkup, by permission of the author, published in *The Prodigal Sun* by Oxford University Press; *In a Sailplane* by James Kirkup, by permission of the author, published in *The Prodigal Sun* by Oxford University Press; *I Fell 18,000 Feet Without a Parachute* by Nicholas Alkemade, adapted from an article by permission of Reader's Digest, © 1958 Reader's Digest; *Changing Places* by David Lodge, reprinted by permission of Martin Secker & Warburg Ltd; *The First to Fly* by Sherwood Harris reprinted by permission of Raines & Raines, New York; *On a Trip with Prince Philip* by Basil Boothroyd from an article in *The Times* of June 10th 1981 and reprinted by permission of Times Newspapers Ltd; *Mary, The Flying Duchess* by permission of the Marquess of Tavistock and the Trustees of the Bedford Estates.

We regret that we have been unable to trace the copyright holders for the following pieces: *The Pioneer* by Neil East, from *A Talent of Silver*; *Flight 539* by John M. Brinnin, from *Poetry Chicago*; *Icarus* by Valentin Iremonger, published by The Dolman Press 1972; *Zeppelin* by Charles Rosendahl and Ernest Lehmann, published by Longmans Green 1937; *50 Great Disasters* by Miles Henslow, published by Odhams 1937.

CONTENTS

Introduction   *xiii*

PART ONE: Balloons and Airships

THE FIRST FLIGHTS

1783, PARIS: ROZIER AND D'ARLANDES	J. M. BACON	3
1783, PARIS: CHARLES AND ROBERT	LESLIE GARDINER	6
1784, LONDON: VINCENT LUNARDI (1)	LESLIE GARDINER	9
1784, SCOTLAND: VINCENT LUNARDI (2)	JAMES LAPSLEY	16
1784: TO SIR THOMAS MANN	HORACE WALPOLE	19
1785, CROSSING THE CHANNEL: BLANCHARD AND JEFFRIES	JOHN JEFFRIES	19
1804: SUPERSTITIOUSNESS OF NAPOLEON	J. M. BACON	25

SOME NINETEENTH CENTURY FLIGHTS

1853: VOYAGE OF *THE GIANT*	J. M. BACON	27
1862: COXWELL AND GLAISHER REACH 36,000 FEET	J. M. BACON	30

1862: SOUNDS FROM LONDON AND PARIS	J. M. BACON	37
1889: FLIGHT OF SPENCER IN INDIA	J. M. BACON	39
1897: THE ANDRÉE EXPEDITION	NILS STRINDBERG	43
A VOYAGE IN THE *GRAF ZEPPELIN*	J. GORDON VAETH	48

TWO AIRSHIP DISASTERS

1930: THE R.101	MILES HENSLOW	62
1937: THE *HINDENBURG*	CHARLES ROSENDAHL	71

PART TWO: Pioneers

THE FATHER OF THE AEROPLANE	GERARD FAIRLIE AND ELIZABETH CAYLEY	81
THE WRIGHT BROTHERS AT KITTY HAWK	FRED C. KELLY	85
FIRST ACROSS THE CHANNEL	LOUIS BLÉRIOT AND SHERWOOD HARRIS	89
TO BEACHEY, 1912	CARL SANDBURG	93
THE CHICAGO MAIL	CHARLES A. LINDBERGH	94
THE FLYING DUCHESS	MARY BEDFORD	101
THE SPIRIT OF ST. LOUIS	CHARLES A. LINDBERGH	119
THE TUTELAGE OF ERNEST K. GANN	ERNEST K. GANN	144
THE TRAIL-BLAZERS		
1. COBHAM AND THE DEATH OF ELLIOTT	ALAN COBHAM	150
THE PIONEER	NEIL EAST	162

2. AMY JOHNSON MAKES AN   AMY JOHNSON AND CONSTANCE   163
    UNEXPECTED LANDING   BABINGTON-SMITH
SHORT-SNORTERS   ERNEST K. GANN   166
ON THE BEAK OF AN   ERNEST K. GANN   167
    ANCIENT PELICAN

PART THREE: Passengers

A TRIP TO PARIS (1)   FREYA STARK   187
A TRIP TO PARIS (2)   EVELYN WAUGH   188
JOYRIDING
  1. IN TEXAS   PAUL CRUME   194
  2. IN GENERAL   KENNETH HUDSON   195
BACK FROM AUSTRALIA   JOHN BETJEMAN   196
JOYRIDING
  3. TEA OVER LONDON   IMPERIAL AIRWAYS, 1933   198
PASSENGERS IN THE U.K.   KENNETH HUDSON   198
PASSENGERS IN THE U.S. (1)   ERNEST K. GANN   199
PASSENGERS IN THE U.S. (2)   KENNETH HUDSON AND   201
                                     JULIAN PETTIFER

AT 30,000 FEET   BERNARD GILHOOLY   203
WAITING ON AIRFIELDS   PETER FLEMING   205
LOVE AT A GREAT HEIGHT   KENNETH TYNAN   207
NIGHT FLIGHT, OVER OCEAN   JOHN UPDIKE   211
PRESIDENT KENNEDY   WILLIAM MANCHESTER   212
    RETURNS TO WASHINGTON
THE MAN FROM LIBERIA   LUDOVIC KENNEDY   221
PROFESSOR SWALLOW AND   DAVID LODGE   226
    PROFESSOR ZAPP
FLIGHT 539   JOHN MALCOLM BRINNIN   235
A TRIP WITH PRINCE PHILIP   BASIL BOOTHROYD   237
COAST TO COAST   WILLIAM GOLDING   241
747 (LONDON—CHICAGO)   ROBERT CONQUEST   244
WHATEVER NEXT?   CLIVE JAMES   247

PART FOUR: A Miscellany of Flights

ICARUS

FROM *THE METAMORPHOSES*   OVID (trans. SAMUEL   255
                            CROXALL)
MUSÉE DES BEAUX ARTS   W. H. AUDEN   258

PARACHUTING

THE FIRST OF THE MANY   J. M. BACON   259
PARACHUTE   LENRIE PETERS   263

GLIDING

STRAIGHT AND LEVEL   PETER SCOTT   264
IN A SAILPLANE   JAMES KIRKUP   267

SPACE

1. THE VOYAGE OF   TOM WOLFE   270
   'FRIENDSHIP 7'
THE ASTRONAUT   JAMES KIRKUP   286
2. ORBITING THE MOON   MICHAEL COLLINS   287

PART FIVE: War

ON THE WESTERN FRONT
   1. PATROLS WITHOUT   CECIL A. LEWIS   301
      ACTION
   2. ACTION   CECIL A. LEWIS   304
AN IRISH AIRMAN FORESEES W. B. YEATS   312
   HIS DEATH

3. THE RED BARON   MANFRED VON RICHTHOFEN   312
FLIGHT TO ARRAS   ANTOINE DE ST. EXUPÉRY   316
DEATH IN THE MORNING (1)   RICHARD HILLARY   320
LOSSES   RANDALL JARRELL   324
DEATH IN THE MORNING (2)   PETER TOWNSEND   325
HESS FLIES IN   RUDOLF HESS   329
WAVELL FLIES OUT   BERNARD FERGUSSON   334
ACROSS THE ATLANTIC   WINSTON S. CHURCHILL   336
FROM CATCH 22   JOSEPH HELLER   341
ALKEMADE TOUCHES DOWN   NICHOLAS ALKEMADE   344

ILLUSTRATIONS

JACKET: The voyage that never was. On 29 June 1785 Vincent Lunardi invited the beautiful actress Mrs Sage and his friend and benefactor George Biggins to make an ascent with him. The picture was painted in anticipation of the event. Unfortunately the balloon proved unable to lift all three, so Lunardi jumped out and sent Biggins and Mrs Sage up on their own (see page 12). They landed without mishap at Harrow. *By Francesco Bartolozzi after John Francis Rigaud.*

SOURCES AND ACKNOWLEDGEMENTS

5 and 7: Royal Aeronautical Society. 12: Science Museum, London. 21: Royal Aeronautical Society. 28: The Illustrated London News Picture Library. 33: The Fotomas Index. 36: The Illustrated London News Picture Library. 40: Caisse Nationale des Monuments Historiques et des Cites, Paris. 44: Arbor House Publishing Co. 45: Andrée Museat, Sweden. 47a: Gamma. 47b and 51: The Illustrated London News Picture Library. 54: Luftschiffbau Zepplin. 66: Musée de l'Air, Paris. 75: The Illustrated London News Picture Library. 83: Anglia Television. 87, 92 and 97: Royal Aeronautical Society. 102: Keystone Press Agency. 120: BBC Hulton Picture Library. 143: Brown Brothers. 159a, b, and 160: BBC Hulton Picture Library. 164: The Illustrated London News Picture Library. 191: The Fotomas Index. 193: KLM. 197: The Illustrated London News Picture Library. 204: Lufthansa. 206: British Airways. 208, 209 and 218: Keystone Press Agency. 238: Camera Press. 246: Keystone Press Agency. 257: Tate Gallery. 261 and 262: Royal Aeronautical Society. 268: Daily Telegraph Colour Library. 270 and 295: NASA. 309: Imperial War Museum. 311: Cecil A Lewis. 313: Camera Press. 315: BBC Hulton Picture Library. 319: The Fotomas Index. 321: National Portrait Gallery. 323: Imperial War Museum. 327: Keystone Press Agency. 337: Imperial War Museum.

INTRODUCTION

Air Journeys is the third (and last) of this trilogy of Journey books, *Railway Journeys* and *Sea Journeys* having preceded it. I compiled *Railway Journeys* because I have loved trains and train travel as long as I can remember; while a lifelong association with the Navy made *Sea Journeys* a natural successor.

About air journeys I was hesitant, never having felt much at home when aloft. My first trip, made at the age of ten in the two-seater of someone's Flying Circus, made me feel very sick. I felt much the same when, after I had joined the Eton College Air Corps because there was no Naval Corps (the Army Corps I felt to be altogether beyond the pale), my instructor, Flight-Lieutenant Grandy (later Marshal of the Royal Air Force, Sir John Grandy) took me looping the loop. And in 1938 I felt extremely sick on my third flight when with four other Etonians we chartered a plane (at a cost of only £3 each) to fly us from Maidenhead to Le Touquet and back on the last whole holiday of my last summer half—a feat we accomplished between noon and 6.00 p.m. with some ten seconds to spare.

On early postwar flights I felt frightened as well as sick, on later ones bored. Furthermore, a journey on a Jumbo jet today, with the heads of one's fellow passengers stretching into the distance like turnips in a field of sheep, seems to me the apogee of discomfort; and if (as I have said elsewhere) you find yourself next to a manic child or compulsive chatterbox, there is nothing you can to do escape.

A particularly gruesome experience of this sort happened to me recently on a night flight from New York to London. I found myself at the (window) end of a row of three seats which had a space in front leading to an emergency exit. The occupants of the other two seats were a pair of identical twins; around fifty, I would say, Dutch-sounding, stocky, smallish, offensively dapper. Before

xiii

take-off they strutted up and down like a pair of poofy turkey-cocks, ignoring all requests from the stewardess to hang up their plastic suit-covers at the other end of the plane. They made a bizarre pair.

In due course we took off. For greater comfort I removed my tie and shoes, adjusted the lighting and began to read. Drinks were ordered and received. But as time went by I became increasingly aware of the elbow of the twin next to me spilling over the seat-rest and digging into my ribs. I stuck it for about half an hour, then said politely, "I wonder if you'd be so kind as to watch your elbow." The twin glared at me, long and hard, incredulous at such a challenge. His brother leaned forward and glared too. But neither spoke and the offending elbow was withdrawn.

I thought no more of the matter, and returned to my book. Half an hour passed and the girls began coming round with the dinner-trays. Then the nearest twin turned to me and said, with all the shock of an exploding bomb, "Your feet are smelling. Please to put your shoes on."

I was too stunned to know how to react. I had been on the go all day in New York, had got very wet in a rainstorm and stepped in two puddles, so perhaps he was right. And presumably a stranger in a plane wouldn't say something so very personal unless it happened to be true. How *awful*! "Poof, poof," said my neighbour, screwing up his nose, "this smell is taking away my appetite for dinner".

There was nothing for it but to comply. Humbly I leaned forwards and put on my shoes. I was not thanked. I ate my dinner quietly and slowly, the twins fast and noisily. There was no elbow trouble. Coffee came and our trays were taken away. I rose and made my way to the loo.

Now it so happens that since a recent nasal operation I have developed a particularly keen sense of smell; and, in order to assess the condition of my feet, I took off both shoes and socks and raised them (somewhat gingerly, I admit) to my nose. They were (to my surprise) pristine, not a whiff emerging of any kind.

Now what would you have done on return to your seat? I know what I *wanted* to do. I wanted to tell my twin what a malicious little swine he was and biff him in the belly. There would have been a fracas in which the other twin would undoubtedly have joined.

Eventually we would have been separated, but what then? The plane was full, so we should still have been obliged to spend the night *à trois*. And with the thought in mind of a full day's work at the BBC, what sort of a night would it be? So I chose the coward's way out, tipped back my seat, and slept fitfully until dawn.

I was not therefore exactly favourably disposed towards air journeys at the outset, and my lack of enthusiasm tended to increase when I found the plethora of available material. Sea captains, train drivers and their passengers rarely find it necessary to set down on paper a record of journeys made. Air travellers have a different perspective. Pilots and passengers, it seems, have only to make a few forays into the atmosphere to assume they have done something unique and remarkable which must be recorded for posterity. The result is a very great deal of very indigestible matter.

However, there is more to air journeys than that; and as my reading progressed I found my way into new, magic worlds. That of balloons, for instance, whose first ascents in France in 1783 mark the beginnings of man's mastery of the air. Only a year later the dashing Vincent Lunardi made the first ascent in England, precursor of others from Liverpool, Glasgow, Kelso and Edinburgh, from where he made a gusty passage across the Firth of Forth. In 1852 Coxwell and Glaisher reached an incredible height of 37,000 feet (10,000 feet higher than Everest) and survived; and who can forget Glaisher's haunting description of the sounds of darkened Paris reaching him in his balloon, " like the breaking of waves against a sandy coast".

After the balloons came the airships, the brainchild of Graf Zeppelin. What strange, fascinating, unreal creatures they were. I see today, as sharply as when I first saw it around 1930 from the lawn of my grandmother's house in Hampshire, the R.100 hovering like a fat cigar above a distant hill. Nor can those of us who were growing up at the time ever forget the news of the disaster to the R.101 and, later, the terrifying pictures of the *Hindenburg* blowing up as she approached her mooring mast in New Jersey.

Before, and increasingly after, the First World War, came the development of heavier-than-air machines, with pioneers like the Wright brothers, Blériot, Alcock and Brown and Charles Lindbergh leading the way. And then in the twenties and thirties came the barnstormers and record-breakers—men and women like Alan Cobham and Jim Mollison, Amy Johnson and Amelia Earheart whose names at one time were household words—and in a class of her own the glorious Flying Duchess, Mary Bedford, whose privately printed diaries are such a delight to read.

Today's generation of travellers, who accept a two-day flight to Australia as commonplace, may find it hard to realise the excitement generated when news came that the record to the Cape, to India, to Australia, had been broken once again. If Mr. Chamberlain could once say that Czecho-Slovakia was a far-away country of which we knew little, how much more intangible and mysterious were the lands that lay beyond the Mediterranean. No wonder that these pioneers returned in triumph to cheering crowds with pictures of the Sphinx and the Nile, of Mashonas and Matabeles, of Table Mountain and the Great Barrier Reef as proofs of worlds elsewhere—and each time less distant than before. It was they who began the process of reducing the world to a pinhead.

It is, however, with passengers rather than pilots that I imagine most readers will identify; and I have been fortunate in being able to call on such lively and distinguished writers as Freya Stark and Evelyn Waugh on early trips to Paris; William Golding travelling across the United States; William Manchester on President Kennedy's last sad journey to Washington; Basil Boothroyd accompanying Prince Philip to Mexico, Kenneth Tynan's lovemaking eight miles high.

As with *Sea Journeys* I was in two minds as to whether to include a section on war, on the grounds that air battles are hardly journeys and rarely interesting unless written by a master hand. In the end I have included a short section, though less about combat than unusual flights—Hess's account of his arrival in England; an extract from St.-Exupéry's Flight to Arras; Churchill returning from Bermuda and nearly making a landfall at Brest; the extraordinary touchdown of Nicholas Alkemade. And it is not for their own sakes that I have included the "kills" of Richard Hillary and Peter Townsend but for the quality of writing that describes them. The scene that Townsend pictures of the young Heinkel pilot and his companions regarding him helplessly "as their flying tumbril bore them . . . down to the sea" stays in the mind, as these last forty years it has obviously stayed in his.

I have not included, as I did in *Railway Journeys* and *Sea Journeys*, a separate section on fiction, though one or two pieces will be found throughout the book. There is a simple reason for this which is that, although long-distance air journeys are quicker than sea journeys and about the same time as train journeys, the immobility of the passengers means that events and relationships take time—and a great many thousand words—to develop. David Lodge's *Changing Places* and Joseph Heller's *Catch 22* are exceptions to the rule that there are few, brief self-contained scenes in air journey fiction.

Once more my most grateful thanks to those who have pointed the way: to A. K. Astbury, Roy Fuller, D. Rowe, Geoffrey Negus, J. M. Bacon, Joy Melville and many others; to Annabel Craig for research and pictures; to Joyce Turnbull for correspondence and permissions; and to my editor Hilary Davies for her continued encouragement and advice.

HIGH FLIGHT

Oh! I have slipped the surly bonds of Earth
    And danced the skies on laughter-silvered wings;
Sunward I've climbed, and joined the tumbling mirth
    Of sun-split clouds,—and done a hundred things
You have not dreamed of—wheeled and soared
and swung
    High in the sunlit silence. Hov'ring there,
I've chased the shouting wind along, and flung
    My eager craft through footless halls of air . . .

Up, up the long, delirious, burning blue
    I've topped the wind-swept heights with easy grace,
Where never lark, or even eagle flew—
    And, while with silent, lifting mind I've trod
    The high untrespassed sanctity of space,
Put out my hand and touched the face of God.

JOHN GILLESPIE MAGEE

BALLOONS
AND
AIRSHIPS

The First Flights

1783, Paris: De Rozier and D'Arlandes

Some eleven months only after the two Montgolfiers were discovered toying with their inflated paper bag, the younger of the two
brothers was engaged to make an exhibition of his new art before
the King at Versailles, and this was destined to be the first occasion
when a balloon was to carry a living freight into the sky. The
stately structure, which was gorgeously decorated, towered some
seventy feet into the air, and was furnished with a wicker car in
which the passengers were duly installed. These were three in
number, a sheep, a cock, and a duck, and amid the acclamations
of the multitude, rose a few hundred feet and descended half a
mile away. The cock was found to have sustained an unexplained
mishap: its leg was broken; but the sheep was feeding complacently,
and the duck was quacking with much apparent satisfaction.

Now, who among mortals will come forward and win the honour
of being the first to sail the skies? M. Pilâtre de Rozier at once
volunteered, and by the month of November a new air ship was
built, 74 feet high, 48 feet in largest diameter, and 15 feet across
the neck, outside which a wicker gallery was constructed, while an
iron brazier was slung below all. But to trim the boat properly two
passengers were needed, and de Rozier found a ready colleague in
the Marquis d'Arlandes. By way of precaution, de Rozier made a
few preliminary ascents with the balloon held captive, and then
the two intrepid Frenchmen took their stand on opposite sides of
the gallery, each furnished with bundles of fuel to feed the furnace,
each also carrying a large wet sponge with which to extinguish the
flames whenever the machine might catch fire. On casting off the
balloon rose readily, and reaching 3,000 feet, drifted away on an
upper current.

The rest of the narrative, much condensed from a letter of the Marquis, written a week later, runs somewhat thus: "Our departure was at fifty-four minutes past one, and occasioned little stir among the spectators. Thinking they might be frightened and stand in need of encouragement, I waved my arm. M. de Rozier cried, 'You are doing nothing, and we are not rising!' I stirred the fire, and then began to scan the river, but Pilâtre cried again, 'See the river; we are dropping into it!' We again urged the fire, but still clung to the river bed. Presently I heard a noise in the upper part of the balloon, which gave a shock as though it had burst. I called to my companion, 'Are you dancing?' The balloon by now had many holes burned in it, and using my sponge I cried that we must descend. My companion, however, explained that we were over Paris, and must now cross it. Therefore, raising the fire once more, we turned south till we passed the Luxemburg, when, extinguishing the flame, the balloon came down spent and empty."

Daring as was this ascent, it was in achievement eclipsed two months later at Lyons, when a mammoth balloon, 130 feet in height and lifting 18 tons, was inflated in seventeen minutes, and ascended with no less than seven passengers. When more than half a mile aloft this machine, which was made of too slender material for its huge size, suddenly developed a rent of half its length, causing it to descend with immense velocity; but without the smallest injury to any of the passengers. This was a memorable performance, and the account, sensational as it may read, is by no means unworthy of credit; for, as will be seen hereafter, a balloon even when burst or badly torn in mid-air may, on the principle of the parachute, effect its own salvation.

REV. J. M. BACON,
The Dominion of the Air

The first manned balloon ascent. On 21 November 1783
Pilatre de Rozier and the Marquis d'Arlandes ascended in
their Montgolfier or Hot Air balloon from the Château de la
Muette near Paris.

1783, Paris: Charles and Robert

The fact that the first manned ascents were done privately and in strict secrecy did not prevent sizeable crowds turning out to watch them. The first public ascent, staged by the Académie Française on 1st December 1783 in the gardens of the Tuileries, drew an estimated two-thirds of the population of Paris.

Professor Charles, "veteran" designer, was the pilot, his balloon, naturally, a "Charlière", financed by public subscription and larger and more elaborate than anything yet built—terrifyingly large, in fact the mere sight of it on its trolley stampeded cattle. Charles was not alone, for a M. Robert, who had devised an outer skin of rubberised silk for the envelope, demanded a passage as the price of his invention. (Some said Charles insisted on him going along, to prove his confidence in it.) The machine itself might truly be called the first real balloon, for it was equipped with a valve to regulate the escape of gas; a gallery for the voyagers, attached to the envelope by twenty-four ropes; sand-ballast and instruments for calculating altitude—practically everything, in fact, that modern balloonists still regard as standard fittings. The "Montgolfière" bore about as much resemblance to it as a Sopwith Camel would to a jet air-liner.

As a spectacle, this first hydrogen ascent suffered from the tedious preliminaries that were so often, in years to come, to infuriate observers and earn many an aeronaut a rough handling from the mob before he even got the chance to get off the ground. The hydrogen bubbled in its own time and hours passed before the fabric showed signs of assuming the right shape. But the Montgolfier brothers were there, to provide a curtain-raiser: they sent up two small air-balloons, which placated the audience, gave Charles a good idea of wind direction and set a problem for the "mathematical persons with proper instruments ... stationed conveniently for the purpose of ascertaining height, rate of going and other particulars".

The sun went down on a balloon far from fully inflated, and the Professor climbed aboard with his passenger and gave the signal to let go. He could not have calculated its buoyancy more

The end of the first successful manned hydrogen balloon
flight, 1 December 1783. Professor Charles and M. Robert
arrive at Nesles, twenty-seven miles from Paris. Robert, on
the left, asks a priest to sign his name as witness to the
landing. Charles, meanwhile, makes a further ascent on his
own. He reached a height of nearly 10,000 feet, but was so
upset by the experience he never flew again.

accurately from the spectator's point of view. It rose slowly into
the sight of thousands, brushed a roof-corner, hung a moment in
suspense, rose lazily once more and sailed into the night. Those
who had waited all day for that moment agreed it had been worth
it. The balloonists came down safely at Nesle two hours later,
having covered the incredible distance of twenty-seven miles. "A
delicious voyage," the Professor called it; so delicious that, although

it was getting on for midnight and his companion had had enough and all the ballast was gone, he jumped back into the car and told the peasants to let go again. The result was an altitude record.

"I sprang like a bird into the air," he recalled. "In twenty minutes I was fifteen hundred toises high, out of sight of terrestrial objects. The globe, which had been flaccid, swelled insensibly; I drew the valve from time to time but still continued to ascend. For myself, though exposed to the open air, I passed in ten minutes from the warmth of spring to the icy cold of winter: a sharp, dry cold, but not too much to be borne. In the first moments I felt nothing disagreeable in the change. In a few minutes my fingers were benumbed by the cold, so that I could not hold my pen." (A tragedy, for the pioneer balloonists, as long as they had a hand free, spent every airborne moment recording their impressions for posterity.)

"I was now stationary as to rising or falling, and moving only in a horizontal direction. I rose up in the middle of the car to contemplate the scenery around me."

What follows is balloonist's licence—it was black night in reality:

"When I left the earth, the sun had set on the valleys; now he rose for me alone; he presently disappeared, and I had the pleasure of watching him set twice on the same day. I beheld for a few seconds the circumambient air, and the vapours rising from the valleys and rivers. The clouds seemed to rise from the earth and collect one upon the other, still preserving their usual form, only their colour was grey and monotonous from the want of light in the atmosphere. The moon alone enlightened them and showed me that I had changed my direction twice.

"Presently I conceived, perhaps a little hastily, the idea of being able to steer my own course. In the midst of my delight I felt a violent pain in my right ear and jaw, which I ascribed to the dilatation of the air in the cellular construction of those organs, as much as to the cold of the external air. I was in a waistcoat, and bare-headed; I immediately put on a woollen cap, yet the pain did not go off until I gradually descended."

The temperature in Professor Charles' balloon dropped from forty-seven degrees at ground level to twenty-one at his highest altitude—which worked out by his reckoning at 9,000 feet, though

8,000 would perhaps have been nearer the mark. On his return to earth he was arrested at the instigation of the local bishop, and spent the rest of the night in gaol.

LESLIE GARDINER,
Man in the Clouds

———◆———

1784, London: Vincent Lunardi (1)

The first balloon ascent in England was made by a handsome young Italian, Vincent Lunardi, secretary to Prince Caramanico, Neapolitan Ambassador to the Court of St. James. Described as "flamboyant yet fastidious, a disarming mixture of modesty and conceit", Lunardi was understandably nervous as the day of the ascent approached. Because of riots occasioned by the failure of a young Frenchman living in England, Moret, to make an ascent in his balloon, Sir George Howard, Governor of Chelsea Hospital, withdrew his permission for Lunardi to ascend from the hospital grounds. At the last moment however he was offered, and accepted, the use of the grounds of the Honourable Artillery Company. The crowds began to gather from early morning.

And now the great day was here, and it found him haggard and irritable, hardly able to dress himself for trembling fingers. The fatigues and anxieties of the past few weeks had brought him to the verge of nervous exhaustion.

Wednesday, 15th September 1784, dawned calm and sunny. Ahead of the balloon staff lay a full programme, and they were on the ground at daybreak, but Lunardi was there before them. Well aware that many a heroic enterprise had gone unacknowledged for want of a proper narrative, he sat in an alcove, pen in hand, rapt in the composition of a potential best-seller.

"The auspicious morning is arrived," he began, "and I will write the occurrences of it as they arise, lest any of those *supposed impossibilities* overtake me, which have lately haunted my designs. I have no apprehension, but of the populace, which is here, as it is everywhere, an impetuous, impatient and cruel tyrant."

The same apprehension was reflected, as the morning wore on, by the large number of empty seats within the ground; but, outside, one of the biggest turn-outs ever remembered in London was shoving and jostling its way to the Artillery Ground. Most of the city shops and offices had closed for the day; the centre of the city seemed deserted; and, on the outskirts, country people swarmed in from all points of the compass. The diary of many a squire in the Home Counties contained entries such as that of Mr. Windham, the politician and friend of Doctor Johnson:

"13th September. Got out of the phaeton at the top of the hill near Burke's (Edmund Burke) and walked down and found them all going to London next day on the same errand as myself, viż., to see Lunardi ascend."

The square inside the Ground—bigger than the biggest *piazza* in Italy, it seemed to Lunardi—appeared to him like "a pavement of human heads". The crowd was estimated in mid-morning to be 150,000 strong—before the day was out it would be the largest ever to attend a sporting event in the history of the world (this record has since been claimed for the Indianapolis Speedway). Lunardi, in a bad attack of eleventh-hour nerves, imagined them all hoping for another fiasco, itching for an excuse to run amok, stab and rob and get their hands round his throat.

Doctor Fordyce, as calmly as though in his own laboratory, shovelled chemicals into his acid tank and stirred the brew. A slow trickle of gas began almost imperceptibly to fill out the folds in the great, shapeless bag of coloured silk, that lay like a collapsed circus tent in the arena. This was the worst time of all: everything prepared, nothing to do but wait and watch while the invisible "inflammable air" bubbled off the "vitriolic mixture" and gently hissed through a narrow pipe. Lunardi's gaze roved round the windows and roofs and scaffolding of the neighbourhood, all crowded with carefree, well-dressed people—some of these seats were costing their occupants ten guineas, but not a penny of it would come his way. Round the balloon all were curiously silent, speaking in whispers as though in church. Except for the confused rumble of mass conversation, rolling in from the mob, no sound could be heard but the slow hissing of hydrogen and the scratching of the inventor's pen.

"They have viewed for hours, with fixed and silent attention, the bustle round the apparatus and the gradual expansion of the balloon," he noted at twelve o'clock. The furthest ranks of the multitude, wedged into narrow streets half a mile away, were calm now—ominously calm, thought Lunardi. Minutes ticked by. The balloon lay inert, Mr. Biggin doubted whether the hydrogen was going in at all. But Fordyce forbade interference, it must be allowed to take its own time. He squatted among the tanks, reaching out a hand to clear an occasional blockage, and looked as though he were prepared to sit there for the next forty-eight hours. Lunardi paced restlessly up and down, declining advice to get some food and rest while he had the chance. He scanned the audience ceaselessly, for the first signs of irritation that would set the mob aflame. His eye took in the façade of one grim fortress blocking off a whole side of his horizon, and he could make out the twin figures of Frenzy and Melancholy that guarded its gates—the press had made great play with the appropriateness of his launching site, next door to Bethlam; as they had done with puns on his name, calling him "Lunarci".

One o'clock arrived, the scheduled time for departure, and still the balloon was nowhere near ready—indeed, as yet, it hardly looked like a balloon to the lay observer. By twenty past, officials were looking worried: the first impatient bellows were drifting in from the crowd and horsemen at the gates were getting involved in scuffles. But all at once came a providential distraction. Bugles blew, the crowd was forced back, the main gates were flung open and, with a flourish of trumpets, in swept a calvacade.

His Royal Highness the Prince of Wales briefly inspected the equipage and its pilots, who afterwards spoke gratefully of his "condescending affability", and took his seat on a balcony in the Armoury House. But it made Colonel Lewis even more anxious to get the show started as soon as possible, for fear of damage to the person of the First Gentleman in Europe. Word went round that the ascent would take place at two sharp, not a moment later.

Friends wept to see the young Italian, pale and tight-lipped, embark to test the buoyancy of the half-filled envelope. "Prince Caramanico," says the minute-by-minute account, "is evidently under some apprehension, I shall remember all my life this unequivocal proof of his friendship."

Biggin joined his friend in the basket and they checked their

Mrs Sage and Mr Biggins ascend from the Royal George
Rotundo in St George's Fields, London, 29 June 1785.
(See caption on page xii).

equipment. The navigation—oars, wings and ballast—was Lunardi's responsibility; Biggin had to look after the animals and "make philosophical observations and experiments". But it was plain that the balloon in its present state would not support the weight of two men. Doctor Fordyce needed another hour at least, Sir Watkyn Lewis, glancing anxiously towards the royal box, wouldn't hear of it. Biggin promptly resolved the argument by stepping out again and wishing his friend *bon voyage*.

The sole remaining pilot was still not satisfied. He held a hurried consultation with Fordyce, and both went away to find a smaller, lighter gallery. At one minute to two he was standing in it, ready at last, waiting for the stroke of the hour, when "a servant brought word that an accident had befallen the balloon, which would prevent the intended voyage."

Fainting with mortification, he tottered out to investigate. It was nothing—a tangled rope, five minutes delay. Back at his controls, he heard the swelling murmur of the multitude. There was no backing out now, he had to go or be torn to pieces where he stood.

At six minutes past two Vincenzo Lunardi flagged the launching signal. The ropes parted, the balloon dragged, scattering onlookers, bumped lightly three times and rose into the air. "The Prince of Wales and the whole surrounding assembly, almost at one instant, took off their hats, hailed my resolution and expressed the kindest and most cordial wishes for my safety and success." Too late, he remembered he had left all his instruments behind.

The burst of cannon, breaking-out of flags and the sight of the blue and red globe lifting steadily into view had a miraculous effect on the rabble beyond the square. "Their shouts passed from incredulity and menace into the most extraordinary expressions of approbation and joy."

Drifting slowly at about forty feet, Lunardi cleared the walls, met a down-draught of air and swooped dangerously close to the sea of upturned heads. Hastily he discarded a couple of sand-bags, breasted the breeze and soared like a falcon to six hundred feet. Now he was free. He brandished his flag, to let the still-incredulous know there really was a man aloft in the sky above English soil, and plied his oars so energetically that one of them broke. In his excitement he trod on the bird-cage and let the pigeon escape—the bewildered bird flew back to the spot he had just left, and spectators fought for its feathers as prized souvenirs.

Carried upward and northward on a light breeze, the balloon passed out of sight of the watching world.

He had a thermometer after all—someone had lashed it to the rigging. And the mercury was draining out of the tube: seventy, sixty, fifty degrees. He shivered, and helped himself to three or four quick nips out of the bottle of wine a well-wisher had strapped on to his hip. Then he rummaged among his provisions—he had loaded up with food for a long journey—but found that the jolting of the car at take-off had mixed the sand with the bread. He managed to clean up the roasted chicken, however, nibbled a leg and tried to persuade his cowering dog to eat the bone.

Moving at the same speed as the breeze, too high to be aware of the slow passage of landmarks—he had lost sight of the little black dot that was his shadow, gliding across field and roof-top—Lunardi had no sensation of motion, either up, down or horizontally. Doctors had warned him of the perils of vertigo, such as affected people when they looked down from a high building, but he felt nothing of it. London, the whole sprawling metropolis, lay directly beneath him—he could distinguish the dome of St. Paul's and the river, broadening out towards the sea. From the angle its furthest suburbs subtended, he calculated that the circle of his horizon—a perfect circle, like the horizon of a calm ocean seen from the bridge of a ship—measured a hundred miles across.

The temperature stood steady at fifty. He was nearly 6,000 feet up, no longer conscious of the cold air, only of "a calm delight". He moved about his cramped small world, stretching his legs, shifting the furniture around, uncorking his flask and drinking, and finishing off the chicken. Then he sat down to write Compagni a letter, just as if he were sitting in his own study.

"Thus tranquil and thus situated, how shall I describe to you a view such as the ancients supposed Jupiter to have of the earth, and to copy which there are no terms in any language? The gradual diminution of objects, and the masses of light and shade, are intelligible in oblique and common prospects. But here every-thing wears a new appearance and has a new effect. The face of the country shows a mild and pleasing verdure, to which Italy is a stranger. The variety of cultivation and the accuracy with which property is divided give the idea ever present to a stranger in England of good civil laws and an equitable administration ... the rivers meandering; the sea glistening with the rays of the sun; the immense district beneath me spotted with cities, towns and villages, pouring out their inhabitants to hail my appearance: you will allow me some merit in not being exceedingly intoxicated with my situation."

Lunardi's impressions of the countryside were echoed by foreign observers a hundred and thirty years later. Two German balloonists, adrift over eastern England in World War I, harped on the same theme: of a vast kitchen-garden, a green and smiling land, dotted with snug hamlets, orchards and multifarious small-holdings—a model of intensive and intelligent husbandry, unlike any other landscape on earth.

Lunardi was so taken with the view that he stopped to enjoy it—or persuaded himself that he did—remaining motionless for half an hour by plying his single oar. Then he let the southerly breeze carry him on and took to his pen again, to scribble a five-page note to the Prince of Caramanico, whose last-minute alarm for his safety still haunted him. Having tied it up in a napkin and dropped it overboard, he took up the wine-flask and downed the rest of its contents, "to the health of my friends and benefactors in the lower world".

There must have been something in the upper air powerfully stimulating to literary composition—unless the effect of a bottle of claret in a rarified atmosphere had something to do with it. Lunardi completed four more lengthy epistles in the next hour, between attending to his navigation and performing "philosophical experiments"...

After tying these missives to articles of his clothing and flinging them to the winds, Lunardi relaxed and dozed and savoured his triumph. Barely an hour earlier, he had been sick with terror at the prospect of a roughing-up by the London mob, of suffering the fate of Moret. One moment, one tremendous bound, had transformed him from clown into demi-god, and a hostile multitude into a race of worshipping ants. Music of the spheres, not catcalls, rang in his ears. On top of the world, free of the cares and passions that molested mankind and giddy with delight, he saw the clouds roll back symbolically as he advanced towards them, like the portals of Heaven, he was traversing Elysian Fields of packed cumulus . . . he fell asleep.

LESLIE GARDINER,
Man in the Clouds

Lunardi came down in a field near Ware in Hertfordshire (where today a stone tablet marks the spot). On return to London he became, as he put it, "the idol of the nation". He was showered with money and presents, fêted by the City companies and the Inns of Court, made a member of the Artillery Company and received at court.

The next year he made ascents from Liverpool, Kelso in the Borders and Edinburgh. From Edinburgh he crossed the Firth of Forth to land in the kingdom of Fife. Here the Gentlemen Golfers of the Royal and Ancient Golf Club at St. Andrews invited him to play a round, but after taking 21 for the first hole he retired. In November and December he made two ascents from the square of St. Andrews Church, Glasgow, dressed in the blue and scarlet regimentals of the Artillery Company. His second ascent took him to the Glen of Campsie, twelve miles away, where he was observed by the local minister, Mr. Lapsley.

1784, Scotland: Vincent Lunardi (2)

Yesterday afternoon, whilst I was walking through my parish, visiting the sick, and rather inclined to be pensive from reflecting upon the scenes of distress to which I had been witness, my attention was suddenly arrested by a confused humming noise, which seemed all at once to spring out of the earth towards the south; but, as my view from that quarter was intercepted by a clump of trees, I walked on, and for two minutes had it not in my power to inquire from what cause it proceeded.

An old woman, who at that moment joined me, hearing the noise at the same time, took some pains to convince me "that it was the buzz of those spirits and elves who before Christmas Eve hold their meetings in sequestered dales, lamenting lost power".

You will easily believe that such a wayward fancy was not agreeable to my present humour. I left her, and hastened to a rising ground, when I now heard distinctly several people shouting aloud, "Yonder he comes! Yonder he comes!" Turning round, I beheld the balloon floating majestically almost over my head. Mr. Lunardi was then standing in his car, and waving his banner. His distance from the earth seemed to be about 300 yards. The people were running from all quarters. Their acclamations were every moment waxing louder and louder; and, in imitation of Mr. Chisholm, were shouting vehemently, "Lunardi come down." I, along with the rest, invited him to descend.

I am rather inclined, however, to think that he did not hear me, owing to the whistling of the wind, which, he said, was very violent during the whole of his excursion. However, as he had resolved not to go far, we were indulged in our request; for, exactly at two o'clock, he dropped his anchor and descended at Easter Mockroft on the banks of the Glassart, on the estate of Sir Archibald Edmistone of Dultreath in the parish of Campsie, nine English miles and a half N.N.E. of Glasgow.

As he descended within less than half a mile where I stood, I immediately hastened to welcome Mr. Lunardi, and to give him all the assistance in my power. The whole country seemed to be alive, running unto him with the same kind intention; and I perceived with pleasure that curiosity was a principle not confined alone to the breasts of the higher born and better educated class of men; for in passing a little cottage I heard a weaver expressing the most vehement desire to see this great sight, and crying to his wife to "take care of the bairns". I believe, however, that she at this time forgot that ever she had promised him obedience, and set out, repeating his commands to the servant, who in her turn exclaimed with rage, that "she wondered what people imagined servants were made of: Let those who got bairns take care of them; for by her faith, she would both see and touch Lunardi with the best of them;" and threw the child from her. Perhaps upon another occasion we might have taken time to tell her that she expressed herself too strongly; but yesterday every thing was her friend.

During my going from the rising ground where I first saw it to the vale where it alighted, I sometimes lost sight of the car, by the gentle-swells which intervened, but never lost sight of the balloon; and as it was suspended some yards from the ground, betwixt the darkness of the day, and the blue mist of the mountains, under whose shade it was, it had the appearance of an object rising out of the sea, resembling the sun when he makes his first appearance in a spring morning out of a thick fog. Before I arrived it assumed a new shape—that of a pear, or inverted cone. Mr. Lunardi then standing in his car, about four feet from the ground, some people assisting him to get out, and others holding the rope in order to prevent him from being dragged along by the strength of the balloon, which was hovering above him.

It was about six minutes after two when I got up. More than 40 people were before me. A vast multitude now assembled from every quarter. The shepherd forsook his flock; the farmer left his plow, and the traveller his journey, so that, in less than a quarter of an hour, there were many hundreds gazing with astonishment at the daring adventurer. Every body was pleased, and every body wished to lend him their aid. Mr. Lunardi hardly had occasion to ask for assistance, nor I to encourage them to give it. In half an hour after two the balloon was emptied, and the netting, basket, and other apparatus, packed up, and all ready to march off the field.

REV. JAMES LAPSLEY

Eventually Lunardi returned to his native Italy. At Naples he made a spectacular ascent in the presence of the King and Queen, and was again showered with honours. Later he went to Spain, and made successful ascents from Madrid and Seville. He then moved to Lisbon, where in 1806 he died "of a decline" at the age of forty-seven.

To Sir Thomas Mann

Strawberry Hill, 30th September 1784

I cannot fill my paper, as they do, with air-balloons; which, though ranked with the invention of navigation, appear to me as childish as the flying kites of schoolboys. I have not stirred a step to see one; consequently, have not paid a guinea for gazing at one, which I might have seen by only looking up into the air. An Italian, one Lunardi, is the first AIRGONAUT that has mounted into the clouds in this country. So far from respecting him as a Jason, I was very angry with him: he had full right to venture his own neck, but none to risk the poor cat, who, not having proved a martyr, is at least better entitled to be a confessor than her master Daedelus. I was even disappointed AFTER his expedition had been prosperous: you must know, I have no idea of space: when I heard how wonderfully he had soared, I concluded he had arrived within a stone's throw of the moon—alas! he had not ascended above a mile and a half: so pitiful an ascension has degraded him totally in my conceit. As there are mountains twice as high, what signifies flying, if you do not rise above the top of the earth? Any one on foot may walk higher than this man-eagle! Well! now you know all that I know—and was it worth telling?

HORACE WALPOLE

1785, Crossing the Channel: Blanchard and Jeffries

Early in 1785, the French balloonist Jean-Pierre Blanchard together with his sponsor, the American physician John Jeffries, set out to cross the Channel from England to France. Dr. Jeffries's *Diary* recounts what happened.

Jan. 7, 1785. This morning, at six o'clock, my little hero Blanchard entered my bed chamber, and told me he believed the wind and

weather were fair, and would do for our intended aerial voyage
from the cliff below the royal castle of Dover, for the continent of
France. Between eight and nine o'clock went with Mr. Hugget,
the pilot, to the pier and pilots' look-out. The pilots were of opinion
that the wind was not decided, and did not extend beyond mid
channel, and that the wind was equally from the French land as
from the English coast. This opinion embarrassed me much,
although I did not think as they did. While I was at the lookout,
the signal gun for our intended voyage was fired, and the flag
hoisted, and soon after several other guns, to give notice to the
adjacent towns, etc. The balloon and net, etc., were carried down
to our apparatus, the balloon hung up, and we began the process
for filling it.

At nine o'clock went to the castle and breakfasted with the
Deputy Governor Lane, after which retired to Capt. Arch. Campbell's apartments to dress for my voyage; after, called to pay my
respects to Capt. James Campbell and his lady, and then went
down to our apparatus, where I found my little heroick Captain,
and the balloon half filled. At half after eleven o'clock let off a
small Mongolfier, which went very well, and took a very good
direction for us. At twelve o'clock filled and sent off from the hands
of Governor Lane our little Devonshire balloon (which had been
the herald of our aerial voyage from London into Kent), and it
took the same course as the Mongolfier had done. At half twelve,
we carried our aerial car and placed it under the balloon, and
began attaching the cords of the net to it. At one o'clock had
completed it, fastened and adjusted in its place the barometer.

We then took in our bladders, other things, and eighty pounds
of ballast, in bags of ten pounds each, compass, chart, loosened
the ropes which had guarded our apparatus, and let the balloon
rise a little, and carry us free of the apparatus, &c.; then fixed our
wings, etc., and balancing the balloon, found our weight too great,
on which we cast out one sack of ballast; still too heavy, and on
the very brink of the cliff cast out a second, then a third and
fourth, and arose so as to clear the cliff, but being rather inclined
to descend, we gradually emptied the fifth sack, and then arose
gradually and most majestically. Exactly at quarter past one
o'clock, we quitted the cliff, and had with us as follows—three
sacks of ballast of ten pounds each, balloon 148 pounds, net 57

7 January 1785: the French aeronaut Jean Pierre
Blanchard and his American sponsor Dr John Jeffries leave
Dover at the start of their crossing of the English Channel.

pounds, aerial car and apparatus 72 pounds, Blanchard's books 34
pounds, Blanchard and his clothes 146 pounds, myself 128 pounds,
sundries 19 pounds.

In a few minutes after our departure, we saluted with our
hands and flags, which they returned with very loud and repeated
shouts and acclamations. Just before entering our car Monsieur B.
had most politely presented me with my colour, a British flag, in
presence of the company and spectators, on which I requested of
Gov. Lane and Capt. Campbell, the commanding officer, leave for
Mr. B. to display his French flag on our departure, which they
very politely granted. At half past one, we had risen considerably,
but appeared to have made very little progress, and that little
rather to the eastward, the wind at our departure being less than

at any part of the morning, and more westerly; the weather very
fine indeed, very clear sun, temperate and warm; the barometer
at starting, 29.7, has now fallen to 27.3.

We had a most enchanting view of the country back of Dover,
&c., for an extent of an hundred miles around, counting 37 towns
and villages, and a formidable view of the breakers on Goodwin
sands, to which we seemed to approach. The coast of France
likewise became very distinct. We passed over many vessels of
various kinds, which we saluted as we passed, and they returned
with shouts and cheers. The balloon extremely distended, and both
tubes extended through their whole length and diameter. There
seemed to be scarce a breath of air on the water under us.
Three-quarters past one, cast both tubes over the sides of the car,
and began to attach the bladders to the hoops of the car. In doing
this, I unfortunately, in reaching behind me, pushed off my colour,
which Mr. Blanchard had placed there for security. 50 minutes
after one, found we were descending fast; emptied one bag of
ballast; not rising, emptied half another, and began to rise again.
Appeared to be about one third of the way from Dover, losing
distinct sight of the castle. At two o'clock, attached the slings to
the circle, one at each end, and the third in the middle for our
feet, to retreat to, like beavers, in case we were forced down into
the water. Found that we were descending again fast. Cast out all
the remaining ballast and bags and all; did not rise. Cast out a
parcel of Mr. B.'s books, and in a minute or two found ourselves
rising again, and that we were full midway between the English
and French coasts.

30 minutes after two, found we were descending again; obliged
to cast out by parcels all our remaining books, and scarcely found
ourselves to arise after it. We had now nothing left but our wings
and apparatus, &c. 40 minutes after two (having passed over a
number of vessels, and being about three-quarters of the way over
from Dover to the French coast, having a most alluring and
enchanting view of it from Blackness, Cape Blanc Nez, quite to
Calais and on to Gravelines) found ourselves descending, and very
rapidly—the part of the balloon next to us having collapsed very
much, apparently for many feet from the lower pole. We cast out
all the little things we could find—apples, biscuits, &c., then one
wing; still descending, we cast away the other wing; but not rising,

cut away the damask curtains around the car, with the gold cord tassels, &c., then stripped off all the silk lining, threw out our bottle of *l'eau de vie*. In its descent it cast out a stream like smoke, with a rushing noise, and when it struck the water, we heard and felt the shock very perceptibly in our car and balloon. I then attempted and succeeded in unscrewing and getting out the moulinet and handle, and cast all over.

Found ourselves still descending, and now approaching the sea, within 120 yards, we proposed and began to strip, Mr. B. first casting away his surtout and coat. I then cast away my coat; then Mr. B. his new coat and long trousers; and we got on and adjusted our cork jackets, and were preparing to get into our slings, when I found the mercury in the barometer falling, and looking around found that we arose, and that the pleasant view of France was opening to us every moment, as we arose to overlook the high grounds. We were now about four miles from the shore, and approaching it fast. 50 minutes after two o'clock, had a fine view of Calais and between twenty and thirty little towns and villages.

We now rose very fast, and to a much greater height than at any time since our first ascent. Exactly at three o'clock, thanks to a kind Providence, we passed over the high grounds from the shore, about midway from Cape Blanc Nez and Calais. At our entrée we were very high, and passed over in a magnificent arch. Barometer had fallen to 23 and three-tenths. Nothing can equal the beautiful appearance of the villages, fields, roads, &c., under us, after having been so long over the water. Mr. Blanchard threw out several packets, each of which was exactly five minutes in reaching the surface of the earth. The weather continued very fine; sun very bright all our voyage; the wind a little increased, and being more westerly than when we first passed from the sea, we were approaching fast the grounds covered with water, on our left, and above and a little to the right of Calais. In a few minutes we changed our course again to the southwest; and found ourselves gradually descending.

In his *Narrative*, Dr. Jeffries describes the successful conclusion of the voyage.

We now found ourselves approaching towards a forest, which, appearing to be more extensive than it was probable we should be able to pass entirely over, we cast away one cork jacket, and soon after it the other, which almost immediately checked and altered the angle of our descent. We had now approached so near to the tops of the trees of the forest as to discover that they were very large and rough, and that we were descending with great velocity towards them; from which circumstances, and from the direction of our course at this time, fearing that the car might be forced into some of the trees so violently as to separate it from the cords that connected it with the net which covered the balloon, I felt the necessity of casting away something to alter our course; happily (it almost instantly occurred to me, that probably we might be able to supply it from within ourselves) from the recollection that we had drank much at breakfast; and not having had any evacuation; and from the severe cold, little or no perspiration had taken place, that probably an extra quantity had been secreted by the kidneys, which we might now avail ourselves of by discharging.

I instantly proposed my idea to M. Blanchard, and the event fully justified my expectation; and, taking down from the circle over our car two of the bladders, for reservoirs we were enabled to obtain, I verily believe, between five and six pounds of urine; which circumstance, however trivial or ludicrous it may seem, I have reason to believe, was of *real utility* to us, *in our then situation*; for by casting it away, as we were approaching some trees of the forest higher than the rest, it so altered our course that, instead of being forced hard against, or into them (as at that instant appeared probable that we should be), we passed along near them in such a manner, as enabled me to catch hold of the topmost branches of one of them, and thereby arrest the farther progress of the balloon, which, almost the instant the car touched the trees, so as to take off a part of its weight, was disposed to ascend again; and in that position continued for a considerable time, waving over our heads, making a very pretty appearance above the woods, until, having for some time held the valve open, a sufficiency of gaz had escaped, to dispose the car to settle on the branches, when, by disengaging, and pushing it from one to another, we found a sufficient space between the trees to admit us

to descend tranquilly to the surface of the ground, a little before
four o'clock, it having been about half after three when I first
stopped the progress of the balloon over the forest; which I have
since been informed, is called the *Forest of Guines*, not far from
Ardres, and near the spot celebrated for the famous interview
between Henry the Eighth, King of England, and Francis the
First, King of France.

> DR. JOHN JEFFRIES,
> *Diary and Narrative of Aerial Voyages
> with Monsieur Jean Pierre Blanchard*

During the next fifteen years, Blanchard made ascents from
most European capitals. In 1793, in the presence of George
Washington, he made the first balloon flight in America at
Philadelphia. He died in Paris in 1809 after a fall from a balloon.

1804: Superstitiousness of Napoleon

The extraordinary fact that the use of the balloon was for many
years discontinued in the French Army is attributed to a strangely
superstitious prejudice entertained by Napoleon. Las Cases (in his
Private Life of Napoleon at St. Helena) relates an almost miraculous story of Napoleon's coronation. It appears that a sum of
23,500 francs was given to M. Garnerin to provide a balloon ascent
to aid in the celebrations, and, in consequence, a colossal machine
was made to ascend at 11 p.m. on December 16th from the front
of Notre Dame, carrying 3,000 lights. This balloon was unmanned,
and at its departure apparently behaved extremely well, causing
universal delight. During the hours of darkness, however, it seems
to have acquitted itself in a strange and well-nigh preternatural
manner, for at daybreak it is sighted on the horizon by the
inhabitants of Rome, and seen to be coming towards their city. So
true was its course that, as though with predetermined purpose,
it sails on till it is positively over St. Peter's and the Vatican,

when, its mission being apparently fulfilled, it settles to earth,
and finally ends its career in the Lake Bracciano. Regarded from
whatever point of view, the flight was certainly extraordinary, and
it is not surprising that in that age it was regarded as nothing less
than a portent. Moreover, little details of the wonderful story were
quickly endowed with grave significance. The balloon on reaching
the ground rent itself. Next, ere it plunged into the water, it
carefully deposited a portion of its crown on the tomb of Nero.
Napoleon, on learning the facts, forbade that they should ever be
referred to. Further, he thenceforward discountenanced the balloon
in his army, and the establishment at Neudon was abandoned.

REV. J. M. BACON,
The Dominion of the Air

Some Nineteenth-Century Flights

1853: Voyage of *The Giant*

A balloon which has become famous in history was frequently used in the researches of the French aeronauts mentioned in our last chapter. This was known as *The Giant*, the creation of M. Nadar, a progressive and practical aeronaut, who had always entertained ambitious ideas about aerial travel.

M. Nadar had been editor of *L'Aéronaut*, a French journal devoted to the advancement of aerostation generally. He had also strongly expressed his own view respecting the possibility of constructing air ships that should be subject to control and guidance when winds were blowing. His great contention was that the dirigible air ship would, like a bird, have to be made heavier than the medium in which it was to fly. As he put it, a balloon could never properly become a vessel. It would only be a buoy. In spite of any number of accessories, paddles, wings, fans, sails, it could not possibly prevent the wind from bodily carrying away the whole concern.

After this strong expression of opinion, it may appear somewhat strange that such a bold theoriser should at once have set himself to construct the largest gas balloon on record. Such, however, was the case, and the reason urged was not otherwise than plausible. For, seeing that a vast sum of money would be needed to put his theories into practice, M. Nadar conceived the idea of first constructing a balloon so unique and unrivalled that it should compel public attention in a way that no other balloon had done before, and so by popular exhibitions bring to his hand such sums as he required. A proper idea of the scale of this huge machine can be easily gathered. The largest balloons at present exhibited in this country are seldom much in excess of 50,000 cubic feet capacity.

Compared with these the *Great Nassau Balloon*, built by Charles
Green, which has been already sufficiently described, was a true
leviathan; while Coxwell's *Mammoth* was larger yet, possessing a
content, when fully inflated, of no less than 93,000 cubic feet, and
measuring over 55 feet in diameter. This, however, as will be seen,
was but a mere pigmy when compared with *The Giant*, which,
measuring some 74 feet in diameter, possessed the prodigious
capacity of 215,000 cubic feet.

But the huge craft possessed another novelty besides that of
exceptional size. It was provided with a subsidiary balloon, called
the *Compensator*, and properly the idea of M. L. Godard, the
function of which was to receive any expulsion of gas in ascending,
and thus to prevent loss during any voyage. The specification of

The two-storey car of M. Nadar's huge balloon, *The Giant*,
(diameter 74 feet, capacity 215,000 cubic feet) on display
at Crystal Palace, London, 1863.

this really remarkable structure may be taken from M. Nadar's own description. The globe in itself was for greater strength virtually double, consisting of two identical balloons, one within the other, each made of white silk of the finest quality, and costing about 5s. 4d. per yard. No less than 22,000 yards of this silk were required, and the sewing up of the gores was entirely done by hand. The small compensating balloon was constructed to have a capacity of about 3,500 cubic feet, and the whole machine, when fully inflated, was calculated to lift 4½ tons. With this enormous margin of buoyancy, M. Nadar determined on making the car of proportionate and unparalleled dimensions, and of most elaborate design. It contained two floors, of which the upper one was open, the height of all being nearly 7 feet, with a width of about 13 feet. Then what was thought to be due provision was made for possible emergencies. It might descend far from help or habitations, therefore means were provided for attaching wheels and axles. Again, the chance of rough impact had to be considered, and so canes, to act as springs, were fitted around and below. Once again, there was the contingency of immersion to be reckoned with; therefore there were provided buoys and water-tight compartments. Further than this, unusual luxuries were added, for there were cabins, one for the captain at one end, and another with three berths for passengers at the other. Nor was this all, for there was, in addition, a larder, a lavatory, a photographic room, and a printing office. It remains now only to tell the tale of how this leviathan of the air acquitted itself.

The first ascent was made on the 4th of October, 1853, from the Champ de Mars, and no fewer than fifteen living souls were launched together into the sky. Of these Nadar was captain, with the brothers Godard lieutenants. There was the Prince de Sayn-Wittgenstein; there was the Count de St. Martin; above all, there was a lady, the Princess de la Tour d'Auvergne. The balloon came to earth at 9 o'clock at night near Meaux, and, considering all the provision which had been made to guard against rough landing, it can hardly be said that the descent was a happy one. It appears that the car dragged on its side for nearly a mile, and the passengers, far from finding security in the seclusion of the inner chambers, were glad to clamber out above and cling, as best they might, to the ropes.

Many of the party were bruised more or less severely, though no one was seriously injured, and it was reported that such fragile articles as crockery, cakes, confectionery, and wine bottles to the number of no less than thirty-seven, were afterwards discovered to be intact, and received due attention. It is further stated that the descent was decided on contrary to the wishes of the captain, but in deference to the judgment of the experienced M. Godard, it being apparently their conviction that the balloon was heading out to sea, whereas, in reality, they were going due east, "with no sea at all before them nearer than the Caspian".

REV. J. M. BACON,
The Dominion of the Air

1862: Coxwell and Glaisher reach 36,000 feet

It was on the 5th of September following that the same two colleagues carried out an exploit which will always stand alone in the history of aeronautics, namely, that of ascending to an altitude which, based on the best estimate they were able to make, they calculated to be no less than seven miles. Whatever error may have unavoidably come into the actual estimate, which is to some extent conjectural, is in reality a small matter, not the least affecting the fact that the feat in itself will probably remain without a parallel of its kind. In these days, when aeronauts attempt to reach an exceptionally lofty altitude, they invariably provide themselves with a cylinder of oxygen gas to meet the special emergencies of the situation, so that when regions of such attenuated air are reached that the action of heart and lungs becomes seriously affected, it is still within their power to inhale the life-giving gas which affords the greatest available restorative to their energies. Forty years ago, however, cylinders of compressed oxygen gas were not available, and on this account alone we may state without hesitation that the enterprise which follows stands unparalleled at the present hour.

The filling station at Wolverhampton was quitted at 1.3 p.m., the temperature of the air being 59° on the ground, and falling to 41° at an altitude of 5,000 feet, directly after which a dense cloud was entered, which brought the temperature down to 36°. At this elevation the report of a gun was heard. Here Mr. Glaisher attempted (probably for the first time in history) to take a cloud-scape photograph, the illumination being brilliant, and the plates with which he was furnished being considered extremely sensitive. The attempt, however, was unsuccessful. The height of two miles was reached in 19 minutes, and here the temperature was at freezing point. In six minutes later three miles was reached, and the thermometer was down to 18°. In another twelve minutes four miles was attained, with the thermometer recording 8°, and by further discharge of sand the fifth aerial milestone was passed at 1.50 p.m., *i.e.* in 47 minutes from the start, with the thermometer 2° below zero.

Mr. Glaisher relates that up to this point he had taken observations with comfort, and experienced no trouble in respiration, whilst Mr. Coxwell, in consequence of the exertions he had to make, was breathing with difficulty. More sand was now thrown out, and as the balloon rose higher Mr. Glaisher states that he found some difficulty in seeing clearly. But from this point his experiences should be gathered from his own words:

"About 1.52 p.m., or later, I read the dry bulb thermometer as minus five; after this I could not see the column of mercury in the wet bulb thermometer, nor the hands of the watch, nor the fine divisions on any instrument. I asked Mr. Coxwell to help me to read the instruments. In consequence, however, of the rotatory motion of the balloon, which had continued without ceasing since leaving the earth, the valve line had become entangled, and he had to leave the car and mount into the ring to readjust it. I then looked at the barometer, and found its reading to be 9¾ inches, still decreasing fast, implying a height exceeding 29,000 feet. Shortly after, I laid my arm upon the table, possessed of its full vigour; but on being desirous of using it I found it powerless—it must have lost its power momentarily. Trying to move the other arm, I found it powerless also. Then I tried to shake myself, and succeeded, but I seemed to have no limbs. In looking at the barometer my head fell over my left shoulder. I struggled and shook my body again, but could not move my arms. Getting my head upright for an instant only, it fell on my right shoulder; then I fell backwards, my back resting against the side of the car and my head on its edge. In this position my eyes were directed to Mr. Coxwell in the ring. When I shook my body I seemed to have full power over the muscles of the back, and considerably so over those of the neck, but none over either my arms or my legs. As in the case of the arms, so all muscular power was lost in an instant from my back and neck. I dimly saw Mr. Coxwell, and endeavoured to speak, but could not. In an instant intense darkness overcame me, so that the optic nerve lost power suddenly; but I was still conscious, with as active a brain as at the present moment whilst writing this. I thought I had been seized with asphyxia, and believed I should experience nothing more, as death would come unless we speedily descended. Other thoughts were entering my mind when I suddenly became unconscious, as on going to sleep. I cannot tell anything of the sense of hearing, as no sound reaches the ear to break the perfect stillness and silence of the regions between six and seven miles above the earth. My last observation was made at 1.54 p.m., above 29,000 feet. I suppose two or three minutes to have elapsed between my eyes becoming insensible to seeing fine divisions and 1.54 p.m., and then two or three minutes more to have passed till I was insensible, which I think, therefore, took place about 1.56 p.m., or 1.57 p.m.

"Whilst powerless, I heard the words 'Temperature' and 'Observation', and I knew Mr. Coxwell was in the car speaking to and endeavouring to rouse me—therefore consciousness and hearing had returned. I then heard him speak more emphatically, but could not see, speak, or move. I heard him again say, 'Do try, now do!' Then the instruments became dimly visible, then Mr. Coxwell, and very shortly I saw clearly. Next, I arose in my seat and looked around, as though waking from sleep, though not refreshed, and said to Mr. Coxwell, 'I have been insensible'. He said, 'You have, and I too, very nearly'. I then drew up my legs, which had been extended, and took a pencil in my hand to begin observations. Mr.

The famous voyage of Coxwell and Glaisher, 5 September 1862.
Glaisher insensible at a height of seven miles.

Coxwell told me that he had lost the use of his hands, which were black, and I poured brandy over them."

Mr. Glaisher considers that he must have been totally insensible for a period of about seven minutes, at the end of which time the water reserved for the wet bulb thermometer, which he had carefully kept from freezing, had become a solid block of ice. Mr. Coxwell's hands had become frostbitten, so that, being in the ring and desirous of coming to his friend's assistance, he was forced to rest his arms on the ring and drop down. Even then, the table being in the way, he was unable to approach, and, feeling insensibility stealing over himself, he became anxious to open the valve. "But in consequence of having lost the use of his hands he could not do this. Ultimately he succeeded by seizing the cord in his teeth and dipping his head two or three times until the balloon took a decided turn downwards." Mr. Glaisher adds that no inconvenience followed his insensibility, and presently dropping in a country where no conveyance of any kind could be obtained, he was able to walk between seven and eight miles.

The interesting question of the actual height attained is thus discussed by Mr. Glaisher: "I have already said that my last observation was made at a height of 29,000 feet. At this time, 1.54 p.m., we were ascending at the rate of 1,000 feet per minute, and when I resumed observations we were descending at the rate of 2,000 feet per minute. These two positions must be connected, taking into account the interval of time between, namely, thirteen minutes; and on these considerations the balloon must have attained the altitude of 36,000 or 37,000 feet. Again, a very delicate minimum thermometer read minus 11.9, and this would give a height of 37,000 feet. Mr. Coxwell, on coming from the ring, noticed that the centre of the aneroid barometer, its blue hand, and a rope attached to the car, were all in the same straight line, and this gave a reading of seven inches, and leads to the same result. Therefore, these independent means all lead to about the same elevation, namely, fully seven miles."

So far we have followed Mr. Glaisher's account only, but Mr. Coxwell has added testimony of his own to this remarkable adventure, which renders the narrative more complete. He speaks of the continued rotation of the balloon and the necessity for mounting into the ring to get possession of the valve line. "I had previously", he adds, "taken off a thick pair of gloves so as to be the better able to manipulate the sand-bags, and the moment my unprotected hands rested on the ring, which retained the temperature of the air, I found that they were frostbitten; but I did manage to bring down with me the valve line, after noticing the hand of the aneroid barometer, and it was not long before I succeeded in opening the shutters in the way described by Mr. Glaisher ... Again, on letting off more gas, I perceived that the lower part of the balloon was rapidly shrinking, and I heard a sighing, as if it were in the network and the ruffled surface of the cloth. I then looked round, although it seemed advisable to let off more gas, to see if I could in any way assist Mr. Glaisher, but the table of instruments blocked the way, and I could not, with disabled hands, pass beneath. My last hope, then, was in seeking the restorative effects of a warmer stratum of atmosphere ... Again I tugged at the valve line, taking stock, meanwhile, of the reserve ballast in store, and this, happily, was ample.

"Never shall I forget those painful moments of doubt and suspense as to Mr. Glaisher's fate, when no response came to my questions. I began to fear that he would never take any more readings. I could feel the reviving effects of a warmer temperature, and wondered that no signs of animation were noticeable. The hand of the aneroid that I had looked at was fast moving, while the under part of the balloon had risen high above the car. I had looked towards the earth, and felt the rush of air as it passed upwards, but was still in despair when Mr. Glaisher gasped with a sigh, and the next moment he drew himself up and looked at me rather in confusion, and said he had been insensible, but did not seem to have any clear idea of how long until he caught up his pencil and noted the time and the reading of the instruments."

The descent, which was at first very rapid, was effected without difficulty at Cold Weston.

REV. J. M. BACON,
The Dominion of the Air

Ascent of M. Poitevin on horseback, Champ de Mars, Paris,
14 July 1850.

1862: Sounds from London and Paris

A day trip over the eastern suburbs of London in the same year seems greatly to have impressed Mr. Glaisher. The noise of London streets as heard from above has much diminished during the last fifteen years, probably owing to the introduction of wood paving. But, forty years ago, Mr. Glaisher describes the deep sound of London as resembling the roar of the sea, when at a mile high; while at greater elevations it was heard as a murmuring noise.

*   *   *

Another wonder detected, equally striking though less uncommon, was of an acoustical nature, the locality this time being over Paris. The height of the balloon at this moment was not great, and, moreover, was diminishing as it settled down. Suddenly there broke in upon the voyagers a sound as of a confused kind of murmur. It was not unlike the distant breaking of waves against a sandy coast, and scarcely less monotonous. It was the noise of Paris that reached them, as soon as they sank to within 2,600 feet of the ground, but it disappeared at once when they threw out just sufficient ballast to rise above that altitude.

It might appear to many that so strange and sudden a shutting out of a vast sound occurring abruptly in the free upper air must have been more imaginary than real, yet the phenomenon is almost precisely similar to one coming within the experience of the writer, and vouched for by his son and daughter, as also by Mr. Percival Spencer, all of whom were joint observers at the time, the main point of difference in the two cases being the fact that the "region of silence" was recorded by the French observers as occurring at a somewhat lower level. In both cases there is little doubt that the phenomenon can be referred to a stratum of disturbed or non-homogeneous air, which may have been very far spread, and which is capable of acting as a most opaque sound barrier.

*   *   *

A description of the very impressive experience of a night sail over London has been reserved, but should not be altogether omitted. Glaisher, writing of the spectacle as he observed it nearly forty years ago, describes London seen at night from a balloon at a distance as resembling a vast conflagration. When actually over the town, a main thoroughfare like the Commercial Road shone up like a line of brilliant fire; but, travelling westward, Oxford Street presented an appearance which puzzled him. "Here the two thickly studded rows of brilliant lights were seen on either side of the street, with a narrow, dark space between, and this dark space was bounded, as it were, on both sides by a bright fringe like frosted silver". Presently he discovered that "this rich effect was caused by the bright illumination of the shop lights on the pavements".

London, as seen from a balloon on a clear moonlight night in August a year ago (1901), wore a somewhat altered appearance. There were the fairy lamps tracing out the streets, which, though dark centred, wore their silver lining; but in irregular patches a white light from electric arc lamps broadened and brightened and shone out like some pyrotechnic display above the black housetops. Through the vast town ran a blank, black channel, the river, winding on into distance, crossed here and there by bridges showing as bright bands, and with bright spots occasionally to mark where lay the river craft. But what was most striking was the silence. At night, after the last bus has ceased to ply, and before the market carts begin lumbering in, the balloonist, as he sails over the town, might imagine that he was traversing a City of the Dead.

It is at such times that a shout through a speaking trumpet has a most startling effect, and more particularly a blast on a horn. In this case after an interval of some seconds a wild note will be flung back from the housetops below, answered and re-answered on all sides as it echoes from roof to roof—a wild, weird uproar that awakes suddenly, and then dies out slowly far away.

Experiments with echoes from a balloon have proved instructive. If, when riding at a height, say, of 2,000 feet, a charge of gun-cotton be fired electrically 100 feet below the car, the report, though really as loud as a cannon, sounds no more than a mere pistol shot, possibly partly owing to the greater rarity of the air, but chiefly because the sound, having no background to reflect it, simply spends itself in the air. Then, always and under all conditions of atmosphere soever, there ensues absolute silence until the time for the echo back from earth has fully elapsed, when a deafening outburst of thunder rises from below, rolling on often for more than half a minute. Two noteworthy facts, at least, the writer has established from a very large number of trials: first, that the theory of aerial echoes thrown back from empty space, which physicists have held to exist constantly, and to be part of the cause of thunder, will have to be abandoned; and, secondly, that from some cause yet to be fully explained the echo back from the earth is always behind its time.

But balloons have revealed further suggestive facts with regard to sound, and more particularly with regard to the varying acoustic properties of the air. It is a familiar experience how distant sounds will come and go, rising and falling, often being wafted over extraordinary distances, and again failing altogether, or sometimes being lost at near range, but appearing in strength further away. A free balloon, moving in the profound silence of the upper air, becomes an admirable sound observatory. It may be clearly detected that in certain conditions of atmosphere, at least, there are what may be conceived to be aerial sound channels, through which sounds are momentarily conveyed with abnormal intensity. This phenomenon does but serve to give an intelligible presentment of the unseen conditions existing in the realm of air.

REV. J. M. BACON,
The Dominion of the Air

◆

1889: Flight of Spencer in India

Thus it came about that in the early days of 1889, in the height of the season, Mr. Percival Spencer arrived at Bombay, and at once commenced professional business in earnest. Coal gas being here available, a maiden ascent was quickly arranged, and duly announced to take place at the Government House, Paral, the chief attraction being the parachute descent, the first ever attempted in India.

M. Nadar on his way up. He was the first balloonist to take
topographical photographs, and edited a journal,
L'Aeronaute, to which Victor Hugo, George Sand, Jules
Verne, Alexandre Dumas and Jacques Offenbach were
subscribers.

This preliminary exhibition proving in all ways a complete success, Mr. Spencer, after a few repetitions of his performance, repaired to Calcutta; but here great difficulties were experienced in the matter of gas. The coal gas available was inadequate, and when recourse was had to pure hydrogen the supply proved too sluggish. At the advertised hour of departure the balloon was not sufficiently inflated, while the spectators were growing impatient. It was at this critical moment that Mr. Spencer resolved on a surprise. Suddenly casting off the parachute, and seated on a mere sling below the half-inflated balloon, without ballast, without grapnel, and unprovided with a valve, he sailed away over the heads of the multitude.

The afternoon was already far advanced, and the short tropical twilight soon gave way to darkness, when the intrepid voyager disappeared completely from sight. Excitement was intense that night in Calcutta, and greater still the next day when, as hour after hour went by, no news save a series of wild and false reports reached the city. Trains arriving from the country brought no intelligence, and telegraphic enquiries sent in all directions proved fruitless. The Great Eastern Hotel, where the young man had been staying, was literally besieged for hours by a large crowd eager for any tidings. Then the Press gave expression to the gloomiest forebodings, and the town was in a fever of unrest. From the direction the balloon had taken it was thought that, even if the aeronaut had descended in safety, he could only have been landed in the jungle of the Sunderbunds, beset with perils, and wihout a chance of succour. A large reward was offered for reliable information, and orders were issued to every likely station to organise a search. But ere this was fully carried into effect messages were telegraphed to England definitely asserting that Mr. Spencer had lost his life. For all this, after three days he returned to Calcutta, none the worse for the exploit.

Then the true tale was unravelled. The balloon had changed its course from S.E. to E. after passing out of sight of Calcutta, and eventually came to earth the same evening in the neighbourhood of Hossainabad, thirty-six miles distant. During his aerial flight the voyager's main trouble had been caused by his cramped position, the galling of his sling seat, and the numbing effect of cold as he reached high altitudes; but, as twilight darkened into gloom, his real anxiety was with respect to his place of landing, for he could with difficulty see the earth underneath. He heard the distant roll of the waters, caused by the numerous creeks which intersect the delta of the Ganges, and when darkness completely shut out the view it was impossible to tell whether he was over land or sea. Fortune favoured him, however, and reaching dry ground, he sprang from his seat, relinquishing at the same moment his hold of the balloon, which instantly disappeared into the darkness.

Then his wanderings began. He was in an unknown country, without knowledge of the language, and with only a few rupees in his pocket. Presently, however, seeing a light, he proceeded towards it, but only to find himself stopped by a creek. Foiled more than once in this way, he at length arrived at the dwelling of a family of natives, who promptly fled in terror. To inspire confidence and prove that he was mortal, Mr. Spencer threw his coat over the mud wall of the compound, with the result that, after examination of the garment, he was received and cared for in true native fashion, fed with rice and goat's milk, and allowed the use of the verandah to sleep in. He succeeded in communing with the natives by dint of lead pencil sketches and dumb show, and learned, among other things, that he had descended in a little clearing surrounded by woods, and bounded by tidal creeks, which were infested with alligators. Yet, in the end, the waterways befriended him; for, as he was being ferried across, he chanced on his balloon sailing down on the tide, recovered it, and used the tidal waters for the return journey.

The greeting upon his arrival in Calcutta was enthusiastic beyond description from both Europeans and natives. The hero of the adventure was visited by rajahs and notables, who vied with each other in expressions of welcome, in making presents, even inviting him to visit the sacred precincts of their zenanas. The promised parachute descent was subsequently successfully made at Cossipore, and then followed a busy, brilliant season, after which the wanderer returned to England.

REV. J. M. BACON,
The Dominion of the Air

1897: The Andrée Expedition

In more ways than one the North Pole proved an irresistible
magnet to the early explorers of land, sea and air. In 1897, the
Swedish explorer August Andrée with two companions, Nils
Strindberg and Knut Fraenkel, attempted to drift over it by
balloon. They set out from Dane's Island, Spitzbergen, but failed
to return. Thirty-three years later, in 1930, Norwegian sailors
on nearby White Island, found their bodies, together with
Andrée's diaries, undeveloped photographic plates (see page 45),
letters from Strindberg to his fiancée, and the accompanying
menu, embedded in the ice.

Strindberg to his fiancée

22nd July, 1897

I wrote my last letter to you the same day we started; you must
have received it, of course. Of what happened since you have
learned from the accounts in the papers, etc., but qúite naturally
I shall describe my personal impressions too. It was grand when
it was at last determined that we should start. Andrée, Fraenkel
and I and Machuron went on shore and looked at the balloon from
the roof of the balloon-house. After we had discussed the possibilities of starting for a while Andrée asked us what we th(ought),
"Shall we try or not?" Fraenkel at first answered evasively, but
then said that (we?) should go on . . . I answered, "I consider that
we ought to try attempt it," and Svedenborg was of the same
opinion. Andrée was serious and said nothing. We all went on
board again. We did not yet know what was to be done, but when
we had come on board Andrée at once said to Ehrensvärd, "Well,
now we have been considering whether the start should be made
or not; my comrades insist on starting, and as I have no fully
valid reasons against it, I shall agree to it, although with some
reluctance. Will you, then, send all hands on shore to begin the
work of dismantling the balloon-house." And then everyone woke
up. The sailors had never worked so willingly before nor had the
carpenters. But now they were happy. I stayed on board awhile
talking to Ehrensvärd and the doctor and getting together my

things and some instruments that were still on board; Andrée went on shore to direct operations.

The harbour now presented a lively picture. Two sealers had just come in and one had been lying there before. The latter had to shift anchorage so as not to be in the way of the balloon. The weather was gloriously beautiful and the wind a fresh S.S.W.

I went ashore and packed a few articles in the car of the balloon and arranged some things here and there. The work of removing the front side of the house went on briskly, and one plank after the other was thrown down. The balloon stood there steady and secure protected against . . .? the winds by the canvas on the fourth and fifth floors. I took some photographs of the work. Then I went on board again with Svedenborg for a moment to fetch some things that had been forgotten, and then I compared chronometers for the last time. When we came on board breakfast was just being served, and we were persuaded to sit down to table in company with the chief and the doctor. The chief took in a bottle of champagne and a toast was drunk to a prosperous journey for us. Everyone enjoyed the breakfast, and when I went on shore again, time did not allow of the others getting anything to eat before the start. We had to satisfy ourselves with sandwiches and ale in the car. When I came on land again the work had made good progress and the balloon was being allowed to lift a little. Some small balloons were let go to test the direction of the wind, which proved favourable. It was quite an inspiring sight when the balloon had been lifted to such a height that the carrying-ring of the gondola left the ground. Andrée gave orders; everyone was willing and helpful and everything went well. I walked about taking photographs up to the last minute.

The balloon had now risen to such a height that the carrying-ring was a good distance above the ground, and was held fast by three ropes. The moment had come to attach the car. When this had been done and a sufficient number of bags of ballast had been taken on board, the time had come to say goodbye. This was done heartily and touchingly but without any signs of weakness. Then Andrée cries, "Strindberg and Fraenkel, are you ready to get into the car?" Yes! and so we got in. Now my thoughts turned for a moment to you and my dear ones at home. How would the journey succeed? And how fast my thoughts came, but I had to

The Andrée Expedition's balloon, *The Eagle*, soon after
landing on an ice floe north of Spitzbergen, 14 July 1897.
The film of this picture was taken by Andrée but remained
undeveloped until it was discovered, along with his body
and those of his two companions, thirty-three years later.

restrain them. I asked Machuron, who stood nearest and whom I
had found most congenial, to give my love to you. I wonder if a
tear did not tremble on my cheek at that moment. But I had to
see that the camera was in order and to be ready to throw out
ballast, etc. And now all three of us stand there on the top of the
car. There is a moment's solemn silence. Machuron says, "*Attendez
un moment! Calme.*" The right moment comes. "Cut away everywhere!" comes Andrée's voice. Three knives cut the three lines

holding fast the carrying-ring and the balloon rises amid the hurrahs of those below; we answer with a "Hurrah for old Sweden!" and then we rose from out the balloon-house. A peculiar sensation, wonderful, indescribable! But one has no time for much thought. I photographed for a while and then we see that we are descending. Ballast is thrown out, but we dip into the sea a moment. Then we rise again. And now everything seems to be going all right. We can still hear the hurrahs at a distance. I take one or two more photographs and then prepare the last card to you, which I intended to throw down on Hollander Naze. But forgot it. Good-night!

The 22nd July, 1897.

*   *   *

Two months later they were still fit enough to enjoy the following

Banquet 18 *Sept.* 97
on an ice-floe immediately east of ??? (*sic*)

Seal steak and ivory gull fried in butter and seal-blubber, seal liver—brain and kidneys. Butter and Schumacher bread.

Wine.   Chocolate and Mellin's-food flour with Albert biscuits and butter.

Gateau aux raisins.

Raspberry syrup sauce.

Port-wine 1834 Antonio de Ferrara given by the King.

Toast by Andrée for the King with royal Hurrah:

The national anthem in unison.

Biscuits, butter, cheese.

A glass of wine.

Festive feeling.

During the day the union-flag waved above the camp.

NILS STRINDBERG
The Andrée Diaries
trans. EDWARD ADAMS RAY

In the steps of Lindbergh. In August 1978, the Americans Larry Newman and Ben Abruzzo, together with Maxie Anderson (who took the picture) made the first trans-Atlantic balloon crossing, from Maine to France. The journey took just over five and a half days.

An Unusual Picnic Lunch. 'The balloon,' says the caption to this drawing in the *Illustrated London News* of 18 August 1906, 'is becoming a formidable rival to the motor-car and this has risen to the dignity of a Society craze. The balloon meets at Ranelagh have been particularly brilliant and interesting, and ladies are proving daring aeronauts.'

A voyage in the *Graf Zeppelin*

Although various attempts at building powered airships with
rigid frames had been made during the nineteenth century, it
was the German Graf von Zeppelin whose work at Lake Constance brought the idea to successful conclusion. And it was the
German military use of airships, or Zeppelins, during the First
World War that led to their commercial development in many
countries afterwards.

Once again the Germans led the field, their two most famous
airships, the *Graf Zeppelin* and the larger *Hindenburg*, making
many flights across the Atlantic to Rio de Janeiro and New York
without incident. Here is an account of the *Graf Zeppelin's* first
voyage to the United States in 1928. Her two senior officers were
among the most famous in airship history. Captain Hugo Eckener
had been *Zeppelin's* chief assistant, and the first officer, Ernst
Lehmann, after a distinguished career as a wartime airship
commander, went on to command the *Hindenburg*.

According to Ernst Lehmann, first officer of the *Graf Zeppelin*,
the worst night an airship ever lived through lay in store for the
LZ-127 on the return leg of its flight to the States.

The ship had arrived at Lakehurst on October 15 with most
of the lower cover of its port stabilizer torn away and with daylight
showing through a rip in the upper surface.While Eckener and his
passengers were being interviewed, the tired craft had been
unloaded of its cargo—which included packages for Abraham and
Straus, Strawbridge and Clothier, Bamberger's, and Gimbel Brothers—and docked alongside the *Los Angeles* in the air-station
hangar.

Tuesday the sixteenth saw the ticker-tape parade in New York
and the beginning of the repairs to the fin at Lakehurst. Working
atop long extension ladders from the floor, sitting in bosun's chairs
slung from the hangar overhead, or crawling in and on the fin
itself, men began to remove the torn and tattered fabric. The
blankets which had been rigged in flight to protect the gas cells
were also taken down.

While the fin was being stripped to its naked girders and
reclothed with new and stronger material, a strange and contagious

enthusiasm was rapidly taking possession of the American public. It was a fascination, sometimes wild and uncontrolled, for the *Graf Zeppelin* and for everything and everybody connected with it.

Highly infectious, this "Zeppelin Fever" spread throughout the country. Souvenirs from the *Graf*, especially pieces of fabric from the fin, were in great demand and brought fantastic prices. Journalists described the LZ-127 as the conqueror of Aeolus, the victor over Neptune. Cartoonists sketched the future in terms of Zeppelin hats, Zeppelin commuters, and a sure sign of the times, Zeppelin speakeasies.

Requests for return passage poured in. Hugh Allen of the Goodyear Tire and Rubber Company, acting as temporary agent for the Zeppelin Company, opened an office on the mezzanine of Thos. Cook & Son at 565 Fifth Avenue. The first transatlantic air ticket agency had been established.

All applications had to be in writing. Hundreds wanted to go. Only a handful could. The choice of passengers was Dr. Eckener's decision. One of the first to be rejected was a young Irishman who wanted to make the flight so that he could parachute from the ship and land on Erin's soil by air.

Meanwhile from Chicago came a loud and steady stream of requests, urgings, and demands that the LZ-127 visit the Midwest. Newspapers of the area were adamant: "We want to see the *Graf Zeppelin!*"

Eckener wanted them to see it too. He considered that it would be a good idea business-wise to show the ship off to Midwestern commercial and industrial leaders. They might become interested in supporting—and this meant financing—the construction of newer, larger and higher-performance Zeppelins to provide the world with a network of regularly flown international airship routes.

But first his command had to complete its repairs. As it did, an average of 20,000 people a day came to see it at Lakehurst. On Sunday, the 21st, an estimated 150,000 jammed into 40,000 automobiles and 10 special trains to descend upon the naval air station. Cars were backed up bumper to bumper for miles. In Lakewood, where taxis were reported refusing the trip at any price, sixteen hundred autos were counted going by in the space of an hour. People who were able to reach the station and find a place to park were relieved of their matches and lighters. Then, under the watchful eye of guards who were there to see that no sparks or fires were touched off anywhere near the hydrogen-filled shape, they were permitted to file through the hangar.

What they saw inside astonished some and overwhelmed others. The bright silvery hull towered high above them, making the visitors look like ants. Its great length stretched, an unbroken picture of parallel girders and aluminized fabric, from the northwest to the southeast end of the dock. Standing amidships one couldn't see bow or stern. It was that big!

One thing attracted every eye and evoked a million comments: the stabilizer.The one which had given so much trouble. The one which had almost destroyed the ship. There it was, in full view of all, its covering in various stages of replacement and repair.

People gazed at the fin, stared at the sleek aerial whale to which it was attached, and left the hangar convinced that seeing the *Graf* that day was the greatest thing that had happened to them in they couldn't remember when.

It took a week or more for the LZ-127 to be repaired and made ready for flight again. This meant that to undertake a Midwestern trip might shove the departure date for Germany back into November.

Eckener didn't like November. "It's the worst month for us to fly the Atlantic," he constantly reminded himself. "It's stormy and it's treacherous."

Still he wanted to take the ship to Chicago if possible. He tried to get off but bad weather over the central states and cross-hangar winds, which prevented him from undocking, forced the cancellation of the flight. Reluctantly he wired his friends in the Midwest OUR VISIT HAS BEEN POSTPONED BUT NOT ABANDONED.

A lot of Chicagoans were disappointed. There was grumbling and some comment that he should have stayed over and made the Midwestern tour even though it meant an Atlantic crossing in November. Eckener held firm.

"Twice we've flown the North Atlantic," he was quick to say. "And each time it was in October, a relatively favorable month. Let's not be overconfident. We still have much to learn."

Air travel of the future? The artist Frank Craig gives his
impression of how it might be, following the successful
maiden flight from Lake Constance of Graf Zeppelin's
newest airship. From the *Illustrated London News* of
27 June 1908.

With this he set the departure for Germany for the evening
of October 28.

The weather that night was cold and clear but the *Graf
Zeppelin* could not get airborne. A cross-hangar wind, the same
kind that had canceled the Chicago trip, was keeping the ship
from being taken out onto the field. The passengers, whose 44
pounds of allowed luggage had been stowed aboard under their
cabin berths, waited impatiently for the wind to slacken or change
direction. Fifty-four sacks of mail had been loaded. So had the
freight, which included copper engravings, a case of silk bearing
designs showing the ship in flight over New York, and a very
special 260-pound bale of cotton (air freight cost $1,300) which

was to be auctioned off in Germany and the proceeds distributed among the Zeppelin crew.

Towards 1.00 a.m. the rising and falling melody sung by the wind whistling around the hangar doors seemed not so loud. A calm was beginning to settle over the air station. This was what everyone was waiting for.

Hans Flemming walked quickly out into the middle of the hangar floor. His voice boomed and echoed: "Passengers on board! All passengers please get on board!"

The shrill trilling of a bosun's pipe told that the ground crew was being formed. Sleepy sailors were beginning to come over to the ship, slip the handling ropes from the rings bolted into the hangar deck, and take up their positions, lines in hand, to walk the *Graf* outside.

At the gangway leading to the main gondola, Knut Eckener was helping and hurrying the last of the twenty-five passengers aboard. Suddenly an attractive young woman rushed out of the crowd, threw her arms around him, and gave him a resounding good-by kiss. As she did she said, "This is from all the women of America." The young bachelor blushed. Ever since his arrival he had been singled out as the hero who fixed the fin. Handsome and blond, he reminded many of Lindbergh. He had been mobbed everywhere he went.

Slowly the hangar's massive twelve-hundred-ton doors began to separate. Driven by electrical motors, they literally inched their way apart. Twenty minutes passed before they were completely open. Meanwhile the gangway was removed, as was the wooden platform on which the aft engine gondola had been resting. The weights and sandbags, too, were taken away. Restrained only by the handling lines held by the three-hundred-man ground crew, the airship was free to float in the hangar. Except that it didn't float. It was "heavy" and wanted to settle to the floor. Two bags of water ballast had to be dumped before the Zeppelin was made light enough to float.

There was the sound of whistles and of authoritative, brief, and smartly given commands from the Navy ground handling officer. The slack was taken up on the lines. Hundreds of enlisted men's black shoes began to shuffle across the block-inlaid hangar floor.

From the lounge passengers looked out into the brightly lighted dock. As the 127's "walk" began, they could see the walls, the faces of friends and spectators, and on the opposite side of the hangar the outlines of the *Los Angeles* and of the small Navy blimps J-3 and J-4. Like a moving panorama, all this seemed to be passing by under the powerful all-revealing beams of lights and floodlights.

All of a sudden the lights were gone. They were outside. Out on the field.

More orders from the ground handling officer. Now the ship was being turned around and pointed into the wind. Eckener walked rapidly back and forth alongside, keeping an alert and critical eye on everything going on. Hans von Schiller did the same. Then, apparently satisfied that everything was ready for take-off, the two men climbed aboard, Eckener into the main gondola, and von Schiller through a hatch towards the stern.

Moments later came the command: "Up Ship!"

The sixty men on the control-car rail pushed. The engines came to life with a roar. The *Graf Zeppelin*, heartened by the powerful surge of lift it felt in the cold dry air, climbed rapidly to cruising height. Then it turned north to give its occupants a night-time view of New York City. From Manhattan the *Graf*, with sixty-four persons aboard, flew the length of Long Island, then to Block Island, Nantucket, and finally to Chatham, Massachusetts, where it left the mainland to begin its Great Circle course to Europe.

For most of the passengers, that first night out was an uncomfortable one. They were on edge to begin with, a result of the long and uncertain wait for the ship to be undocked. The hour of departure—1.55 a.m. on the twenty-ninth—plus the sight-seeing cruise over New York kept them up for most of the night. And when they finally did go to bed, they were too cold to sleep.

Fifty gallons of antifreeze had been put in the engines and in the water ballast. But the passenger cabins were unheated. Two brown camels-hair blankets, with a big black LZ-127 stenciled on each, had been provided for each berth. They weren't enough. Coats, jackets, and other clothing were piled atop the beds in none-too-successful attempts to keep warm during the night.

The travelers made quite a picture the next morning when

The *Graf Zeppelin*, named after its creator, taking shape. The next ring of the huge rib-cage lies waiting on the hangar floor.

they gathered in the lounge. Any pretense at formality had disappeared. For who could be formal wearing heavy socks, leather jackets, white wool sweaters, or anything else, regardless of style, as long as it was warm? Three U.S. Navy officers were along as nonpaying invited guests of Dr. Eckener and Luftschiffbau-Zeppelin. Commander M. R. Pierce, Lt. T. G. W. Settle, and Lt. C. E. Bauch, had brought along the fur-lined clothing which they wore aboard the *Los Angeles*. Doubtless they were the best prepared and the most comfortable. But by far the most picturesque was the gentleman who showed up wearing the raccoon coat.

There was plenty to talk about that morning. The lights of New York. The coffee and rolls served by the steward at four. The cold. The clouds and fog at daybreak. And the stowaway.

A blond nineteen-year-old boy, Clarence Terhune, had been uncovered by von Schiller. The young man, a caddy at the Rye Country Club, had slipped aboard at Lakehurst and stowed away among the bags of mail. A teen-age adventurer, this lad, attired in a bright red shirt, boasted of having stowed away on the maiden voyage of the Matson Line's steamer *Malolo*, of having crashed the gates at the Dempsey and Tunney fights, and of having hitchhiked across the length and breadth of the United States.

Eckener wasn't a bit happy to see the boy. He said very little to him and turned his unwelcome passenger over to Flemming, who soon had Terhune sweeping the floor and washing dishes. "When the papers hear of this," the captain frowned, "they'll make him a hero. Then we'll have to fight off stowaways on every trip we make."

The Zeppelin man was right. For a week Clarence Terhune would be front-page news. "So typically American" was how the Europeans thought of him. He received offers from publishers and editors for his firsthand impressions of the crossing. He was invited by many German families to be their houseguest. He even, so some said, received offers of matrimony. If it was fame that Clarence Terhune wanted, he had it, briefly.

But if his goal was to be first to stow away on a transatlantic flight, he was a victim of history. An airship rigger named W. W. Ballantyne and a Scottish kitten sneaked aboard the British R-34 on its flight to Long Island in 1919. Ballantyne had been driven out of hiding on that crossing by the smell of the gas cells, and

Wopsey, the feline stowaway, by the noise of the engines.

The morning wore on. At 10.15 the steamer *Laconia*, churning a spume-marked trail through the North Atlantic's grayish waters, radioed that a dirigible had just passed it. The ship's position: ninety miles southwest of Cape Sable, the lower tip of Nova Scotia.

Farther and farther towards the northeast the Zeppelin droned. The farther north it progressed, the warmer the outside air became. A front was surely waiting ahead, a front that the Lakehurst weather map had failed to show. The isobars, or lines of equal pressure, on the chart had shown a giant high-pressure system of good weather extending from the American coast to the shores of Ireland. According to this map, the *Graf Zeppelin* should have had smooth sailing all the way across. But the year was 1928. Weather-reporting stations in the North, particularly those which could advise of cold fronts with their accompanying air masses pushing down from the Arctic, were few in number and far between. Many cold fronts were apt to be missed and not reported. The ship was rapidly nearing one of these.

It came upon the line of cold- and warm-air demarcation shortly after noontime. A chicken lunch, catered by Louis Sherry of New York and prepared by a master chef borrowed for the flight from the North German Lloyd steamship line, was being finished in the lounge. A few dishes slipped to the floor and a bottle or two of whisky overturned as the ship's nose entered and rose in somewhat turbulent air. After ten or fifteen seconds the LZ-127 righted itself, returned to an even keel, and continued making its way along as if nothing had happened. From the windows, passengers and officers could look back and see a wall of gray-black clouds being rapidly left behind.

The wind had shifted, changing from the northwest to the southwest. This gave the *Graf* a direct on-the-tail push and a very good ground speed. At two that afternoon a radio message from D-E-N-N-E reported the ship making 103 miles an hour over the water. The sky had cleared and become a friendly and radiant blue.

Not for long, however. An overcast began to form, a thick gray canopy which hung a thousand feet or so above the ocean's restless surface. For a while Eckener made his way under this cover of clouds. When their base lowered to the water, he climbed the ship and flew above them. But when they reached three thousand feet in height, he plowed ahead into the bank itself.

He had no reason to be concerned about flying blind through this drab and milky horizonless mass of saturated air. He knew his approximate position and his ground speed, then about eighty knots. He was at a safe altitude. The air was relatively smooth. And he could be sure that the *Graf Zeppelin* was the only aircraft anywhere around in the sky.

"This is a typical Newfoundland fog," he thought to himself. "If we hold to our present course, we should find ourselves getting out of it about 150 miles south of Cape Race."

The ship moved on with no hint that any trouble lay ahead.

Suddenly—it was about 5.00 p.m.—the *Graf* began to buck and lurch and then to twist and roll. The nose went up. Then it pitched back down. The bow moved widely from left to right, yawing incessantly and twisting and turning in a turbulent dance staged in the murkiness of a fog-filled sky.

For those accustomed to flying in an airplane in severe turbulence, of course the airship's pitching, yawing and rolling motion seemed comparatively mild. There was none of the sudden and violent riding of up- and downdrafts, their effects being absorbed by the Zeppelin's length and size. Inherently and incessantly the ship tried to return to its normal flying attitude. Constantly it sought to steady itself. That the LZ-127 was in the midst of a violent storm was mainly apparent to the passengers by what they saw out the windows, by the sensations which they felt as heavy gusts struck the hull, and by the irregular beat and hum which they heard coming from the large wind-driven generator located at the extreme aft end of the gondola.

Actually there was probably more genuine concern in the control room than in the passenger spaces. The experienced Zeppelin men knew that no large dirigible should normally carry on as their ship was doing.

Eckener had ordered half speed. The pounding of the struggling engines had dropped to a lower-pitched grumble of throttled-back horsepower. Even so, with the rpm's reduced, the unpredicted aerial ballet continued.

If anything, it got worse. The girders creaked. The whole structure groaned in loud complaint.

Standing in the catwalk, one could see the ship bend—up to two feet—as its structure flexed and gave in response to the pounding it was taking.

The officers on the bridge were thankful that the *Graf* had this resiliency built into it. Nevertheless they wore worried looks. Even Eckener found himself beginning to wonder if the LZ-127 would be torn apart in the air. Their minds kept going back to two things. One was the ship's unusually long and thin profile, a design which critics had predicted would snap in half in severe weather. The other was the location of the main gondola so far forward. For better balance of forces and structural strength, should it have been placed, instead, closer to the center of the ship?

As the men in the control room stared ahead, to the side, and below for some explanation of what was going on, Eckener suddenly remarked, "I think we're over land. This turbulence must be the result of gale winds beating against the cliffs of Newfoundland. Somewhere there must be a hole in this stuff. We've got to find it and take a look at what lies below."

Moments later he gave a start: "Look! There's one!" Then, seeing it close in before the others could find it, he added, "I'm not sure but I think I saw rocks down there."

For several minutes those near him stared, peered, and imagined as they tried to make their eyes adjust to see what Nature was hiding outside. At first they couldn't make out a thing. Just fog. Then they began to catch momentary glimpses of the ocean's surface, angrily streaked with the foam of tossing whitecaps. Finally they came to a large gap in the shroud of water vapor obscuring their view.

Sure enough, there *were* rocks below. The *Graf Zeppelin* was flying over a steep, rugged, and primitive shoreline. But how could this be? How could they have wandered two hundred miles off their course?

A drift reading gave the answer. The navigator checked the ship's movement over the water. "Wind southeast, seventy miles!" he called out.

Eckener could hardly believe his ears. And the navigator his eyes. Yet confirmation was had simply by looking out the window. Pointed into the wind at half its normal engine power, the airship could be seen to be drifting rapidly tailfirst towards the northwest.

Inexplicably the *Graf Zeppelin* had suddenly come upon unpredicted winds of hurricane force. One of the early clues to the speed-up of low-pressure systems as they move over the Gulf of St. Lawrence had been accidentally discovered. The steersman was given a new heading, one which, as wind and time allowed, would gradually take the *Graf* in a northeasterly direction away from the storm. But although they knew that they were off the triangular-shaped coast of Newfoundland, they weren't sure just where. The watch out the windows continued as searching eyes tried to identify the geography over which they were passing. Night had fallen but a full moon, the same that had illuminated their Lakehurst take-off, was trying to break through. For a brief time it did, spreading shimmers of bright reflected light over the open water, the wet and glistening rocks, and the many small islands below.

Finally in the darkness a definite fix was possible. The welcome sight of a lighthouse beam could be seen describing flashing circles in the sky. It lay off to the right. "That's probably Trinity Bay," Flemming commented. "If so, then we've reached the northeast coast."

Not long after that the *Graf Zeppelin* was over the waters of the Atlantic once more.

It had begun to get cold again in the lounge. The passengers were tired and restless. They hardly touched their supper of pâté de foie gras, caviar canapés, and Westphalian ham. They played with the chow puppy which was aboard. And they looked out at the blackish white-topped waters boiling beneath. The waves were high as houses. By nine that evening the salon was largely deserted. Most of the twenty-four men and one woman had gone to bed. But those who did stay up were well rewarded by what they saw.

White spots began to appear on the boiling seas. Ice floes! At first there were just a scattered few. Then as the minutes passed, they became larger and more numerous. Some could be seen slamming violently into another with a resounding crash followed by a spray of ice slivers and particles. Behind the floes came icebergs. Ten or fifteen of them. Small ones, yet big enough to have steep walls, jagged peaks, and rugged pits and crevices.

The night progressed. Gradually the laboring Zeppelin pulled away from the zone of blinding fog, violent turbulence, low-hanging clouds, hurricane winds, and rain mixed with snow. Slowly it left behind a weather situation which the St. John's, Newfoundland, radio station saw fit to describe as "a wild night".

With the coming of daybreak, things improved rapidly. The wind abated and shifted around behind the tail. Sea and air began to moderate. Radio contact, which had been broken since about four o'clock the previous afternoon, was re-established. Then came the most encouraging sign of all, the sun. Although surface vessels were still having a rough time of it in the running sea, conditions had changed so much in the air that the engines were stopped one at a time to be checked and rested. The airship was halfway home by that time.

From mid-ocean the *Graf Zeppelin* uneventfully proceeded to the Bay of Biscay, crossed the coast at the mouth of the Loire River, and headed across a fog-draped France for its Friedrichshafen hangar. It arrived over Lake Constance shortly after four in the morning on November 1 but circled until seven, waiting for visibility to improve and for the ground crew to assemble. Then it slowed to a stop over the field, dropped its handling lines. and valved off hydrogen. Quickly the ship was brought to the ground.

Eckener looked out the window at the welcoming crowd. Despite lack of sleep on the crossing, he was cheery and smiled happily at everyone. He wasn't saying much, however, simply "Good morning." He watched while his passengers, all dutifully enrolled in the Transoceanic Air Passengers Club, disembarked. And he looked on with disgust at the mob of teen-age girls who rushed stowaway Terhune off his feet, hugging him, and carrying him to the Zeppelin Company offices, where the American consul at Stuttgart was waiting to shake his hand and give him his passport.

With the passengers off, the mail—101,683 pieces of it—was unloaded. Then the cargo. And the bale of cotton. It would go by rail to Bremen to be paraded through the streets on a truck carrying German, American, and city flags. Thousands would stand on the corners and sidewalks to see the procession. When auctioned off, it would bring $3,500 for the benefit of the *Graf Zeppelin's* crew. Finally it would be presented to the City Museum as perhaps the most celebrated cotton bale in history.

The night of the ship's return a banquet was held at Friedrichshafen's Kurgarten Hotel to celebrate the 71-hour and
4,500-mile flight from America. Eckener, of course, was the principal speaker. A man who always played down his difficulties and
who didn't like to talk about battles with the elements or close
calls in the air, he surprised the guests by saying:

"This last trip made me think of God. I never regarded it as a
small thing to cross the ocean in an airship, but never until now
had I quite realized what it meant."

He admitted that the LZ-127 had been caught in a weather
situation which at times threatened to break it in two. "We have
not yet conquered the ocean," he added. "But we know now that
we have a good ship. It had to be good to endure that storm!"

And Hugo Eckener could safely make that statement. For
despite misgivings regarding the ship's new and unusual design,
the *Graf Zeppelin* had emerged from its critical Newfoundland
trial without damage. Not a girder had collapsed. Not a wire had
snapped. Not a rip had been made in the outer cover.

Ludwig Dürr had built his airship well.

J. GORDON VAETH,
Graf Zeppelin

Two Airship Disasters

1930: The R.101

Britain never embraced airships in the whole-hearted way that Germany did. Her commitment to them may be said to have begun and ended in 1930 with the R.101's inaugural flight of the Empire service to India.

From the time she was moored, in the morning of October 2, until the eve of her departure, the roads to Cardington poured in their streams of traffic. Hour by hour the people of Britain collected in their crowds to see the latest wonder of the skies. They too were proud of her in a way they could not have defined, and few among them did not envy the lucky passengers and crew their historic journey.

Throughout that day, and the day following, lorries arrived, and baggage and cases were transferred to the lift in the tower. Finally, on October 4, R101 was ready to leave, and by midday the important passengers began to arrive. Lord Thomson, Secretary for Air—Air Vice Marshal Sir W. Sefton Brancker—Wing Commander R. B. B. Colmore—Lt.-Col. V. C. Richmond—Major C. H. Scott, Assistant Director of Passenger Airship Development.

Fifty-four in all, passengers and crew, and surely there was never so notable a gathering for such an event. Veterans of airship travel, pioneers of rigid-airship design, men who had worked together for years for the development and perfection of lighter-than-air craft. All were to share the honour of the first official flight in the mighty craft which represented the culmination of all their ideas. In fact, it can be truthfully said that when the last man walked aboard, from the balcony of the tower through the hatchway into the nose of the ship, the heart, soul, and brains of

British airship science were collected in that silver envelope.

The eve of the great adventure was at hand. Pressmen in their telephone booths were sending last paragraphs across the world. Tiny figures could be seen behind the glass windows of the promenade decks, waving to their friends and relations on the ground below.

As the light of the autumn evening began to fail, and the shadow of the giant ship merged with the gloom of the ground, the hum of machinery was heard from above. White—red—green-white, the navigation lights sprang out from the twilight, marking the extremities of the great envelope, and the lamps in the passengers' quarters glowed comfortably along the hull. A sigh seemed to rise from the crowd below, and then a hush fell as zero hour approached.

Gradually, one by one, the five engines burst into life. Stabs of flame from the exhausts increased the spectacle of awe. The rumble and roar of 2,400 horse-power shook the air. A cheer went up. The flight had begun.

Slowly at first, and then more swiftly as she turned into her course and gathered speed, R101 decreased in size. Came a final twinkle of the control tower telegraph bell, and all that was left was the beat and drone of engines. The red, green, and white lights merged with the stars—and might well have been stars but for their movement. Suddenly quiet after their cheering, the crowd stood still to watch, until there was nothing left to watch. Nothing, that is, save two oblong patches of light behind which, impossible though it seemed men were walking, talking, and laughing. Then even the lights disappeared into the distance. R101 had gone.

*   *   *

Looking down from where they stood at the windows, the passengers watched as the fields swung round below them. Ahead and astern the mighty engines beat their rhythmic note. The stars were out, and the world seemed very far away. Car lights pointed out the roads, illuminating hedges, trees, and telegraph poles as they sped about their business; but soon, as the distance increased, all earthly things lost shape, and but for occasional dabs of light there might well have been no earth at all. The great ship droned on into the night, and one by one the passengers turned from the windows, finding more interest in the novel and luxurious surroundings than the vault of darkness outside.

Rain began to fall as they passed over London, but its noise was slight, and barely heard above the drumming of the engines. A few spots appeared on the windows, and soon they were running with water, blown with the wind, but if anything this only served to increase the atmosphere of comfort in the gaily lighted passenger quarters. The select company sat and chatted from the depths of softly upholstered chairs and settees. The door of the smoking-room opened and closed as stewards came and went. Ice tinkled against glass, and aromatic clouds of blue smoke coiled lazily upwards from the tips of glowing cigars. The scene might well have been set in any of London's West-end clubs for all a stranger would have known. Only occasional scraps of conversation—guesses as to height and speed—inquiries about weather conditions—marked the difference between that half-hour before dinner, and the half-hour before dinner in any one of the houses several hundred feet below.

The weather report received on board before leaving Cardington was more than fair. At the most R101 would encounter winds of twenty to thirty miles per hour. There was no other feeling than that of extreme confidence amongst passengers, crew, and officers. The ship was behaving splendidly, and for all the emotion shown by those in charge, or at work on their various jobs, they might have done nothing more adventurous in their lives. London was reached at about 8 p.m., and eight minutes later the second weather report came through by radio from Cardington.

"Over London. All well," R101 radioed Cardington at 8.21 p.m., giving details of winds and clouds. "Course now set for Paris. Intend to proceed via Paris, Tours, Toulouse, and Narbonne."

Puzzled, no doubt, by the weather report which indicated a turbulent area over southern France, the airship's commander had chosen a course which he estimated would carry them round the disturbance. He was certainly not to know the true facts of the position—that R101 was already trapped in the middle of a wide circle of winds, and that sooner or later she would have to battle through them, no matter what course she took. Those conditions had not existed when the ship slipped her mast about two and a half hours earlier. However, as her radio message shows, all was well on board, and there was not the least anxiety felt about the weather ahead. Conversation sparkled as the rain beat down unheeded outside, and R101 throbbed her majestic way through the night, past London, on towards Sussex and the coast.

"Crossing coast in vicinity of Hastings," crackled the airship's radio shortly after half-past nine. "It is raining hard and there is a strong south-westerly wind . . . Engines running well at cruising speed giving 54.2 knots . . . Gradually increasing height so as to avoid high land. Ship is behaving well generally and we have begun to recover water ballast."

Forward from the passengers' quarters, in the control room, one of the officers was busily engaged checking the airship's drift, making fullest use of their last sight of the English coast. The commander, having despatched the radio message was standing by. Beside him the height coxswain, eyes on the altimeter, hands on the elevator wheel. The coastline passed astern and R101 droned out over the Channel.

Seeing the altimeter needle drop to 900 feet, the commander took the wheel from the height coxswain, and pulled the ship up to 1,000 feet.

"Do not let her go below 1,000 feet," he said; and he handed the wheel back to the coxswain. Every man of the nine officers and thirty crew not only knew his job but was ready and willing to turn his hands to anything for the care and welfare of the ship. Even the commander, veteran in airship experience, would not have been found wanting for the most menial task. Competent, cool, confident, all were as much at home riding the clouds as they would have been with the simplest task on land.

"Crossing the French coast at Pointe de St. Quentin," announced R101's radio at 11.36. "Wind 245 true, thirty-five miles per hour."

And as the great ship of the skies left the dark waves behind her, heading through the night for Paris, the cheerful company of passengers drifted away from their tables to glance through the windows, or to stroll about the smoking-room for a leisurely half-hour before turning in. Stewards cleared away the table-cloths, and the first day of airship routine drew to its close. The atmosphere of comfort and goodwill on board was perfect, and, more than

The comfort of airship travel. Dinner in the *Graf Zeppelin*.

satisfied with R101's behaviour, the commander despatched a further radio message at midnight:

"2400 G.M.T. 15 miles S.W. of Abbeville. Average speed thirty-three knots. Wind 243 degrees (West South West), thirty-five miles per hour. Altimeter height 1,500 feet. Air temperature 51° Fahrenheit. Weather—intermittent rain. Cloud nimbus at 500 feet. After an excellent supper our distinguished passengers smoked a final cigar, and having sighted the French coast have now gone to bed to rest after the excitement of their leave-taking. All essential services are functioning satisfactorily. The crew have settled down to watch-keeping routine."

But the altimeter, perfect and accurate as it may be, takes no account of what goes on beneath it. Over the Channel, when the commander took over the wheel and pulled the ship up to 1,000 feet, there was exactly that distance between her and the choppy waves below. But the sea had given way to land, and rising up

through the darkness, claiming the lion's share of the height shown
on the dial, were hills, rising ground, and trees. The commander
could see none of these when he despatched his midnight message.
Only his maps could tell him— and they were lying, because the
wind had already blown R101 off her course.

Droning along through cloud and rain, all unknown to those
on board, the airship headed nearer and nearer to the boundaries
of the stormy circle in which she was flying; and below her the
French peasants ran from their houses to see her pass—nearer
and nearer to them as she crossed the hilly country.

"Less than half her own length from the ground," said one
who saw her pass to the west of Poix aerodrome soon after
midnight. And then:

"What is my true bearing?" asked the commander by radio at
one minute to one.

The appeal, flashed out through the night, was picked up by
radio stations at Le Bourget, Valenciennes, and Croydon. Bending
over their direction-finding gear, tuning in to the airship's radio
note, the operators took rapid bearings of her position and com-
municated with one another.

"One kilometre north of Beauvais," came the reply. And at
approximately 2 a.m. R101 thundered over Beauvais, rousing the
inhabitants with the roar of her engines. They came running from
their beds to see her as she battled her way through the wind and
rain. Windows rattled up and doors were flung open, and men
came rushing into the streets and market square to watch her go.
She passed the town and flew on over the fields, and the ground
still rose beneath her. A shepherd heard her engines as he lay in
his hut, and he saw her lights appear, as he said, "like the lights
of a passing train."

But the excitement was only on the ground. Up in the airship
the passengers slept, oblivious to the commotion below. The hands
of the clock in the control car crept on to 2 a.m. The new watch
came on duty. Seated on one of the luxurious settees, alone in the
blue and gold smoking-room, Mr. Leech, a foreman engineer, was
enjoying a brief period of relaxation after an inspection of the
engines. On the table before him stood a syphon and some glasses,
last traces of the cheerful and carefree evening spent by the
company of distinguished guests. The flight so far had been bumpy,

but everything was running according to plan. Second by second
the minutes ticked away, and the giant ship droned on past
Beauvais ... 2.3 ... 2.4 ... 2.5 ... 2.6 ...

Suddenly there was a lurch. The ship was diving. The glasses
and the syphon fell to the floor. The peaceful mood of that solitary
occupant of the smoking-room was rudely disturbed as he was shot
along the settee.

But there was no cause for alarm. In bad weather an airship
will often go into a steep dive before she can be checked ... 2.7
... Mr. Leech picked up the glasses and the syphon and replaced
them on the table. He slid the table back to its proper position as
the ship regained her normal angle ... 2.8 ... Another lurch, a
violent lurch ... a jangle of telegraph bells ... the door of the
smoking-room swung open ... Beyond the door there was a great
flame.

*   *   *

Sleeping peacefully, dreaming, if at all, of the morrow—of sunrise
over verdant mountain slopes—the passengers of the giant R101
were jolted into terrible wakefulness as the ship crunched into the
soft, wet earth. In that split second which preceded the tragedy
the control telegraphs had tinkled their message. The engines were
already slowing ... stopping ... a member of the crew was already
on his way to release emergency ballast. But he never got there.
It was all too late.

Only at the very last moment did those in the control-car
realise that R101's journey was ended, but even they had no idea
of the awfulness of what was to follow. Orders were given but
there was no time to carry them out. Church, a rigger who was on
duty in the car, was already leaving after his watch when he
received the command to release emergency water ballast. But
the ship was diving. Church was thrown clear of the wreck but he
died in hospital from his injuries. He was barely able to reiterate
his last order. He did not recover sufficently to remember more.

Mr. Disley, the electrician, was also asleep when the ship began
her plunge to doom. The lurch awakened him, and he too felt her
recover. Like Mr. Leech in the smoking-room close by, however,
he did not attach any great significance to the dive.

"It did not seem long at the bottom," he said afterwards. "It just appeared that it was only a matter of the coxswain changing the elevator from one way to the other."

But then, as the ship regained her level keel, the chief coxswain passed the switchboard. He had, apparently, just left the control-car, and was on his way aft with his message.

"*We are down, lads,*" he said.

He said it quite simply and without excitement—and he passed on down the ship towards where the crew were sleeping. He never reached them.

There was no panic. There was no reason for panic then. All that could be done in the brief instant before the ship grounded, was done. None guessed the horror that was to follow. In the port midship gondola, Alfred Cook, an engineer, had just come on watch. Blake the engineer, whom he had relieved, had reported everything Okay and climbed back into the ship to sleep. Cook made a quick, preliminary inspection of the engine and instruments with his torch. Then, all at once the ship dived, and simultaneously the telegraph rang . . . "*Slow.*" Ringing back in the usual way to the control car, Cook slowed his engine. And as he did so the ship dived again. There was nothing unusual about the dive, but coupled with the order to slow his engine, Cook had a feeling that something serious was happening. They had been cruising uninterruptedly since leaving Cardington. He leaned across the car to peer out into the night, and at that instant R101 struck. He stopped the engine immediately, but as he did so the whole car fell away from the ship. A few minutes earlier, and it would have been Blake, not he, who fell to safety.

From the starboard midship engine gondola another engineer had just walked back to sleep, relieved by engineer Savoury. Savoury had not even the warning of his control telegraph before it happened. Engines were being rung to slow from the control car, but there was not sufficient time for all the orders. Savoury was standing in the darkness by his engine when the dive came. He was hurled backwards against the starting engine. There was a flash of scorching flame which singed and half blinded him. That was all.

Aft, in the rear engine-car, one of those unaccountable freaks of fortune was taking place. Mr. Bell, like other engineers on watch, was due to be relieved at 2 a.m. But his relief, Mr. Binks, was late. He arrived in the car at about five minutes past two, and they talked. Second by second the precious minutes ticked away. They were still talking when the telegraph rang . . . "*Slow.*" The ship was diving. They looked at each other. And then, within a second of obeying the order came the crash. The engine car sank . . . dragged along the ground . . . the bottom tore away . . . flames belched in through the opening.

There was no more warning than that. Those in the control tower were still passing out orders, and ringing their quick precise messages, when the ground loomed out of the darkness. The R101 was down—or would be down in a matter of seconds. The altimeter needle, moving slowly round the dial as the ship sank, told the tale only too plainly. It was disaster, of course, but more of a failure than disaster. None could foresee that wave of flame from which practically nothing was to escape. The engines were at slow, or slowing. The airship's speed was almost nil as she neared the ground. Had her gasbags been filled with helium instead of hydrogen it is unlikely that even one of the fifty-four would have sustained any injury worth speaking of. But in those gasbags was five and a half million cubic feet of the most explosive of all substances.

Awakened by the lurch, and hearing the coxswain's words, Mr. Disley reached for the switches. Instantaneous and urgent thought impelled him to "kill" all live circuits. He had time to pull one switch only. He did all he could. Many men less quick could not have achieved that much. But it was in vain:

"I heard a crash and a series of explosions," he said. "There were blinding flashes all round, and the next thing I knew was that the ship was on fire. She flared up in an instant, from stem to stern, and I cannot tell how the fire started, but I think it began amidships rather than in the bows.

"The fire was awful—awful. It is impossible to describe it. It was just one mass of flame, roaring like a furnace. My one idea was to get out of the ship. I threw myself at the fabric covering and tried to break through but could not.

"Then I sat down, and I found myself sitting on wet grass. I was under the airship, you understand, and the fabric was already torn where I sat. So I crawled on the ground following the tear, until I found myself outside. I went along to see if I could get anybody out, but nothing could be done. It was all over in a minute."

   Those who had run into the streets of Beauvais to see the giant liner's majestic passing, heard the sudden lull of her engine noise. They saw a red glow of fire spread over the trees and houses. They felt the air tremble from the thud of distant explosions. The shepherd, who had turned from watching the sky to look over his sheep, was horrified to see the dark night suddenly filled with flame. The flash of explosions lighted up the sky, and where the airship had been was nothing but a dancing, crimson blaze. At eight minutes past two the colossus, R101, pride of all Britain, and keynote of world news, was fighting her way stolidly and bravely through the elements and darkness. At nine minutes past two she lay, a roaring inferno, crumpled across the fringe of a wood in the heart of the French countryside.

MILES HENSLOW,
Loss of the R101
from *50 Great Disasters and
Tragedies that shook the World*

1937: The *Hindenburg*

The take-off of the *Hindenburg* for the first scheduled North Atlantic flight in the 1937 series took place on May 3rd, at 8 p.m. Central European Time, from the new Rhein-Main World Airport, in ideal weather conditions. On board were thirty-six passengers representing five nationalities. The Danish Minister of Transportation, who was to have made the trip with one of his officials, had to cancel his reservation at the last moment. In command of the ship was Captain Max Pruss whose airship experience dates back to the world war; in his crew were included two other captains, Albert Sammt and Heinrich Bauer. As Director of the Deutsche Zeppelin Reederei, Captain Lehmann came along on this 1937 inaugural trip; also Captain Anton Wittemann of the *Graf Zeppelin*. Although the normal crew of the *Hindenburg* was about forty, a considerable number of younger airship men was carried in addition for training purposes, bringing the total crew up to sixty-one. Among them were Dr. Rudiger, the first doctor ever to be carried regularly in the crew of any commercial aircraft, and the first airship stewardess, Mrs. Imhof. There were, then, ninety-seven persons on board the *Hindenburg* on this trip.

Within a short time the city of Cologne was reached, the shadowy outline of its famous cathedral silhouetted against the city's lights. The course then proceeded as customary via Holland to the North Sea; there thunderstorms over the Channel made it advisable to detour to the north. For a while the weather remained unpleasant but not severe, with bad visibility; neither the French nor English Coasts were sighted. Over the ocean the ship took a course somewhat more northerly than that generally taken by steamers at this time of the year. On the afternoon of May 5th, the coast of North America was first sighted near Newfoundland. Large horseshoe-shaped ice fields pushed their way into the sea and closer to the shore numerous icebergs of varied and fantastic forms floated about. For the benefit of the passengers, the ship flew low over the crystal-like, glittering ice forms.

Now the ship's course was changed to a generally southerly direction, passing the lighthouse at Cape Race and several lonely coastal cities. As had been experienced on practically the entire trip, head winds persisted, now blowing at 45 to 50 miles-per-hour velocity at flying levels. However there was no turbulence during the flight, merely the slowing down of the ship's speed over the surface because of opposing winds. It was noon on May 6th before Boston was reached; by three o'clock the ship was over New York City and then soon headed southward for the vicinity of Lakehurst. Although the scheduled time of arrival set many months in advance had been 6 a.m. on May 6th, the prevalence of head winds had caused Captain Pruss to radio that he would delay the landing time until 6 p.m. that day. Hence although the ship arrived over the Lakehurst field at about a quarter past four, no attempt was made to land before the announced time of 6 p.m. since the arrangements necessarily involved not only the ground crew at a designated time but also all those officials who are customarily associated with the official entry of a foreign commercial vessel.

Meanwhile, a weather "front" accompanied by rain and thunderstorms was moving in from the westward. Cruising in an area a few miles south and southeast of Lakehurst, the *Hindenburg* awaited the passage of this front at Lakehurst, then proceeded westward coming in behind the front. Although the ground crew stood in readiness at six o'clock, heavy rain and a thunderstorm made it advisable for the ship to stay clear until the weather improved. As the thunderstorm passed and the rain practically ceased, I sent a radio message to Captain Pruss recommending that he come on in and land. Hence, at about 7 p.m., Eastern Daylight Saving Time, the *Hindenburg* came into view and passed over the station on a northerly course at an altitude of 500 to 600 feet to have a look at surface conditions. The ground crew consisted of some ninety Navy enlisted personnel together with a proportionate number of naval officers, and 138 civilians recruited from the vicinity, practically all of whom had at one time or another been employed at the station and hence were familiar with airships and their landing and mooring. After circling, the *Hindenburg* came back over the station, adjusted her trim and static conditions by valving hydrogen and dropping ballast in perfectly normal fashion, headed into the wind, descended to about 200 feet altitude, backed down on her engines to check the headway of the ship, and at 7.21 dropped her manila landing ropes to the ground. It was raining almost imperceptibly and while the light of the sinking sun was dimmed by the overcast cloud condition, the weather was definitely improving.

On board, all members of the crew were at their landing stations, eager to land and reservice their proud ship and be off again on schedule eastward over the Atlantic. In the passageways near the gangway, the passengers' baggage had been assembled ready to be passed out immediately upon reaching the ground. In the spacious lounge rooms near the open observation windows, most of them on the starboard side with their passports and papers ready for examination there by the boarding officials, were crowded nearly all the passengers trying to recognize friends on the ground and watching the landing operation.

The ground crew at once grabbed the ship's landing lines, connected them to corresponding ground lines and began the operation of hauling them taut as the first step in the landing maneuver. From the very nose of the ship, the steel mooring cable, by which the ship was to be pulled in to its connection on the mooring mast, began to make its appearance. Following the passage of the thunderstorm, the wind had become light and variable, scarcely two miles-per-hour velocity on the surface and only some six knots at the ship's altitude; the direction there was some 90° different from that on the surface. Before the slack of the landing ropes could be taken in by the ground crew, a light gust from the port side caused the ship to move very very slowly to starboard and also gradually tightened the port manila landing rope.

At 7.25, or just four minutes after the landing ropes had been dropped, I saw a burst of flame on top of the ship just forward of where the upper vertical fin attaches to the hull. It was a brilliant burst of flame resembling a flower opening rapidly into bloom. I knew at once that the ship was doomed, for nothing could prevent that flame from spreading to the entire volume of hydrogen with which she was inflated. There was a muffled report and the flames spread rapidly through the after quarter of the ship. In the control room, the officers were not aware that anything was wrong until they felt a shudder through the ship that reminded them of the snapping of a landing rope, but a quick glance assured them that it was something else. As the stern section of the ship lost its buoyancy in the fire, it began to settle to the ground on almost an even keel, ablaze throughout and sending huge pillars of flame and smoke to great heights, particularly as the fuel oil began to burn.

As the stern settled, the forward three-quarters of the ship, still having its buoyancy, pointed skyward at an angle of about 45°. Through the axial corridor of the ship, in reality a huge vent extending along the very central axis, the flame shot upward and forward as though it were going up a stack. Although the travel of the flame was actually progressive, it spread forward so rapidly and so quickly encompassed the entire length of the ship that to some it may have seemed almost instantaneous. The forward section was not long in following the stern to the ground, and within less than a minute from the first appearance of the fire, the ship had settled, not crashed, on to the ground and lay there

The end of the *Hindenburg*, and of the airship era. On
6 May 1937 the flagship of Germany's fleet burst into
flames when about to moor at Lakehurst, New Jersey.

writhing and crackling from the hottest flame that man knows.

The feelings of those on the ground are difficult to describe.
Visitors who stood in the assigned visiting space several hundred
yards away were stricken dumb or fled in horror at this amazing
spectacle. In order not to be caught under the burning ship, the
ground crew were ordered to run from the immediate vicinity.
But even before the ship had touched the ground, they had dashed
back to effect such rescues as might be possible. In the ground
crew were many men who were not only acquainted with many
of those on board the ship but were also familiar with the parts
of the ship where passengers and crew were located. To such places

they went immediately. On board the ship there was little time
for warning or help. Some were surprised in their cabins or at
their posts of duty and never knew what overtook them. Others
heard shouts from within and from without the ship to jump
through the windows and many of the survivors got out by this
method. At first glance, it seemed impossible that human beings
could come out alive from such an inferno. As I stood off to one
side, spellbound by this most unexpected tragedy, I saw the flames
eat rapidly along the fabric sides of the hull greedily devouring
the illustrious name "Hindenburg" letter by letter.

It is unfortunate that most of the passengers were gathered on
the starboard side and that they and perhaps others on board did
not realize that the wind on the surface was blowing directly onto
the port beam and hence was driving the flames to starboard.
Realization of this fact might have saved a few more lives. I do
not recall when I have been so startled as when I saw Chief
Steward Kubis, Watch Officers Ziegler and Zable, and several
others, suddenly emerge from the burning mass of wreckage totally
unharmed. There were of course some miraculous escapes, not all
of which will ever be recorded. One of the elderly women passengers,
as though led by a guardian angel, left the ship by the regular
hatchway with the calmness of a somnambulist, receiving only
minor burns. Others hearing the call to them to jump, went through
the open windows and were then led to safety. Mr. George Grant,
a British shipping man, escaped without a single scratch or burn
by jumping through a window, and then as he was picking himself
up to run away from the fire, suffered the great misfortune of
having another person leap from the same window and land
squarely in the middle of his back injuring him severely. Probably
the most miraculous escape was that of Werner Franz, a 14-
year-old cabin boy. As he jumped through a hatch in the bottom
of the ship and reached the ground, the searing flames began to
choke him. Just at that moment, a water tank opened up immediately above him discharging its entire contents upon him and
bringing him to his senses. Just then he spied an opening in the
wreckage free from flames, worked his way through it and emerged
into the open air from this fiery furnace totally unharmed and
thoroughly drenched. Another who escaped without injury was
Captain Anton Wittemann. Nelson Morris, an American passenger

and an experienced airship traveler, jumped through a window on the starboard side and then with his bare hands snapped the red hot structural members about him as though they were twigs and fought his way clear of the burning wreck with only minor burns.

Those in the control car, as had every member of the crew, stuck to their posts in accordance with the highest traditions. As the forward section of the ship settled to the ground, it rebounded slightly from the resiliency of the forward landing wheel. Then and only then came the word: "Now everybody out." There had been plenty of quick thinking in the control car during those seconds of descent. The normal impulse would have been to drop water ballast to ease the impact of the ship with the ground, but those in the control car in an instant decided not to drop it but to let the weight of that water remain in the ship as long as possible to bring the burning hull to the ground in the shortest space of time. In my opinion, this was one of the outstanding events in the whole disaster.

Captain Pruss was badly burned, but not so badly as Captain Lehmann who nevertheless was able to stagger away from the ship. Largely because there were many tons of fuel oil still remaining on board, the fire raged for more than three hours despite the efforts of all available fire fighting apparatus. Thirteen out of thirty-six passengers perished or died subsequently from injuries; of the sixty-one crew members twenty-two fell victims to this awful fire and one civilian member of the ground crew died of burns. To anyone having seen the tragedy, it seems remarkable indeed that out of 97 persons on board, 62 of them or nearly two-thirds have survived. Sad as was the loss of every one of them, no loss will be more keenly felt in the airship world than that of that outstanding pioneer Ernst Lehmann who succumbed to burns.

The above, written by Lehmann's great friend, Commander Charles Rosendahl, forms the last chapter of Lehmann's autobiography, *Zeppelin*, which his death prevented him from completing.

PIONEERS

The father of the aeroplane

Miss Phil stood by the circular opening, almost a glass-less window, built in the garden wall of The Green. Through it she could see out over the Dale, that long valley with slopes either side reaching to the trees of wooded Wyedale. People from the village were beginning to gather by the gate into the Dale, for word had got around that Sir George Cayley was to conduct an exciting experiment that very morning.

Miss Phil felt extremely nervous, knowing what this meant to George. In a way it was the culmination of at least the first part of his life-work, but, although she hated the thought, and although they had never put it into so many words, it could well be his last triumph. After all, in this year 1852, George was seventy-nine years of age, and although he showed little physical and no mental signs of growing old, yet by the very nature of things he could not expect to go on very much longer.

It was a nice day, with a little breeze and a few fluffy white clouds. What wind there was came from east to west, and Miss Phil knew that George had been forced to wait for such a day. He needed a steady, not gusty, breeze coming across the valley from one side or the other, a wind which the wings of his man-carrying glider could use in taking off from one slope towards the other.

The little crowd was encroaching on the field. They could see George's flying machine, beautiful in the sunshine, and they wanted to get a closer view. George had anticipated that and instructed the Brompton staff to keep their inquisitive friends at a safe distance.

Miss Phil felt a little sick. She wondered how George's coachman felt, with a chance of a place in history so soon to be his. She looked out and saw him there, standing beside George as they examined the machine for the last time to make sure that all was

in order. Her eyes searched the Brompton group for a sign of Lady
Sarah, but she was not to be seen. "Scarcely surprising," said Miss
Phil to herself, "after all, she is over eighty, and a very tired and
sick old lady." However, this meant that she herself could join
George on the hill.

Miss Phil got herself through the opening in the wall but not
without difficulty. She remembered the days when she and George
as children had played in that garden, scrambling through that
opening at full speed in a game of chase. They had often used the
garden at The Green as a change from the maze at Brompton, but
at seventy-four she found getting through the gap an adventure
in itself.

She went briskly towards the group beside George's machine
and stood behind him, well aware that he was conscious of her
nearness. She began, silently, to pray as the coachman climbed
into the boat-like nacelle. She heard George giving him his final
instructions and thought how strained they both looked.

George stood back, testing the wind by wetting his finger, and
holding it up. He gave the order to start, and as he did so his left
hand reached backwards. She took it, and pressed it.

The machine, on its tricycle undercarriage with those delicate
wheels George had invented, was drawn forward by an eager team
of young Brompton men.

She and George stood erect. She felt his hand tightening on
hers.

For an agonising moment it appeared that the machine would
not rise. And then suddenly it was off the ground, and rising fast.
Then it levelled out in free flight. Miss Phil found herself shouting
she knew not what. She also found herself alone. She saw George
giving a very fair imitation of a gallop as he followed the machine.
Miss Phil went after him, as she had so meekly done all her life,
but this time still shouting; they were far out-distanced by the
glider as it soared over the valley towards the other bank. It was
already perhaps two hundred yards ahead of them.

Then abruptly George stopped, and she nearly ran in to him.
She looked up quickly. He was staring at the machine with an
agony of apprehension in his eyes. The glider had dipped threat-
eningly . . . A moment later it levelled out again, but it had lost
height and was coming down, reasonably gently but much too fast;

In 1973 the test pilot Derek Piggott simulated the historic
experimental flight organised by Sir George Cayley, 'father'
of the aeroplane, in 1852. Piggott's flight took place near
Cayley's home at Brompton Vale in Yorkshire.

even she could see that.

It hit the far bank of the Dale too hard. It did not smash up,
but it seemed to crumple a little.

George was off again, and she followed him. The watchers were
all running with them now, intent on helping their friend the
coachman.

To their great relief they saw him step from the nacelle,
apparently unhurt. As they slowed to a walk the coachman came
running towards them. He reached his master, and his eyes still

betrayed his fright. For a moment he was quite unable to speak and Miss Phil felt the greatest sympathy for him. But suddenly the words came with a rush.

"Please, Sir George, I wish to give notice. I was hired to drive and not to fly."

But George was grasping his hand, tears of joy in his eyes. And everyone in the little crowd was laughing excitedly, scarcely realising that they had been privileged to see the first flight ever made by a fully-grown man in a heavier-than-air machine, the first flight ever made in an aeroplane.

Miss Phil turned away and walked quietly back towards the gate to the Dale, on her way to the Low Hall. She knew that George would be absorbed in his work, worrying out the lessons to be learned from the flight. Instead of enjoying the triumph of the first conquest of the air, he would be seeking to improve his gliding aeroplane and to adapt it to power-driven aerial navigation.

No doubt he would come and tell her all about it in the evening.

Miss Phil had witnessed the first free flight of a glider fitted with inherent lateral and longitudinal stability, adjustable fin and tailplane, nacelle with undercarriage, and pilot operated flying controls—in other words, all the basic features of every aeroplane flying today. But in fact this was the second glider Sir George Cayley designed and constructed which flew with a human passenger.

In the spring of 1848 the Dale had also been crowded by Brompton inhabitants there to witness an historic occasion. The machine was smaller than the 1852 glider, and a local boy of ten was its occupant. Most unfortunately his name has not been recorded and is lost to posterity, as is that of the coachman.

The experiment was entirely successful. The machine soared over the valley and landed gently as intended. A tactless local approached the delighted Sir George.

"But what is the good of it, Sir George?" he asked.

Quick as a flash came the retort:

"What is the good of a new-born baby?"

Sir George treated this only as a test flight. The boy was very light in weight, and only a flight with a fully-grown man would prove that aerial navigation was possible. For that Sir George had to wait until 1852.

Sir George was first described as the "Father of the Aeroplane", by W. S. Henson in a letter written to him in 1846. No doubt it gave him pleasure. No doubt he would today be more than gratified at the universal acceptance of Henson's tribute. But he would also have been horrified at mankind's misuse of his invention.

GERARD FAIRLIE AND ELIZABETH CAYLEY,
The Life of a Genius

The Wright Brothers at Kitty Hawk

From Orville Wright's Diary
Thursday, December 17, 1903

When we got up, a wind of between 20 and 25 miles was blowing from the north. We got the machine out early and put out the signal for the men at the station. Before we were quite ready, John T. Daniels, W. S. Dough, A. D. Etheridge, W. C. Brinkley of Manteo, and Johnny Moore of Nag's Head arrived. After running the engine and propellers a few minutes to get them in working order, I got on the machine at 10.35 for the first trial. The wind according to our anemometer at this time was blowing a little over 20 miles (corrected) 27 miles according to the Government anemometer at Kitty Hawk. On slipping the rope the machine started off increasing in speed to probably 7 or 8 miles. The machine lifted from the truck just as it was entering on the fourth rail. Mr. Daniels took a picture just as it left the trucks.

I found the control of the front rudder quite difficult on account of its being balanced too near the center and thus had a tendency to turn itself when started so that the rudder was turned too far on one side and then too far on the other. As a result the machine would rise suddenly to about 10 feet and then as suddenly, on turning the rudder, dart for the ground. A sudden dart when out about 100 feet from the end of the track ended the flight. Time about 12 seconds (not known exactly as watch was not promptly stopped). The flight lever for throwing off the engine was broken, and the skid under the rudder cracked.

After repairs, at 20 minutes after 11 o'clock Will made the second trial. The course was about like mine, up and down but a little longer . . . over the ground though about the same in time. Distance not measured but about 175 feet. Wind speed not quite so strong.

With the aid of the station men present, we picked the machine up and carried it back to the starting ways. At about 20 minutes till 12 o'clock I made the third trial. When out about the same distance as Will's, I met with a strong gust from the left which raised the left wing and sidled the machine off to the right in a lively manner. I immediately turned the rudder to bring the machine down and then worked the end control. Much to our surprise, on reaching the ground the left wing struck first, showing the lateral control of this machine much more effective than on any of our former ones. At the time of its sidling it had raised to a height of probably 12 to 14 feet.

At just 12 o'clock Will started on the fourth and last trip. The machine started off with its ups and downs as it had before, but by the time he had gone three or four hundred feet he had it under much better control, and was traveling on a fairly even course. It proceeded in this manner till it reached a small hummock out about 800 feet from the starting ways, when it began its pitching again and suddenly darted into the ground. The front rudder frame was badly broken up, but the main frame suffered none at all. The distance over the ground was 852 feet in 59 seconds. The engine turns was 1071, but this included several seconds while on the starting ways and probably about a half second after landing. The jar of landing had set the watch on the machine back, so that we have no exact record for the 1071 turns. Will took a picture of my third flight just before the gust struck the machine. The machine left the ways successfully at every trial, and the track was never caught by the truck as we had feared.

After removing the front rudder, we carried the machine back to camp. We set the machine down a few feet west of the building, and while standing about discussing the last flight, a sudden gust of wind struck the machine and started to turn it over. All rushed to stop it. Will, who was near the end, ran to the front, but too late to do any good. Mr. Daniels and myself seized spars at the rear, but to no purpose. The machine gradually turned over on us.

When Orville put his camera on a tripod for Mr. Daniels to take a picture of the first flight, he had it aimed at a point short

Wilbur Wright and his sister Katherine making a dual
flight at Pau, 1908.

of the end of the sixty-foot starting rail. He said to Daniels something like this: "When I turn the wings to a flying angle I'll leave the track and should be about two feet off the ground when directly in front of the camera. That's the time to press the button." The picture turned out perfectly balanced, exactly as Orville had hoped.

Except for the accident to the plane after the four flights were over, the brothers would have tried after lunch to fly to the Kitty Hawk weather station four miles away. Their gasoline tank, made by a tinner in Dayton, was only a foot long by three inches in diameter and contained about half a gallon. Since the machine with operator weighed only about 750 pounds, one filling of the tank would have lasted, they estimated, eighteen minutes and taken them at least nine or ten miles.

A surprising thing was that despite the historic importance of the demonstrations that man could fly, there was no trace of excitement at the scene of the flights, least of all by the Wrights themselves. They had done only what they had been fully expecting to do; and the others present did not then realize what an event they had witnessed.

Another astonishing thing about those first flights was that Wilbur and Orville each wore a stiff, white starched collar and a necktie! Indeed, they *always* wore white starched collars, whether in their bicycle shop or at Kitty Hawk. The natives there used to say they must be men of means, they were so well dressed. Neither was ever known to wear a sweater or flannel shirt. Whenever they went to Kitty Hawk they took enough clean collars to last them all the time they were there.

The telegram to their father, written by Orville, said: SUCCESS FOUR FLIGHTS THURSDAY MORNING ALL AGAINST TWENTY-ONE-MILE WIND STARTED FROM LEVEL WITH ENGINE POWER ALONE AVERAGE SPEED THROUGH AIR THIRTY-ONE MILES LONGEST 59 SECONDS INFORM PRESS HOME CHRISTMAS.

Carrie Grumbach remembered vividly, forty-five years after the event, what happened when the message was received at 7 Hawthorne Street. As it was late afternoon, already growing dark, she had lighted the gas in the kitchen and was starting to get supper. The doorbell rang and it was a messenger with a telegram for the Bishop. Carrie signed for it and took it upstairs to him. In a little while he came down and said to Carrie, "Well, they've made a flight." He was always calm and showed no excitement, but he looked pleased. Just then Miss Katharine came home, Carrie remembered, and when she saw the telegram she asked Carrie to delay supper while she took the telegram to her brother Lorin. (Soon afterward Lorin took the message to the office of the Dayton *Journal* and showed it to the city editor, Frank Tunison, who also represented the Associated Press, but he didn't think a flight of less than a minute worth a news item and seemed annoyed over being bothered about such nonsense. No reference to the flight appeared in the *Journal* the next morning.)

At the supper table, Carrie said, the Bishop and Miss Katharine were in high spirits, not because of the historic importance of the first official announcement that man could fly, but because now the boys would be home for Christmas. That meant that Mr. Wilbur would be on hand to stuff the Christmas turkey.

Stuffing the turkey had always been Wilbur's privilege, and the way he did it was something special. He made a ceremony of it, with all the ingredients arranged before him just so, and solemnly he'd rub his hands as if about to perform a piece of magic.

ed. FRED C. KELLY,
Miracle at Kitty Hawk

First across the Channel

In 1909, the London *Daily Mail* offered a prize of £1,000 to the first aviator to fly the English Channel. By mid-summer the two front-runners were both Frenchmen, Hubert Latham (of English descent) and Louis Blériot, who both waited near Calais for suitable conditions for take-off. Latham had already made one attempt which had ended in the sea. Blériot was on crutches as the result of burns received when his engine caught fire on an earlier flight.

A gale kept Latham and Blériot on the ground on July 24 and it looked very unlikely that a break would come the next day. For some reason, Alfred Le Blanc, a business associate of Blériot who had come along to help, had a sleepless night and finally got up in the early hours of the morning of July 25th. It seemed to him that the weather was improving, so he awakened Blériot. While Latham and his crew slept on, Blériot and Le Blanc drove from the hotel in Calais where they stayed to Les Baraques, where the plane was kept in a garage. At 4 a.m. Blériot threw down his crutches and was helped into his plane. "I won't want them again until I come back from England," he told his crew. A few minutes later he took off. He made a fifteen-minute trial flight around Calais, then landed at the jumping-off spot for England and waited for the sun to come to fulfill the conditions laid down by the *Daily Mail*, which were that the flight had to take place between sunrise and sunset. What happened next was routine—almost uneventful—but it thrilled the world and meant that things could never again be the same. Here, in Blériot's own words, is his exclusive account for the *Daily Mail* of the first flight across the English Channel:

At 4:30 we could see all around. Daylight had come. M. Le Blanc endeavored to see the coast of England, but could not. A light breeze from the southwest was blowing. The air was clear.

Everything was prepared. I was dressed as I am at this moment, a khaki jacket lined with wool for warmth over my tweed clothes and beneath engineer's suit of blue cotton overalls. My close-fitting cap was fastened over my head and ears. I had neither eaten nor drunk anything since I rose. My thoughts were only upon the flight, and my determination to accomplish it this morning.

4:35! *Tout est prêt!* Le Blanc gives the signal and in an instant I am in the air, my engine making 1,200 revolutions—almost its highest speed—in order that I may get quickly over the telegraph wires along the edge of the cliff. As soon as I am over the cliff I reduce my speed. There is now no need to force my engine.

I begin my flight, steady and sure, towards the coast of England. I have no apprehensions, no sensations, *pas du tout*.

The *Escopette* has seen me. She is driving ahead at full speed.

She makes perhaps 42 kilometers (about 26 miles per hour). What matters? I am making at least 68 kilometers (42 miles per hour).

Rapidly I overtake her, travelling at a height of 80 meters (about 260 feet).

The moment is supreme, yet I surprise myself by feeling no exultation. Below me is the sea, the surface disturbed by the wind, which is now freshening. The motion of the waves beneath me is not pleasant. I drive on.

Ten minutes have gone. I have passed the destroyer, and I turn my head to see whether I am proceeding in the right direction. I am amazed. There is nothing to be seen, neither the torpedo-destroyer, nor France, nor England. I am alone. I can see nothing at all—*rien du tout!*

For ten minutes I am lost. It is a strange position, to be alone, unguided, without compass, in the air over the middle of the Channel.

I touch nothing. My hands and feet rest lightly on the levers. I let the airplane take its own course. I care not whither it goes.

For ten minutes I continue, neither rising nor falling, nor turning. And then, twenty minutes after I have left the French coast, I see the green cliffs of Dover, the castle, and away to the west the spot where I intended to land.

What can I do? It is evident that the wind has taken me out of my course. I am almost at St. Margaret's Bay and going in the direction of the Goodwin Sands.

Now it is time to attend to the steering. I press the lever with my foot and turn easily towards the west, reversing the direction in which I am travelling. Now, indeed, I am in difficulties, for the wind here by the cliffs is much stronger, and my speed is reduced as I fight against it. Yet my beautiful aeroplane responds. Still I fly westwards, hoping to cross the harbor and reach the Shakespear Cliff. Again the wind blows. I see an opening in the cliff.

Although I am confident that I can continue for an hour and a half, that I might indeed return to Calais, I cannot resist the opportunity to make a landing upon this green spot.

Once more I turn my aeroplane, and, describing a half-circle, I enter the opening and find myself again over dry land. Avoiding the red buildings on my right, I attempt a landing; but the wind catches me and whirls me round two or three times.

At once I stop my motor, and instantly my machine falls straight upon the land from a height of 20 meters (65 ft.). In two or three seconds I am safe.

Soldiers in khaki run up, and a policeman. Two of my compatriots are on the spot. They kiss my cheeks. The conclusion of my flight overwhelms me. I have nothing to say, but accept the congratulations of the representatives of the *Daily Mail* and accompany them to the Lord Warden Hotel.

Thus ended my flight across the Channel. The flight could be easily done again. Shall I do it? I think not. I have promised my wife that after a race for which I have entered I will fly no more.

Blériot (in flying gear and with moustache) with his crashed plane near Dover Castle after his famous cross-Channel flight, 19 July 1909.

Latham was shattered. Waking up around 4.30 a.m. to see what the weather was like, Levavasseur had seen Blériot fly over the beach and take his departure for England. He quickly got Latham up, but by the time the Antoinette was ready to go the wind was too strong. The Calais correspondent for the *Daily Mail* describes the scene in the Latham camp:

As I look back upon the crowded hours of the morning, I see against a background of radiant faces and enthusiastic crowds a tall, slim figure with bent head and quivering lips and hands clenched in unavailing regret for lost opportunity. It is the figure of Hubert Latham ... He looked like a man on the verge of a nervous breakdown. His back was curved almost to a hump. There were deep lines around his mouth. His eyes were narrowed to a slit. More than once he brushed away a tear. The extreme tension of the past fortnight had told upon him severely, and this bitter blow coming at the end of it was having its natural, its inevitable effect.

SHERWOOD HARRIS,
The First to Fly

It was this flight, says one writer, which "did more than any other to impress the world's governments with the vital importance of aviation".

TO BEACHEY, 1912

Riding against the east,
A veering, steady shadow
Purrs the motor-call
Of the man-bird
Ready with the death-laughter
In his throat
And in his heart always
The love of the big blue beyond.

Only a man,
A far fleck of shadow on the east
Sitting at ease
With his hands on a wheel
And around him the large gray wings.
Hold him, great soft wings,
Keep and deal kindly, O wings,
With the cool, calm shadow at the wheel.

CARL SANDBURG,
Complete Poems

The Chicago Mail

The world knows the name of Charles Lindbergh for his famous
Transatlantic flight in the *Spirit of St. Louis*. But that epic trip
would never have been possible without the experience he had
gained as a U.S. mail pilot, flying all kinds of planes in all
weathers. This trip took place in September 1926.

Night already shadows the eastern sky. To my left, low on the
horizon, a thin line of cloud is drawing on its evening sheath of
black. A moment ago, it was burning red and gold. I look down
over the side of my cockpit at the farm lands of central Illinois.
Wheat shocks are gone from the fields. Close, parallel lines of the
seeder, across a harrowed strip, show where winter planting has
begun. A threshing crew on the farm below is quitting work for
the day. Several men look up and wave as my mail plane roars
overhead. Trees and buildings and stacks of grain stand shadowless
in the diffused light of evening. In a few minutes it will be dark,
and I'm still south of Peoria.

How quickly the long days of summer passed, when it was
daylight all the way to Chicago. It seems only a few weeks ago,
that momentous afternoon in April, when we inaugurated the
air-mail service. As chief pilot of the line, the honor of making the
first flight had been mine. There were photographs, city officials,
and handshaking all along the route that day. For was it not a
milestone in a city's history, this carrying of the mail by air? We
pilots, mechanics, postal clerks, and business executives, at St.
Louis, Springfield, Peoria, Chicago, all felt that we were taking
part in an event which pointed the way toward a new and
marvelous era.

But after the first day's heavy load, swollen with letters of
enthusiasts and collectors, interest declined. Men's minds turned
back to routine business; the air mail saves a few hours at most;
it's seldom really worth the extra cost per letter. Week after week,
we've carried the limp and nearly empty sacks back and forth
with a regularity in which we take great pride. Whether the mail
compartment contains ten letters or ten thousand is beside the

point. We have faith in the future. Some day we know the sacks
will fill.

We pilots of the mail have a tradition to establish. The
commerce of the air depends on it. Men have already died for that
tradition. Every division of the mail routes has its hallowed points
of crash where some pilot on a stormy night, or lost and blinded
by fog, laid down his life on the altar of his occupation. Every
man who flies the mail senses that altar and, consciously or
unconsciously, in his way worships before it, knowing that his own
next flight may end in the sacrifice demanded.

Our contract calls for five round trips each week. It's our
mission to land the St. Louis mail in Chicago in time to connect
with planes coming in from California, Minnesota, Michigan, and
Texas—a time calculated to put letters in New York City for the
opening of the eastern business day.

Three of us carry on this service: Philip Love, Thomas Nelson,
and I. We've established the best record of all the routes converging
at Chicago, with over ninety-nine percent of our scheduled flights
completed. Ploughing through storms, wedging our way beneath
low clouds, paying almost no attention to weather forecasts, we've
more than once landed our rebuilt army warplanes on Chicago's
Maywood field when other lines canceled out, when older and
perhaps wiser pilots ordered their cargo put on a train. During the
long days of summer we seldom missed a flight. But now winter
is creeping up on us. Nights are lengthening; skies are thickening
with haze and storm. We're already landing by floodlight at
Chicago. In a few more weeks it will be dark when we glide down
onto that narrow strip of cow pasture called the Peoria air-mail
field. Before the winter is past, even the meadow at Springfield
will need lights. Today I'm over an hour late—engine trouble at
St. Louis.

Lighting an airport is no great problem if you have money to
pay for it. With revolving beacons, boundary markers, and floodlights, night flying isn't difficult. But our organization can't buy
such luxuries. There's barely enough money to keep going from
month to month.

The Robertson Aircraft Corporation is paid by the pounds of
mail we carry, and often the sacks weigh more than the letters
inside. Our operating expenses are incredibly low; but our revenue

is lower still. The Corporation couldn't afford to buy new aircraft. All our planes and engines were purchased from Army salvage and rebuilt in our shops at Lambert Field. We call them DHs, because the design originated with De Haviland, in England. They are biplanes, with a single, twelve-cylinder, four-hundred-horse-power Liberty engine in the nose. They were built during the war for bombing and observation purposes, and improved types were put on production in the United States. The military DH has two cockpits. In our planes the mail compartment is where the front cockpit used to be, and we mail pilots fly from the position where the wartime observer sat.

We've been unable to buy full night-flying equipment for these planes, to say nothing of lights and beacons for the fields we land on. It was only last week that red and green navigation lights were installed on our DHs. Before that we carried nothing but one emergency flare and a pocket flashlight. When the dollars aren't there, you can't draw checks to pay for equipment. But it's bad economy, in the long run, to operate a mail route without proper lights. That has already cost us one plane. I lost a DH just over a week ago because I didn't have an extra flare, or wing lights, or a beacon to go back to.

I encountered fog, that night, on the northbound flight between Marseilles and Chicago. It was a solid bank, rolling in over the Illinois River valley. I turned back southwest, and tried to drop my single flare so I could land on one of the farm fields below; but when I pulled the release lever nothing happened. Since the top of the fog was less than a thousand feet high, I decided to climb over it and continue on my route in the hope of finding a clear spot around the air-mail field. Then, if I could get under the clouds, I could pick up the Chicago beacon, which had been installed at government expense.

Glowing patches of mist showed me where cities lay on the earth's surface. With these patches as guides, I had little trouble locating the outskirts of Chicago and the general area of Maywood. But a blanket of fog, about 800 feet thick, covered the field. Mechanics told me afterward that they played a searchlight upward and burned two barrels of gasoline on the ground in an effort to attract my attention. I saw no sign of their activities.

After circling for a half hour I headed west, hoping to pick up

Lindbergh in his barnstorming days. With fellow pilot Bob Gurney at Lambert Field, St Louis, 1924. Lindbergh had a penchant for practical jokes and once made Gurney ill by filling his water jug with kerosene.

one of the beacons on the transcontinental route. They were fogged in too. By then I had discovered that the failure of my flare to drop was caused by slack in the release cable, and that the flare might still function if I pulled on the cable instead of on the release lever. I turned southwest, toward the edge of the fog, intending to follow my original plan of landing on some farmer's field by flarelight. At 8.20 my engine spit a few times and cut out almost completely. At first I thought the carburetor jets had clogged, because there should have been plenty of fuel in my main tank. But I followed the emergency procedure of turning on the reserve. Then, since I was only 1500 feet high, I shoved the flashlight into my pocket and got ready to jump; but the power surged into the engine again. Obviously nothing was wrong with the carburetor—the main tank had run dry. That left me with reserve fuel for only twenty minutes of flight—not enough time to reach the edge of the fog.

I decided to jump when the reserve tank ran dry, and I had started to climb for altitude when a light appeared on the ground—just a blink, but that meant a break in the fog. I circled down to 1200 feet and pulled out the flare-release cable. This time the flare functioned, but it showed only a solid layer of mist. I waited until the flare sank out of sight on its parachute, and began climbing again. Ahead, I saw the glow from a small city. I banked away, toward open country.

I was 5000 feet high when my engine cut the second time. I unbuckled my safety belt, dove over the right side of the fuselage, and after two or three seconds of fall pulled the rip cord. The parachute opened right away. I was playing my flashlight down toward the top of the fog bank when I was startled to hear the sound of an airplane in the distance. It was coming toward me. In a few seconds I saw my DH, dimly, less than a quarter of a mile away and about on a level with me. It was circling in my direction, left wing down. Since I thought it was completely out of gasoline, I had neglected to cut the switches before I jumped. When the nose dropped, due to the loss of the weight of my body in the tail, some additional fuel apparently drained forward into the carburetor, sending the plane off on a solo flight of its own.

My concern was out of proportion to the danger. In spite of

the sky's tremendous space, it seemed crowded with traffic. I shoved my flashlight into my pocket and caught hold of the parachute risers so I could slip the canopy one way or the other in case the plane kept pointing toward me. But it was fully a hundred yards away when it passed, leaving me on the outside of its circle. The engine noise receded, and then increased until the DH appeared again, still at my elevation. The rate of descent of plane and parachute were approximately equal. I counted five spirals, each a little farther away than the last. Then I sank into the fog bank.

Knowing the ground to be less than a thousand feet below, I reached for the flashlight. It was gone. In my excitement when I saw the plane coming toward me, I hadn't pushed it far enough into my pocket. I held my feet together, guarded my face with my hands, and waited. I heard the DH pass once again. Then I saw the outline of the ground, braced myself for impact, and hit—in a cornfield. By the time I got back on my feet, the chute had collapsed and was lying on top of the corn tassels. I rolled it up, tucked it under my arm, and started walking between two rows of corn. The stalks were higher than my head. The leaves crinkled as I brushed past them. I climbed over a fence, into a stubble field. There I found wagon tracks and followed them. Ground visibility was about a hundred yards.

The wagon tracks took me to a farmyard. First, the big barn loomed up in haze. Then a lighted window beyond it showed that someone was still up. I was heading for the house when I saw an automobile move slowly along the road and stop, playing its spotlight from one side to the other. I walked over to the car. Several people were in it.

"Did you hear that airplane?" one of them called out as I approached.

"I'm the pilot," I said.

"An airplane just dove into the ground," the man went on, paying no attention to my answer. "Must be right near here. God, it made a racket!" He kept searching with his spotlight, but the beam didn't show much in the haze.

"I'm the pilot," I said again. "I was flying it." My words got through that time. The spotlight stopped moving.

"*You're the pilot?* Good God, how—"

"I jumped with a parachute," I said, showing him the white bundle.

"You aren't hurt?"

"Not a bit. But I've got to find the wreck and get the mail sacks."

"It must be right near by. Get in and we'll drive along the road a piece. Good God, what went wrong? You must have had *some* experience! You're sure you aren't hurt?"

We spent a quarter hour searching, unsuccessfully. Then I accompanied the farmer to his house. My plane, he said, had flown over his roof only a few seconds before it struck the ground. I asked to use his telephone. The party line was jammed with voices, all talking about the airplane that had crashed. I broke in with the statement that I was the pilot, and asked the telephone operator to put in emergency calls for St. Louis and Chicago. Then I asked her if anyone had reported the exact location of the wreck. A number of people had heard the plane pass overhead just before it hit, she replied, but nothing more definite had come in.

I'd hardly hung up and turned away when the bell rang—three longs and a short.

"That's our signal," the farmer said.

My plane had been located, the operator told me, about two miles from the house I was in. We drove to the site of the crash. The DH was wound up in a ball-shaped mass. It had narrowly missed a farmhouse, hooked one wing on a grain shock a quarter mile beyond, skidded along the ground for eighty yards, ripped through a fence, and come to rest on the edge of a cornfield. Splinters of wood and bits of torn fabric were strewn all around. The mail compartment was broken open and one sack had been thrown out; but the mail was undamaged—I took it to the nearest post office to be entrained.

CHARLES A. LINDBERGH,
The Spirit of St. Louis

The Flying Duchess

One of the most remarkable aviators of the period between the two world wars was Mary, Duchess of Bedford. She was a woman of exceptional talents. She ran a surgical hospital at her home at Woburn Abbey, and was a trained theatre nurse and radiologist. She was a keen ornithologist, both at Woburn and wherever in the world her travels took her. She was a skilled salmon fisher and expert shot—one entry in her diary records a stand at Woburn where she killed forty-two pheasants and two rabbits in forty-eight shots!

When she was sixty-one and growing deaf, she took up flying. Soon it became an obsession. She used her Puss-Moth as other people used cars—to fish in Devon, shoot and birdwatch in Scotland, see the Grand National at Aintree, visit Harrogate for an eclipse of the sun. Her diaries are quite unlike anything else in aviation literature.

June 17th, 1926

To-day I took my first flight from the Croydon Aerodrome to Woburn in a 2-seater "Moth" (open) machine travelling at 70 air m.p.h., Mr. Sydney St. Barbe pilot. There was a little wind, but not enough to make things unpleasant, and I enjoyed my new experience enormously. I did not experience the slightest feeling of apprehension, nausea, or cold, in fact all is pleasant except the noise. The aeronaut must be grateful to the Romans for their straight roads, for they and open sheets of water must make things easy for the pilot in clear weather, and when, as we did, we came straight down Watling Street. It is curious that, though I have not a good "head" for looking down precipices, as when climbing Mont Blanc and the Ortler, I experienced no discomfort whatever in this respect and could look over the edge of my machine from the first. I suppose it is confidence in one's pilot and mechanics. My only apprehension (as I could only communicate by signs with the pilot) was that we should land in the Bison field (which from above looked particularly attractive!) instead of in the safer but less open parts of the Park! It was very wonderful realising for the first time that one was supported by nothing but air.

The Duchess of Bedford with her personal pilot,
Captain C. D. Barnard, 1931.

Left Woburn at 1 p.m. for my first long flight abroad in the Hon. Geoffrey Cunliffe's "Moth," with Captain C. D. Barnard as pilot. Jemima, Mrs. Glendining, and the Liddells came to see me off, and we departed amidst much photography. Except that we had a south-west wind, it was perfect weather for starting. We had to land at Croydon for a few minutes and again at Lympne, where one of the big air liners was just starting off. Woburn to Croydon, 30 minutes; Croydon to Lympne, 50 minutes. My luggage on the "Moth" consisted of two, small suit-cases, a small attaché case on my knee, a hat in a bag, and a little leather hand-bag. For the rest, Captain Barnard had his suit-case, and we carried as much extra petrol and oil as space permitted. The suit-cases (3) on either side of my legs and a couple of oil tins at the end left just comfortable room and, on occasions later, kept me warmer, I think than I should have been without them. My maid and courier travelled by the usual routes, and were to meet me as often as circumstances permitted.

It seemed to take an amazingly short time crossing the much-dreaded Channel, and I have never done it more supremely comfortably. The different system of cultivation on the French side is very marked from the air, and the small strips of different-coloured land reminded one forcibly of the puzzle boxes made of different-coloured strips of wood. There is an absence of hedges, cattle, and the little round ponds which are such a conspicuous feature in English aerial travel. Captain Barnard swooped low to show me places of interest, such as the Cathedrals of Abbeville and Beauvais, and after two hours' flying from Lympne we arrived, to my great regret, at the Le Bourget Aerodrome in bright sunshine, and were immediately pounced upon by photographers. Capt. B. having expatiated upon the admirable restaurant arrangements for travellers at Le Bourget, took me thither, only to find all in the hands of painters and builders, so I waited outside whilst he put the "Moth" to bed and watched aeroplanes constantly coming and going. We stayed at the Ritz Hotel, and our road from Le Bourget might have led to Hades itself, for there were funeral processions by the score.

April 22nd

Owing to various delays, we did not leave Le Bourget till 12.15. Rather late, as it happened, as we had hoped to get to Biarritz and had a long flight before us. We flew over Versailles, which I saw for the first time. We dipped down to Chartres and its Cathedral and landed for petrol at Tours at 2.30 p.m. A fine, big aerodrome, but with very bad surface. Paris to Tours 2 hours 15 minutes. We left again at 3.30 p.m., often following the long straight roads which seemed to dwarf our Roman roads. After a time we rose up to 5,000 feet and over above sea-level, which I did greatly enjoy, as the view is so vast and the earth looks such a very long way away! I afterwards learnt that it was because we were getting rather short of petrol. After flying at this height for some time the engine stopped and I wondered why. I was to be enlightened shortly by my pilot, who said, "I don't know why the engine stopped like that; I think it must have been an air-lock." We had, as was ever to be our fate, a strong headwind against us, and he then told me we should only just reach the aerodrome, and asked if I minded coming down quickly from a height, "because some people did". As the petrol gave out at that moment, my reply was not of much importance, and we did come down quickly by some amazing corkscrew, but landing very neatly at the bottom. All experiences being new to me and having implicit faith in my pilot, even when short of petrol, I had done nothing but enjoy myself. Landed at 6.20 p.m. It had taken us 2 hours and 50 minutes from Tours.

We had reascended but a short time when we saw very ominous-looking fog over the sea, but we persevered for a time with misgivings, till we came close to the shore, and then decided upon a retreat to Bordeaux.

We were high up in sunshine above the fog, which looked like the Arctic Ocean with tumbled masses of snow and ice. We had rather a race to keep ahead of it going back to the aerodrome, which we reached in safety at 7.55 p.m., after another 55 minutes' flight. It was a long time before we could get a car from the town, but it was a beautiful evening, and we dined on arrival, about 9.45 p.m., and went to bed.

April 23rd

We left Bordeaux at 10 a.m., and whilst my pilot was getting

the "Moth" ready, I wandered into the fir wood and saw the little
cups hanging on the fir trees for collecting resin. Why these and
cork trees stand the cutting of bark which their respective indus-
tries entail has always been a mystery to me, seeing that if the
bark of a tree at home is gravely injured, it invariably proceeds
to die.

To-day we had a lovely flight, *most* thrilling, not on account
of adventures, but it was all so new and weird and wonderful. We
retraced our route of the previous evening to the great forest of
Les Landes, which borders the coast for some seventy miles. We
scudded along the sandy shore with the sea on our right and the
vast forest on the left. We were only some 20 to 30 feet above the
sand, and at this height one can recognise the birds so far as the
pace at which one travels allows and of which under these circumstances one is conscious. Flying high, pace is largely a matter of
the air-speed meter, and one is hardly conscious of it. Here and
there in the sand dunes were little settlements, and one wondered
what the people lived by and on. Fishing I was told, but no boats
were in evidence so far as I could see.

We arrived at Biarritz Aerodrome at 11.30 a.m., but before
landing had a look at the town. The aerodrome is small but
picturesque, and I was told few aeroplanes landed there.

Seated in the bright dining-room at luncheon with the gay
crowd, my pilot, whose thoughts were evidently elsewhere,
remarked, "To-morrow we go over the Pyrenees, and if the engine
fails we crash or else come down where we cannot get away from."
I said, "Yes; it is strange how calmly one can look forward to it,"
and asked whether he tried to forget or to remember it. "I am
always thinking of it," he said. "A pilot who is not always thinking
of it is no use;" and I expect he is right. However, the matter was
not to concern us much on the morrow, for on

April 24th

I woke to find it raining and the weather in general looking
particularly hopeless, and such as I am getting used to expect
when I travel to Southern Europe. I looked out at the hour which
we had fixed for starting and saw my pilot's shoes, suit, etc., lying
in waiting outside his door, and gathered that he also had made
up his mind that it was unnecessary to rise, though later I found

that this little weakness was not always to be accounted for by the weather! Later on the rain stopped, and Captain Barnard suggested having a short flight along the lower Pyrenees, which of course I jumped at.

It was my first view of mountains from the air and a very beautiful one. We flew over the picturesque town of San Sebastian and along the coast and back over the lower Pyrenees. All of which more than compensated for being detained a day at Biarritz. Just as we were approaching the aerodrome and about 3,000 feet up, a voice from the rear asked if I would "like to try a little spin and nose dive"; he said it made some people giddy, but as I felt my education would not be complete without it, I said, "Yes," and away we went. I saw the earth once in the middle of it, but how anybody ever guides an aeroplane out of a spin I am at present at a loss to understand. I suppose most people are more or less giddy the first time while it is going on, but as the aeroplane straightened, so did I. As Capt. Barnard called it "rather jolly" later, I hope I too may get to think so. The inhabitants at the aerodrome, unused to spectacular displays, as we found on landing, concluded we were done for! In the afternoon we took a long drive up the beautiful Valley of the Nive to St. Jean, and our only regret was that one could not see it in sunshine. A pilot friend of Capt. Barnard's, Mr. Hamilton, dined with us. (Afterwards drowned in an attempt to cross the Atlantic.)

April 25th

The weather looked worse than ever in the morning, dark and gloomy over the mountains, raining and blowing at Biarritz. We went up to get the "Moth" ready, but with little hope of starting that day. I strolled out to buy an umbrella and a warmer garment for crossing the mountains when the time came, but it all looked pretty hopeless.

In the afternoon the clouds were higher and my pilot's hopes of getting away rose with them, so we packed with a view to taking another flight in the neighbourhood if we could not go farther. Once up at the aerodrome things began to look more hopeful. Whilst my pilot was attending to the machine in the morning, I had helped the woman who lived at the aerodrome to pluck five Dotterels, which I had never seen in the flesh before, i.e. in the hand. We started off feeling none too hopeful about the weather, but as we approached the mountains the weather cleared and only an occasional cloud near the tops caused my pilot anxiety and had to be dodged. When nearly at our highest point, the sun came out and the scenery was wonderful beyond description, and I am indeed thankful that I have had the courage to fly before my course is run. Not that any great courage is needed actually to fly, for I had always longed to do it, but one has to run the gauntlet of one's friends and relations, who think it silly and foolhardy and done from a desire to show off.

I remember as a child of less than eight years being taken to see a flying machine which had crashed on the South Downs near Amberley after the owner was said to have flown "the height of a house", the sequel being that he committed suicide from disappointment. I cannot actually say that my desire to fly dated from then, but at least I have always wished it were within my reach since aviation became possible for anyone, and I can certainly say that from the time I took my first flight from Croydon Aerodrome no qualm for my personal safety has ever possessed me except for Herbrand's sake. Incidentally, the poor little pilot who took me up on that occasion afterwards crashed at his own aerodrome and fractured his skull, shoulder, collar-bone, finger, and leg, but was flying again before I left on this trip, four months later. Of such stuff are pilots made! (Mr. St. Barbe.)

But to return to my trip. On the Spanish side all was sunshine and blue sky. As a rule one sees no birds at the height at which we fly, but after reaching our highest altitude we saw an Egyptian Vulture which, owing to its colour, was conspicuous far below. We swooped down to it, but it pitched on the mountain-side and would not rise again; we did, however, flush a flock of about 20 Common Vultures, which seemed much scared at the sight of the "Roc" above them. They kept alighting as we swooped at them, and evidently did not like us at all. We reached Burgos in 2½ hours, first circling round over the town to see the Cathedral and other points of interest. We found Smith and Vetter awaiting us. The latter, who has travelled with me for close upon 40 years and is seventy-six, does not appreciate the uncertainties of my new method of travel. The hotel was comfortable, but as *all* sanitary arrangements were *in* my bedroom, I could but hope the drains were well trapped! We strolled out to see the Cathedral, but as it was getting dark, a better view had to be postponed to the morning.

*   *   *

Next year the Duchess and Captain Barnard flew to Italy, and then in June 1928 they attempted to break the London–Karachi record.

June 9th 1928

After months of postponement, change of plans, etc., etc., Captain Barnard's flight to India in the Fokker "Princess Xenia", on which I am to accompany them, is to come off, and I left Henlow Aerodrome in my "Moth", with Captain Hope, as my pilot, in the afternoon. Being a somewhat stormy day and Captain Hope unacquainted with Park landings, he elected to leave from an aerodrome, and Jemima and my two Matrons came to see me off. We had a bumpy journey and one big bump over the N. Downs, which my pilot subsequently made the most of to the reporters at Lympne, so that with further embellishment from them my sorrowing friends and relations were greeted next morning with startling headlines in the newspapers: "Duchess nearly thrown out of her aeroplane", "nearly killed", etc., etc.

I arrived, however, in safety at Lympne, all unconscious of my "perilous escape", and spent the night or such hours of it as our very early start permitted, at a Hythe hotel.

June 10th

I left the hotel in the dark at 4 a.m. for the aerodrome, where a small group of people, including Miss A. Stone and the irrepressible reporter, came to see us off; the persistency of the latter made it almost impossible to talk to one's own friends. The morning was fairly fine, but with an unpropitious wind for taking off with our heavily loaded machine. We started at 4.25 a.m., but the machine was a long time getting up, and we learnt subsequently that we had removed some of the telegraph wires and narrowly escaped disaster, also incidentally provided much further food for the reporters. However, the machine righted itself and we were soon over the Channel. The weather was indifferent till we had passed over Belgium and part of Germany, but then cleared up, and we had a lovely flight over and along the course of the muddy Danube, with snow mountains on one side of us. We landed at Sofia at 6.10 p.m., having done our first 1,200 miles.

As it would have been difficult to get to the aerodrome from the town by 4.30 a.m. next morning, I accepted the offer of a sofa as bed in one of the married officers' sitting-rooms. Unfortunately, it was their only living-room, so supper had to come first, cooked and served by his wife. It was not ready till 9 p.m. and the room was not cleared till 10 p.m. I was offered the kitchen sink to wash in, and my host promised to call me at 4 a.m. the following morning. However, I was pretty well ready before he arrived, and dressing was not a long business, as the kitchen tap did not even provide any washing water. I found later that I had also two unwashed and unshaven pilots to keep me company. My host spoke a little English, but his wife none at all.

June 11th

We left the aerodrome at 4.30 a.m. Had some lime-juice cordial for breakfast. We were soon over the mountains and then followed the Maritza River towards Constantinople. Not long after Sofia we passed Philippopolis, which was recently damaged by earthquake, but at 5,000 feet one could not see much damage, and as my host told me last night that the houses were only cracked, I suppose the "awful destruction" was the usual Press exaggeration, as the tall buildings would be the first to go.

Just as we were nearing Constantinople, Captain Barnard asked me to make some time and distance calculations. A cruel moment to do so, as it was all so wonderfully beautiful and interesting. I left my seat to get a look on the other side, but was immediately called to order by, "Have you finished that, Your Grace?" I say called, but all communications on the "Foker" had to be in writing, so back to my sums I went, and consoled myself with the hope that calculations would not be wanted on the return journey.

It was all a dream of beauty over the azure-blue Sea of Marmora, then over the wonderful sandy mountains and over the narrowest part of the Gulf of Ismid; once in the mountains we followed the Baghdad Railway all the time. At one time we rose up to 10,000 feet to the snow-line before reaching Adana. Over the desert we flew at 7,000 to 8,000 feet, and it was delightfully cool.

We reached Aleppo at 3 p.m., having flown 997 miles. Here the French officers gave me a tiny room in their quarters, filled with the bare necessities of life, which did not include any sort or kind of curtain or blind to the two large windows which took up most of the room. We had not had much to eat and still less to drink, but (here again) I had to wait for the normal dinner-hour, when for the first time I was entertained as the sole lady guest at an Officers' Mess. They assured me that the water was not fit to drink and I was given the alternative of getting drunk on champagne or going thirsty, and "thirsty" I did "go", from now onwards till I became a well-roasted and acclimatised Persian. At times "one's tongue clave to the roof of one's mouth" and one felt one could not talk. Mr. Eustace Miles had provided me with some of his concentrated vegetarian foods for travellers, but they were not for the traveller in the desert in the month of June. As Capt. B. said we *must* start at dawn, I offered to call him, as he and Mr. Alliott were next door, but when I did proclaim the first streak of dawn, it was not at all popular, and he arrived very much out of temper a half-hour after I did, at the hanger, declaring that I had called them an hour too soon by Aleppo time. But by then the sun was high in the heavens and dawn is dawn anywhere, whatever the clocks may say. My own bed had been too extraordinarily lumpy to make it attractive, but I felt sorry for the poor major culprit, as he had had a tiring day.

June 12th

Once more we were off on our flight, this time following the Euphrates nearly from the start. At one time Mesopotamia on one side and Syria on the other, then through Iraq. Desert, the acme of desolation all the way, still amazingly interesting, and but for thirst we were perfectly cool and comfortable. Now and again we saw trains which crawled along the Baghdad Railway; the mirage was ever with us, providing us with vast lakes to look at, which vanished or receded as we drew near them. Now and again there was a tiny collection of mud huts, and one wondered on what the inhabitants could possibly live. We passed extinct volcanoes, and near Babylon went through a mild sandstorm. The rivers and their tributaries were a wonderful turquoise-blue or emerald green.

We passed near the site of the Garden of Eden. Had I been in Eve's place I should certainly have succumbed to temptation in order to be expelled if I could have found the apples, though it may not be so terrible in winter as it looked in the month of June; those who cherish the allegory had better not visit this Biblical Paradise.

> On leaving Bushire, in Iran, their engine blew up and they had to wait ten weeks for a new one. On August 22nd they left for Karachi.

Darkness came on as we neared Karachi, and we landed by flares. A crowd had assembled to greet us, but I was soon whisked off to Government House, where I stayed with the Thomases. We had had a 13-hours' flight, but I was not a scrap tired. Mrs. Thomas and her sister gave me a very kind welcome, and I was soon provided with dinner, of which I was rather in need. It was a strange contrast to the life I had been leading for the last ten weeks and more, particularly with my luncheon to-day, which had consisted of the drumstick of a chicken, eaten without knife and fork, and a hunk of dry bread. Here I was surrounded by luxury and domestics waiting upon us, and the portraits of all the old Governor-Generals of Sind looking down upon us from the walls. I felt desperately shabby in my surroundings, but the genial Mrs. Thomas was not one to make one conscious of one's shortcomings. My wardrobe was at the lowest ebb. I had taken plenty of underclothing with me, but the upper strata, which had to meet the eyes of those in Persia who looked for London's latest creations, would have made my maid blush. An iron was not to be had, and the local laundries did not seem to have one either, so one thought for as long as circumstances permitted before sending blouses and dresses to the wash. I was therefore soon decked out in Czechoslo-vakian shoes bought at Ispahan, artificial silk stockings from

Abadan with long cashmere tops coming below my skirt, some thin
white silk knickers ordered by Mr. Parkyn at Bushire, a skirt
made by an Armenian woman at Bushire and copied from the
upper part of a pyjama suit to which she attached a pleated skirt
(rather a successful garment in the end), some unironed home-
made shirts and a solar topee. And thus attired did I find myself
at Government House, Karachi! Mercifully it had only been at
Mohammerah that I met womenkind elsewhere, but if one goes
a-flying in these early days, one has to take the rough with the
smooth.

Friday, August 23rd

I was awakened by the screams of the once familiar Green
Parrots. A late breakfast-lunch was the order of the day, and when
Mr. Thomas appeared on the scene, he greeted me with the news
that our new propeller had gone all to pieces on the flight and
would not be fit to use again. This meant that we should either
have to get our old one from Bushire and try it, or else send for
a new one from home and wait another four to five weeks. The
steamer for Bombay was leaving that afternoon; had I missed it,
I should have had to wait a week for the Bushire propeller and
another week before we knew if it would answer. If it did not,
then one would have to be obtained from home.

Hospital work was going to pieces and our time for Scotland
getting very near. I think I should have waited for the Bushire
propeller had I been in an hotel, but like everyone else since our
breakdown at Bushire EXCEPT MR. PARKYN, Mr. Thomas evidently
thought the whole expedition a risky and foolish one for me, and
advised me to go home by sea. So much did he put on the pressure
that his kind little wife fled down the verandah after him and
very obviously scolded him, and then came back to me and said,
"Of course, Duchess, if you would like to wait, we should be only
too delighted, etc., etc." But I had to decide on the spot, so there
was nothing for it but to go—a cruel disappointment after all
these weeks of waiting for our engine. It was the middle of the
Monsoon, so I did not anticipate a pleasant voyage.

The next year (1929) Captain Barnard and the Duchess made
a record-breaking flight to Karachi and back in just under
ninety-one hours flying time. Huge crowds greeted them at
Croydon airport and there was a telegram from the King. The
following year they made another record-breaking flight, to the
Cape and back in twenty days; there was an even bigger crowd
at Croydon and another telegram from the King. This extract
from the Duchess's diary is a good example of the sort of
adventures that intercontinental fliers of those days faced.

April 24th

We left Dodoma at 4.5 a.m., with a lot of heavy cloud about
and not at all a promising outlook. The country at first was densely
wooded, but with fewer tall single trees and more thorn and scrub;
later, near L. Micularna, it is low scrub and barren ground. There
were Egrets everywhere near water, thousands of them, also large
flocks of Storks, but less than of Egrets. We passed big herds of
Giraffes, and near L. Victoria there was an amazing amount of
Big Game: Rhino and Hippo, Gnus, Zebras, Elands, Hartebeests,
Waterbucks, Beisa Antelopes, Ostriches, and a host of smaller fry
which we were flying too quickly to identify. It was an amazing
experience to see all this great zoological collection, fleeing before
us in every direction. Unfortunately, just as we were passing them
all, Mr. Little indicated that pumping was urgently required. My
special task was to pump the contents of the big extra tank of
petrol into the wing tanks daily, an operation which meant a
quarter-hour's pumping every hour till it was empty, 270 gals., I
believe. A thousand pumps took just about a quarter-hour.

Not long after passing Nature's Zoological Garden, and whilst
still on the shores of L. Victoria, Capt. B. handed me his "Printator"
slate on which he had written, "There is a leak in our oil supply
and we shall have to make a forced landing to examine it. Do you
think it was hard ground where we saw all that game?" I replied
that where Zebras and Ostriches were it ought to be, but did not
look like it, though I did not see any splashing.

However, he continued to fly straight on, and in a short time
another note came down. "We may just reach Kisumu, but it will
be a matter of minutes."

So over the waters of Lake Victoria and other impossible landing-places the old *Spider* sped on, till we had apparently only a pint of oil or less left, but we managed to reach Kisumu at 10.30 a.m. We landed safely on this pretty little landing-ground, right on the Equator, and there found that the oil supply was going strong, but that the oil gauge had gone on strike and given quite needless anxiety. It is rather interesting to experience just how one feels when one knows that the end may come at any moment. My own experience is that with a little determination panic can be lived down if one has no responsibility on one's shoulders. It would be a very different business if one had; also, probably, if one knew one's fate rested in unreliable hands; but knowing as I did that if a crash was to occur it could not have been avoided, it *is* possible to divert the thoughts to other channels and accept "Che Sara Sara".* It is the more easy if there is as much to interest oneself in as there was on this occasion. Beyond the ordinary anxiety of forced landings in England, of which I have had my share, the worst time I ever had was in the Mistral on the Riveria, and for actual test of one's principles of refusing to be seized with panic, I give this the palm.

It was not at all disagreeably hot, even at Kisumu, and an English lady, whom I spoke to, told me that it was never at all "unbearable". It is a very different story from what one hears in the Persian Gulf.

The women in these parts (they are very black) are extraordinary figures. From the habit of carrying their babies on their backs, they develop a seat for their infants on that part of their persons on which, in the normal course of events, they would sit themselves. I suppose they can straighten out to sit down, but they do not look like it, and I noticed that temporarily they rested themselves when the infant was *in situ* with their hands on their knees. The babes cling on by putting their hands round under the armpits, the fingers in front pointing upwards.

Having satisfied ourselves as to the oil supply, the next thing was to get to Juba in the only four hours of daylight left to us, and we took off again at 11.20 a.m. (E.T.).

---

*Whatever will be, will be. The Bedford family motto.

We were over Uganda about half-hour later, but our bad luck
as regards weather pursued us, and we kept on running into very
heavy storms and bad visibility. Between us and Juba lay a range
of mountains and the blackest of clouds, and a deluge of
thunder-storms seemed to be raging on them. Capt. B. had a try
at getting through, but daylight was fading, and he swung round
to the flatter country below. I wondered what was going to happen,
but the luck which failed us in the matter of weather on this flight
seemed to be playing with us, and when it had made us sufficiently
uncomfortable always provided a way out. The N'mule landing-
ground was not far off, and to that we went. We were immediately
surrounded by a weird collection of natives dressed in girdles of
beads only, very black, but very cheerful-looking, and apparently
quite as much amused by my appearance as I was by theirs. The
pilot's book of directions said that shelter might be obtained
through the native doctor. So I wrote a note, which Captain
Barnard managed to dispatch to this official. After a long wait, a
man who spoke English and dressed as an Englishman appeared,
and said the doctor had left two years ago, but that there was a
hut, apparently intended for sheltering stray aeronauts, to which
he would conduct us. So by the light of an electric torch we followed
a native guide for over a mile along a path with many pitfalls
with long grass crops on either side. Our guide told us that it was
not safe to walk after dark without a lantern, as there were lions
about which were wont to spring out on foolish virgins and others
who had none. They were not likely to attack those carrying
lanterns, but merely roared to instil a proper respect. At last, after
what seemed a very long mile, we reached our shelter—a stone
hut which had neither doors nor windows (i.e. only frames) and
was thatched with grass or reeds. Some little camp bedsteads, a
table, and some chairs were unearthed from somewhere, and as
each little bedstead was erected, my exhausted companions flung
themselves down upon them. The hut had two compartments, but
no door between. Our supper was to come from $4\frac{1}{2}$ miles away,
so there was no prospect of seeing it for some hours. The bedsteads
were provided with mosquito curtains, but no other bedding, and
as the hut was but dimly lit by three candles, I followed my
companions' example, and rolling up my skirt as a pillow, crawled
in under the mosquito curtains, hoping to get some sleep. I had

dozed rather fitfully till 11 p.m., when supper arrived. It consisted of two chickens, which I imagine must have been captured and cooked after our arrival; at all events knives would not penetrate them, so we resorted to fingers and teeth. Supper over, we crawled on to our charpoys once more and I watched the fireflies dancing up and down outside, and only longed to hear a lion roar to complete the romance, but they were not broadcasting that night.

We were evidently all very much on the alert for dawn, for as soon as the first signs of it appeared there was a stirring in the next room, and we were ready some time before we could rouse anyone to carry our suit-cases from the native huts. The pathway by day was less formidable than by night.

In July of that year the Duchess sacked Captain Barnard "as he has too many other engagements", and Flight Lieutenant Allen became her personal pilot instead. On a trip with him to Spurn Head the Duchess was involved in a comic incident.

August 30th, 1932

I flew up to Spurn Head to see what prospect there was of doing any bird-watching there. As we landed in a field some five miles on the Spurn Head side of Withernsea, I hoped that perhaps I might find it fairly undisturbed. A considerable number of people, however, swarmed down on us to look at the aeroplane, so we lunched on the bank, hoping they would soon get bored with their inspection.

The inspecting crowd, however (especially with a holiday element in it), is not readily satisfied, and having seen you land is prepared to wait indefinitely to see you take off, so I walked off, leaving my pilot in charge.

I had no sooner done so than I came across five Green Sandpipers in a bit of marshy ground, and was congratulating myself on the prospect of a highly interesting afternoon, as one rarely sees more than one or at most two together. I had walked for about twenty minutes when the Flight-Lieut. came flying round me, obviously anxious to attract my attention. I was then on the public road just in front of what was apparently the only occupied building of the War Department buildings, deserted since the War. He then dropped a note on the road, scribbled on a fragment of paper out of his notebook and wrapped in less than a quarter of the front sheet of *The Times*, to tell me that he was going to inspect the Withernsea Hotel. I picked it up in the presence of two or three bystanders, thew away the piece of *The Times*, read the note, and walked on up the shore. I had just spotted another interesting Wader from the sand-dunes, when a man whom I took for a merchant seaman officer, walked close in front of me with a terrier. As he upset my bird, I went down and sat on a breakwater till he was out of sight, and then strolled on again, only to meet him again, and again he passed without speaking. As he had entirely dispersed every bird within a mile of me, I walked over to the Humber shore, where again I found him dogging me, so, as time was getting short, I returned to the aeroplane, and as he was only a few yards behind and I was getting pretty exasperated I turned round and said, 'Good morning." He then informed me that he was a Customs Officer, and that I had been seen to pick up a *parcel* dropped from an aeroplane, and that he had a right to demand to see it. I told him what was in it, and that I had thrown it away, in spite of which he informed me very unnecessarily three times, "Well, I've taken the number of yer aeroplane, d'ye see? and shall report yer," which trouble I saved him by reporting *him* for dogging me for two hours without speaking, but it did not reward me for having my rather hardly earned bird-watching completely spoilt.

In 1933, Flight-Lieutenant Allen was killed in a flying accident, and his friend, Flight-Lieutenant Preston, took his place. With him the Duchess went on a flying holiday to North Africa in 1934.

April 23rd

We left the Canaries for Marrakech. When some twelve miles off Fuera Ventura, the engine showed very decided signs of going on strike again. Flight-Lieut. Preston, by various mishandlings of the throttle and dives, tried to rouse it to a sense of its duties, but without success, and for a time we had the interesting experience of feeling quite certain that our flying career was about to end in a very rough sea. However, the engine did not, as we expected, entirely fail, and Flight-Lieut. Preston turned round and said, "I think we may reach land." With a prospect of wild mountains and rocks and an irregular sandy spit on which there was a lighthouse, I told him I thought the sea was preferable, and apparently he thought so too when he saw it closer, and he turned out to sea again. By this time the engine had picked up more or less, and we were able to regain height. It gave us another little threat of collapse when Flight-Lieut. Preston turned off one tank to try to locate the trouble, and thereafter behaved itself for the remaining hour, which enabled us to reach Cabo Juby. I am persuaded that, when faced with apparently certain death in this way, one does not experience the terror which those who do not live to tell are supposed to feel. Flight-Lieut. Preston's wife told me later that she had asked him what it felt like when he thought his last hour had come, and he replied, "Well, it's come at last." This is exactly what I felt; Flight-Lieut. Preston was engaged in trying various devices to restart the engine, but I, who had nothing to do but consider the situation, felt a little disappointment that our flight would be wasted and that they would hear nothing about it at home; but I thought it quite an agreeable way of finishing up compared with most ends which are the lot of man, and certainly the one I had most desired; for, with not a boat in sight and a very rough sea, the process could not have lasted long. At all events I should have gone down knitting a prosaic sock and the reporters would have pictured me clinging round Flight-Lieut. Preston's neck and imploring him to save me! Only our height, 6,000 feet, saved us, as we dropped over 4,000 feet.

I write this with other similar experiences in the past to confirm my opinion.

On March 22nd, 1937 the Duchess (who had first gone solo in 1930) took off from Woburn to complete her two hundred hours solo flying. She was seventy-two. Her route, via Buntingford and Cambridge, should have brought her back to Woburn within the hour. But she was never seen again. A month later parts of her plane were found washed ashore on the east coast. She had no cause to fly over the North Sea; and there are many who think that, having lived a full and richly rewarding life, she had chosen her moment, and method, of ending it.

The Spirit of St. Louis

Charles Lindbergh's solo journey from New York to Paris in 1928 rightly caught the imagination of the world. On a personal level it was a far greater achievement than that of Alcock and Brown, who were the first to fly the Atlantic, in 1919. He had only his own resources to keep him awake and, by the time he reached their starting-point in Newfoundland, he had already been airborne ten hours.

More than this, in linking by air for the first time the most famous city of the old world with the most famous city of the new, he anticipated, more than any other flight since Blériot, the era of intercontinental air travel.

The Twelfth Hour

Here, all around me, is the Atlantic—its expanse, its depth, its power, its wild and open water. Is there something unique about this ocean that gives it character above all other seas, or is this my imagination? Flying swiftly through that gap in the mountains was like diving into a cold pool. One moment you look on water from the warm dryness of land. The next, you look at land from the enveloping wetness of water. In a few seconds your standards, your sensations, your viewpoint, have all undergone a major change. You've stepped suddenly into a different frame of life and values. A minute ago, I was a creature of the land, thinking of the ocean ahead, stripping for that final plunge. Now, I'm a creature of the ocean, sensing the exhilarating coolness of the water, thinking of the continent behind. This feeling penetrates my mind and body as though I'd actually made a dive, as though there were a major change in time, in air, in existence, between one side of that narrow gap and the other.

Charles Lindbergh with the *Spirit of St Louis* at Roosevelt
Field before taking off for Paris.

Now, I'm giving up both land and day. Now, I'm heading
eastward across two oceans, one of night and one of water. From
the ocean of water, I may still turn back to that receding coast;
but I can't turn back to the shore of day. Even in an airplane I
could never reach it.

I look at the black silhouette of the mountains behind me. On
Avalon Peninsula, fields exist where I could land with little
damage, now that a third of my fuel is gone—but never after
nightfall. I've been holding on to such fields with my mind—holding
on to the field at Long Island when mists looked thick ahead;
holding on to the Maine coast, just over the horizon to my left;
holding on to Newfoundland as a final point of refuge on my route.
Now, the last of these is slipping from my grasp. The last gate is

closing behind me. I study the face of each instrument. I switch off first one magneto and then the other. The tachometer needle barely moves. There's no sign of roughness. If I were landing from a test flight, I could suggest no adjustment to the most meticulous mechanic.

Suppose that in another hour the engine does begin to miss or the oil pressure drop? Of course I'd turn back. There'd be no sensible alternative. And the engine might keep going until I reached St. John's. But what then? A scattering of lights on the black earth below, the vague outline of mountains against the stars; beyond that, night would cover cliffs and boulders as water covers shoals. It would be a crash wherever I came down—on land or on sea.

I look back again at the lowering silhouette of the mountains, still sharp against the western sky. That is America. What a strange feeling—America at a distance! It's as though I were saying, "That's the earth"—far away, like a planet. There are no more reassuring islands ahead; no more test stretches of salt water. I've given up a continent and taken on an ocean in its place—irrevocably.

The Thirteenth Hour

I'm flying with my head thrown back, looking up through the skylight at the handful of stars above me, glancing down at intervals to make sure my compass heading is correct. When you can see stars close to the horizon it's easy to hold on course. They draw you toward them like a beacon on the earth. But looking straight up for guidance is like dangling at the end of a rope; it's almost impossible to keep from turning slightly.

The stars blink on and off as haze thickens in places and then thins out again. I hold on to them tightly, dreading the blind flying that lies ahead the moment I let them go, hoping I can climb above the haze into the crystal blackness of the higher night—hoping, climbing, and yet sinking deeper with every minute that I fly.

Soon haze becomes so thick that, except for those dim points of light, it might as well be cloud. At any moment those stars may blink their last and die, leaving me stranded thousands of feet below the surface, like a diver whose life line has been cut. I'd thought I could climb above the fog and leave it beneath me, a neat and definite layer. Now, I realize what a formidable enemy it is. Its forces have been in ambush all around me, waiting only for the cool of night to show their form.

Why try to hold on to those stars? Why not start in now on instruments? After all, they were put there so I could fly through fog. This game of hide and seek with a half-dozen stars is child's play. But if I start flying blind, God only knows how many hours of it lie ahead. It might go on through the entire night—the monotony of flying with my eyes always on the instrument board; the strain of flying by intellect alone, forcing the unruly senses of the body to follow the doubted orders of the mind—the endless bringing of one needle after another back to its proper position, and then finding that all except the one my eyes hold tight have strayed off again. The *Spirit of St. Louis* is too unstable to fly well on instruments. It's fast, and it has a greater range than any plane that flies; but it's high-strung, and balanced on a pin point. If I relax pressure on stick or rudder for an instant, the nose will veer off course.

And there's the question of staying awake. Could I keep sufficiently alert during long, monotonous hours of flying with my eyes glued to the instruments, with nothing more to stimulate my mind than the leaning of a needle? It was difficult enough to stay awake over the ice fields southwest of Newfoundland, when my eyes could travel the whole horizon back and forth, and with the piercing light of day to stir my senses. How would it be with fog and darkness shutting off even the view of my wing tips?

The Fourteenth Hour

It's hard to be an agnostic up here in the *Spirit of St. Louis*, aware of the frailty of man's devices, a part of the universe between its earth and stars. If one dies, all this goes on existing in a plan so perfectly balanced, so wonderfully simple, so incredibly complex that it's far beyond our comprehension—worlds and moons revolving; planets orbiting on suns; suns flung with apparent recklessness through space. There's the infinite magnitude of the universe; there's the infinite detail of its matter—the outer star, the inner atom. And man conscious of it all—a worldly audience to what if not to God?

The Fifteenth Hour

I glance at the chart on my lap. Of course I've shortened the night by flying with the earth's rotation. And I've been bending more and more eastward as I follow the great-circle route, cutting each meridian at a greater angle than the last, changing course a degree or two clockwise every hour through the day and night. When I took off from New York, I pointed the *Spirit of St. Louis* northeast; and when the sky cleared, the morning sun beamed down on an angle from my right. But when I reach Paris, I'll be heading south of east, and heavenly bodies will be rising on my left. After all, it's late in May. That's probably where the moon should be for a pilot on the great-circle route.

I'd almost forgotten the moon. Now, like a neglected ally, it's coming to my aid. Every minute will bring improving sight. As the moon climbs higher in the sky, its light will brighten, until finally it ushers in the sun. The stars ahead are already fading. The time is 10:20. There have been only two hours of solid darkness.

Gradually, as light improves, the night's black masses turn into a realm of form and texture. Silhouettes give way to shadings. Clouds open their secret details to the eyes. In the moon's reflected light, they seem more akin to it than to the earth over which they hover. They form a perfect setting for that strange foreign surface one sees through a telescope trained on the satellite of the world. Formations of the moon, they are—volcanoes and flat plateaus; great towers and bottomless pits; crevasses and canyons; ledges no earthly mountains ever knew—reality combined with the fantasy of a dream. There are shapes like growths of coral on the bed of a tropical sea, or the grotesque canyons of sandstone and lava at the edge of Arizona deserts—first black, then gray, now greenish hue in cold, mystical light.

I weave in and out, eastward, toward Europe, hidden away in my plane's tiny cockpit, submerged, alone, in the magnitude of this weird, unhuman space, venturing where man has never been, irretrievably launched on a flight through this sacred garden of the sky, this inner shrine of higher spirits. Am I myself a living, breathing, earth-bound body, or is this a dream of death I'm passing through? Am I alive, or am I really dead, a spirit in a spirit world? Am I actually in a plane boring through the air, over the Atlantic, toward Paris, or have I crashed on some worldly mountain, and is this the afterlife?

The Sixteenth Hour

Fifteen hundred miles behind. Two thousand one hundred miles to go. I'm halfway to Europe; not halfway across the ocean or halfway to Paris, but halfway between New York and Ireland—and Ireland seems like Europe, though it's really an island lying well out in the Atlantic. If I can reach Ireland in daylight and in clear weather, it should be easy sailing from there on.

After I flew out through that gap in the mountains at St. John's, Ireland became, subconsciously, more of an objective than Paris in my mind. If I could reach Ireland, Paris would follow, I felt, just as I consciously always took for granted that if I could reach Paris, Le Bourget would follow. Now, I'm nearer to Ireland than to New York!

A long flight always divides up into such mileposts. They help pass time and distance—the first state, the first shore line, the first hundred miles, the first thousand—there's always some objective reached to give the feeling of accomplishment. My log of them is filling. In it I've placed the continent of North America, Newfoundland, three stretches of salt water, the first day, and the blackness of the first night. Next, still quite far away, will be the dawn.

*   *   *

There's the moon, a little higher, and too far north. I've let the plane veer off course again. If only those compasses would steady down, I could stop cramping my neck to see the stars, and rest. That's what I want most now—to rest. Why try to hold a steady course? There's no accuracy to navigation anyway, with the compasses swinging, and after all those detours of the night. If I keep the *Spirit of St. Louis* pointing generally eastward, that should be enough; that will bring me closer to Europe. Why bother with careful navigation when it's so much easier to sit quietly and rest? After the night has passed, I can hold a straight course. It will be easier when the sun's up. Until then why should I worry about a trivial five or ten degrees?—Ten degrees isn't much of an angle—I can't possibly miss the whole continent of Europe—What difference does it make if I strike the shore line a little farther from course than I planned?

I shake myself violently, ashamed at my weakness, alarmed at my inability to overcome it. I never before understood the meaning of temptation, or how powerful one's desires can become. I've got to alert my mind, wake my body. I can't let anything as trifling as sleep ruin the flight I spent so many months in planning. How could I ever face my partners and say that I failed to reach Paris because I was sleepy? No matter how inaccurate my navigation, it must be the best I can carry on. Honor alone demands that. The more my compasses swing, the more alert I must stay to compensate for their errors. If my plane can stay aloft, if my engine can keep on running, then so can I.

I cup my hand into the slipstream, diverting a strong current of air against my face, breathing deeply of its gusty freshness. I let my eyelids fall shut for five seconds; then raise them against tons of weight. Protesting, they won't open wide until I force them with my thumb, and lift the muscles of my forehead to help keep them in place. Sleep overcomes my resistance like a drug.

My fingers are cold from the slipstream. I draw my mittens on again. Shall I put on flying boots? But I'd have to unbuckle the safety belt and take my feet off the rudder pedals, and do most of the work with one hand. The *Spirit of St. Louis* would veer off course and I'd have to straighten it out a dozen times before I got the boots on. It's too much effort. I'd rather be a little cold.

I draw the flying suit's wool collar across my throat. Should I put the windows in now? Why not shut off the world outside, relax in the warmth of a closed cockpit, and gain that last mile or two of speed from streamlining? Those windows, resting idly in their rack, pushing down on the plane with their three or four pounds of unused weight, still rankle in my mind—fifty miles of range thrown away. There's still time to save more than half of it, still time to make them pay a profit on their passage. But the same argument that kept them out before steps forward and wins its case again. If I shut myself off even partially from outside air and clouds and sky, the lure of sleep may prove beyond resistance. The coolness of the night is a guard against it; the clarity of moonlit clouds helps to overcome it; the exhaust of the engine, barking in through open windows, serves to ward it off.

The Seventeenth Hour

Now, I've burned the last bridge behind me. All through the storm and darkest night, my instincts were anchored to the continent of North America, as though an invisible cord still tied me to its coasts. In an emergency—if the ice-filled clouds had merged, if oil pressure had begun to drop, if a cylinder had started missing—I would have turned back toward America and home. Now, my anchor is in Europe; on a continent I've never seen. It's been shifted by the storm behind me, by the moon rising in the east, by the breaking sky and warmer air, and the possibility that the Gulf Stream may lie below. Now, I'll never think of turning back.

I let the *Spirit of St. Louis* bore its way on eastward. Unless the clouds below me break too, there's nothing to do until the sun rises except hold my heading, shift fuel tanks, and fill in the log each hour. The mixture control is well advanced, and the engine's throttled down as far as it's advisable to go. There's no need to watch dials carefully. Earlier in the night if their needles had forecast trouble, the sooner I noticed it and turned back the better chance I had of reaching land. Now, no matter what the needles show, I'll continue on my course as long as engine can hold plane in air. Before, I'd been flying away from safety. Now, every mile I cover brings me closer to it.

The Eighteenth Hour

The minute hand has just passed 1:00 a.m. It's dawn, one hour after midnight. But it's one hour after midnight only on the clock, and back at the longitude of New York where I set it before take-off in the morning—yesterday morning, it is, now. The clock simply shows the number of hours I've been in the air. It relates only to my cockpit and my plane, not to time outside. It no longer marks the vital incidents of day—dawn, and noon, and sunset. My flight is disconnected from all worldly measures. It passes through different frames of time and space.

With this faint trace of day, the uncontrollable desire to sleep falls over me in quilted layers. I've been staving it off with difficulty during the hours of moonlight. Now it looms all but insurmountable. This is the hour I've been dreading; the hour against which I've tried to steel myself. I know it's the beginning of my greatest test. This will be the worst time of all, this early hour of the second morning—the third morning, it is, since I've slept.

I've lost command of my eyelids. When they start to close, I can't restrain them. They shut, and I shake myself, and lift them with my fingers. I stare at the instruments, wrinkle forehead muscles tense. Lids close again regardless, stick tight as though with glue. My body has revolted from the rule of its mind. Like salt in wounds, the light of day brings back my pains. Every cell of my being is on strike, sulking in protest, claiming that nothing, nothing in the world, could be worth such effort; that man's tissue was never made for such abuse. My back is stiff; my shoulders ache; my face burns; my eyes smart. It seems impossible to go on longer. All I want in life is to throw myself down flat, stretch out—and sleep.

I've struggled with the dawn often enough before, but never with such a background of fatigue. I've got to muster all my reserves, all the tricks I've learned, all remaining strength of mind, for the conflict. If I can hold in air and close to course for one more hour, the sun will be over the horizon and the battle won. Each ray of light is an ally. With each moment after sunrise, vitality will increase.

*   *   *

Shaking my body and stamping my feet no longer has effect. It's more fatiguing than arousing. I'll have to try something else. I push the stick forward and dive down into a high ridge of cloud, pulling up sharply after I clip through its summit. That wakes me a little, but tricks don't help for long. They're only tiring. It's better to sit still and conserve strength.

My mind strays from the cockpit and returns. My eyes close, and open, and close again. But I'm beginning to understand vaguely a new factor which has come to my assistance. It seems I'm made up of three personalities, three elements, each partly dependent and partly independent of the others. There's my body, which knows definitely that what it wants most in the world is sleep. There's my mind, constantly making decisions that my body refuses to comply with, but which itself is weakening in resolution. And there's something else, which seems to become stronger instead of weaker with fatigue, an element of spirit, a directive force that has stepped out from the background and taken control over both mind and body. It seems to guard them as a wise father guards his children; letting them venture to the point of danger, then calling them back, guiding with a firm but tolerant hand.

When my body cries out that it *must* sleep, this third element replies that it may get what rest it can from relaxation, but that sleep is not to be had. When my mind demands that my body stay alert and awake, it is informed that alertness is too much to expect under these circumstances. And when it argues excitedly that to sleep would be to fail, and crash, and drown in the ocean, it is calmly reassured, and told it's right, but that while it must not expect alertness on the body's part, it can be confident there'll be no sleep.

The Nineteenth Hour

When I leave a cloud, drowsiness advances; when I enter the next, it recedes. If I could sleep and wake refreshed, how extraordinary this world of mist would be. But now I only dimly appreciate, only partially realize. The love of flying, the beauty of sunrise, the solitude of the mid-Atlantic sky, are screened from my senses by opaque veils of sleep. All my remaining energy, all the attention I can bring to bear, must be concentrated on the task of simply passing through.

The Twentieth Hour

The nose is down, the wing low, the plane diving and turning. I've been asleep with open eyes. I'm certain they've been open, yet I have all the sensations of waking up—lack of memory of intervening time, inability to comprehend the situation for a moment, the return of understanding like blood surging through the body. I kick left rudder and pull the stick back cornerwise. My eyes jump to the altimeter. No danger; I'm at 1600 feet, a little above my chosen altitude. In a moment, I'll have the plane leveled out. But the turn-indicator leans over the left—the air speed drops—the ball rolls quickly to the side. A climbing turn in the opposite direction! My plane is getting out of control!

The realization is like an electric shock running through my body. It brings instant mental keenness. In a matter of seconds I have the *Spirit of St. Louis* back in hand. But even after the needles are in place, the plane seems to be flying on its side. I know what's happening. It's the illusion you sometimes get while flying blind, the illusion that your plane is no longer in level flight, that it's spiraling, stalling, turning, that the instruments are wrong.

There's only one thing to do—shut off feeling from the mind as much as your ability permits. Let a wing stay low as far as bodily senses are concerned. Let the plane seem to maneuver as it will, dive, climb, sideslip, or bank; but keep the needles where they belong. Gradually, when the senses find that the plane is continuing on its course, that air isn't screaming through the cowlings as it would in a dive, that wings aren't trembling as they would in a stall, that there's really no pressure on the seat as there would be in a bank, they recover from their confusion and make obeisance to the mind.

As minutes pass and no new incident occurs, I fall into the

state of eye-open sleep again. I fly with less anguish when my conscious mind is not awake. At times I'm not sure whether I'm dreaming through life or living through a dream. It seems I've broken down the barrier between the two, and discovered some essential relationship between living and dreaming I never recognized before. Some secret has been opened to me beyond the ordinary consciousness of man. Can I carry it with me beyond this flight, into normal life again? Or is it forbidden knowledge? Will I lose it after I land, as I've so often lost the essence of some midnight's dream?

The Twenty-second Hour

Will the fog never end? Does this storm cover the entire ocean? Except for that small, early morning plot of open sea, I've been in it or above it for nine hours. What happened to the high pressure area that was to give me a sunny sky? The only storms reported were local ones in Europe!

I remind myself again that I didn't wait for confirmation of good weather. Dr. Kimball said only that stations along the coast reported clearing, and that a large high-pressure area was moving in over the North Atlantic. He didn't say there'd be no storms. The weather's no worse than I expected when I planned this flight. Why should I complain of a few blind hours in the morning? If the fog lifts by the time I strike the European coast, that's all I should ask. The flight's been as successful as I ever hoped it would be. The only thing that's seriously upset my plans is the sleepless night before I started—those extra twenty-three hours before take-off.

Of course no one thought the weather would break enough to let me start so quickly. But why did I depend on what anyone thought? Why did I take any chance? I didn't have to go to a show that evening. I didn't have to go to New York. This is the price for my amusement, and it's too high. It imperils the entire flight. If this were the first morning without sleep instead of the second, blind flying would be a different matter, and my navigation on a different plane.

*   *   *

The fog dissolves, and the sea appears. Flying two hundred feet higher, I wouldn't have seen it, for the overcast is just above me. There's no sun; only a pocket of clear air. Ahead, is another curtain of mist. Can I get under it this time? I push the stick forward. Waves are mountainous—even higher than before. If I fly close to their crests, maybe I can stay below the next area of fog.

I drop down until I'm flying in salt spray whipped off whitecaps by the wind. I clip five feet above a breaker with my wheels, watch tossing water sweep into the trough beyond. But the fog is too thick. It crowds down between the waves themselves. It merges with their form. A gull couldn't find enough ceiling to fly above this ocean. I climb. The air's rougher than before, swirling like the sea beneath it. I open my throttle wider to hold a margin of speed and power.

Before I reach a thousand feet, waves show again, vaguely—whitecaps veiled and unveiled by low-lying scuds of fog. I nose down; but in a moment they're gone, smothered by mist. I climb.

*   *   *

While I'm staring at the instruments, during an unearthly age of time, both conscious and asleep, the fuselage behind me becomes filled with ghostly presences—vaguely outlined forms, transparent, moving, riding weightless with me in the plane. I feel no surprise at their coming. There's no suddenness to their appearance. Without turning my head, I see them as clearly as though in my normal field of vision. There's no limit to my sight—my skull is one great eye, seeing everywhere at once.

These phantoms speak with human voices—friendly, vaporlike shapes, without substance, able to vanish or appear at will, to pass in and out through the walls of the fuselage as though no walls were there. Now, many are crowded behind me. Now, only a few remain. First one and then another presses forward to my shoulder to speak above the engine's noise, and then draws back among the group behind. At times, voices come out of the air itself, clear yet far away, traveling through distances that can't be measured by the scale of human miles; familiar voices, conversing and advising on my flight, discussing problems of my navigation, reassuring me, giving me messages of importance unattainable in ordinary life.

The Twenty-third Hour

Sea, clouds, and sky are all stirred up together—dull gray mist, blinding white mist, patches of blue, mottling of black, a band of sunlight sprinkling diamond facets on the water. There are clouds lying on the ocean, clouds just risen from its surface, clouds floating at every level through twenty thousand feet of sky; some small, some overpowering in size—wisps, masses, layers. It's a breeding ground for mist.

I fly above, below, between the layers, as though following the interstices of a giant sponge; sometimes under a blue sky but over an ocean veiled by thick and drifting mist; sometimes brushing gray clouds with my wings while my wheels are almost rolling in the breakers' foam. It's like playing leapfrog with the weather. These cloud formations help me to stay awake. They give me something on which to fix my eyes in passing, but don't hold my stare too long. Their tremendous, changing, flashing world removes monotony from flight.

*   *   *

Sunlight flashes as I emerge from a cloud. My eyes are drawn to the north. My dreams are startled away. There, under my left wing, only five or six miles distant, a coastline parallels my course—purple, haze-covered hills; clumps of trees; rocky cliffs. Small, wooded islands guard the shore.

But I'm in mid-Atlantic, nearly a thousand miles from land! Half-formed thoughts rush through my mind. Are the compasses completely wrong? Am I hopelessly lost? Is it the coast of Labrador or Greenland that I see? Have I been flying north instead of east?

It's like waking from a sound sleep in strange surroundings, in a room where you've never spent a night before. The wallpaper, the bed, the furniture, the light coming in the window, nothing is as you expected it to be.

I shake my head and look again. There can be no doubt, now, that I'm awake. But the shore line is still there. Land in mid-Atlantic! Something has gone wrong! I couldn't have been flying north, regardless of the inaccuracy of my compasses. The sun and the moon both rose on my left, and stars confirmed that my general direction was toward Europe. I know there's no land out here in mid-ocean—nothing between Greenland and Iceland to the north, and the Azores to the south. But I look down at the chart for reassurance; for my mind is no longer certain of its knowledge. To find new islands marked on it would hardly be stranger than the flight itself.

No, they must be mirages, fog islands sprung up along my route; here for an hour only to disappear, mushrooms of the sea. But so apparently real, so cruelly deceptive! *Real* clouds cover their higher hills, and pour down into their ravines. How can those bluffs and forests consist of nothing but fog? No islands of the earth could be more perfect.

The Twenty-fourth Hour

Here it's well into midday and my mind's still shirking, still refusing to meet the problems it undertook so willingly in planning for this flight. Are all those months of hard and detailed work to be wasted for lack of a few minutes of concentrated effort? Is my character so weak that I can't pull myself together long enough to lay out a new, considered course? Has landing at Le Bourget become of so little import that I'll trade success for these useless hours of semiconscious relaxation? *No; I must, I will* become alert, and concentrate, and make decisions.

There are measures I haven't yet used—too extreme for normal times. But now it's a case of survival. Anything is justified that has effect. I strike my face sharply with my hand. It hardly feels the blow. I strike again with all the strength I have. My cheek is numb, but there's none of the sharp stinging that I counted on to wake my body. No jump of flesh, no lash on mind. It's no use. Even these methods don't work. Why try more?

But Paris is over a thousand miles away! And there's still a continent to find. I must be prepared to strike a fog-covered European coast hundreds of miles off course; and, if necessary, to fly above clouds all the hours of another night. How can I pass through such ordeals if I can't wake my mind and stir my body? But the alternative is death and failure. Can I complete this flight to Paris? Can I even reach the Irish coast? *But the alternative is death and failure! Death! For the first time in my life, I doubt my ability to endure.*

The stark concept of death has more effect than physical blow or reasoned warning. It imbues me with new power, power strong enough to communicate the emergency to my body's senses, to whip them up from their lethargy and marshall them once more—in straggling ranks, but with some semblance of order and coordination. *It's life, life, life itself at stake.* This time I'm not just saying so. *I know it.*

The Twenty-sixth Hour

Is there something alive down there under my wing? I thought I saw a dark object moving through the water. I search the surface, afraid to hope, lest I lose confidence in vision. Was it a large fish, or were my eyes deceiving me? After the fog islands and the phantoms, I no longer trust my senses. The *Spirit of St. Louis* itself might fade away without causing me great surprise. But—yes, there it is again, slightly behind me now, a porpoise—the first living thing I've seen since Newfoundland. Fin and sleek, black body curve gracefully above the surface and slip down out of sight.

The ocean is as desolate as ever. Yet a complete change has taken place. I feel that I've safely recrossed the bridge to life—broken the strands which have been tugging me toward the universe beyond. Why do I find such joy, such encouragement in the sight of a porpoise? What possible bond can I have with a porpoise hundreds of miles at sea, with a strange creature I've never seen before and will never see again? What is there in that flashing glimpse of hide that means so much to me, that even makes it seem a different ocean? Is it simply that I've been looking so long, and seeing nothing? Is it an omen of land ahead? Or is there some common tie between living things that surmounts even the barrier of species?

Can it be that the porpoise was imaginary too, a part of this strange, living dream, like the fuselage's phantoms and the islands which faded into mist? Yet I know there's a difference, a dividing line that still exists between reality and apparition. The porpoise *was* real, like the water itself, like the substance of the cockpit around me, like my face which I can feel when I run my hand across it.

* * *

It's twenty-six and a half hours since I took off. That's almost twice as long as the flight between San Diego and St. Louis; and that was much the longest flight I ever made. It's asking a lot of an engine to run twenty-six hours without attention. Back on the mail, we check our Liberties at the end of every trip. Are the rocker-arms on my Whirlwind still getting grease? And how long will it keep on going if one of them should freeze?

I shift arms on the stick. My left hand—being free, and apparently disconnected from my mind's control—begins aimlessly exploring the pockets of the chart bag. It pulls the maps of Europe halfway out to reassure my eyes they're there, tucks my helmet and goggles in more neatly, and fingers the shiny little first-aid kit and the dark glasses given me by that doctor on Long Island. Why have I let my eyes burn through the morning? Why have I been squinting for hours and not thought of these glasses before? I hook the wires over my ears and look out on a shaded ocean. It's as though the sky were overcast again. I don't dare use them. They're too comfortable, too pleasant. They make it seem like evening—make me want to sleep.

I slip the glasses back into their pocket, pull out the first-aid kit, and idly snap it open. It contains adhesive tape, compact bandages, and a little pair of scissors. Not enough to do much patching after a crash. Tucked into one corner are several silk-covered, glass capsules of aromatic ammonia. "For use as Smelling Salts," the labels state. What did the doctor think I could do with smelling salts over the ocean? This kit is made for a child's cut

finger, or for some debutante fainting at a ball! I might as well
have saved its weight on the take-off, for all the good it will be to
me. I put it back in the chart bag—and then pull it out again. If
smelling salts revive people who are about to faint, why won't
they revive people who are about to fall asleep? Here's a weapon
against sleep lying at my side unused, a weapon which has been
there all through the morning's deadly hours. A whiff of one of
these capsules should sharpen the dullest mind. And no eyes could
sleep stinging with the vapor of ammonia.

I'll try one now. The fumes ought to clear my head and keep
the compass centered. I crush a capsule between thumb and
fingers. A fluid runs out, discoloring the white silk cover. I hold it
cautiously, several inches from my nose. There's no odor. I move
it closer, slowly, until finally it touches my nostrils. I smell nothing!
My eyes don't feel the slightest sting, and no tears come to moisten
their dry edges. I inhale again with no effect, and throw the
capsule through the window. My mind now begins to realize how
deadened my senses have become, how close I must be to the end
of my reserves. And yet there may be another sleepless night
ahead.

The Twenty-seventh Hour

I'm flying along dreamily when it catches my eyes, that black
speck on the water two or three miles southeast. I realize it's there
with the same jerk to awareness that comes when the altimeter
needle drops too low in flying blind. I squeeze my lids together
and look again. A boat! A small boat! Several small boats, scattered
over the surface of the ocean!

Seconds pass before my mind takes in the full importance of
what my eyes are seeing. Then, all feeling of drowsiness departs.
I bank the *Spirit of St. Louis* toward the nearest boat and nose
down toward the water. I couldn't be wider awake or more keenly
aware if the engine had stopped.

Fishing boats! *The coast, the European coast, can't be far away!*
The ocean is behind, the flight completed. Those little vessels,
those chips on the sea, are Europe. What nationality? Are they
Irish, English, Scotch, or French? Can they be from Norway, or

from Spain? What fishing bank are they anchored on? How far
from the coast do fishing banks extend? It's too early to reach
Europe unless a gale blew behind me through the night. Thoughts
press forward in confused succession. After fifteen hours of solitude,
here's human life and help and safety.

The ocean is no longer a dangerous wilderness. I feel as secure
as though I were circling Lambert Field back home. I could land
alongside any one of those boats, and someone would throw me a
rope and take me on board where there'd be a bunk I could sleep
on, and warm food when I woke up.

The first boat is less than a mile ahead—I can see its masts
and cabin. I can see it rocking on the water. I close the mixture
control and dive down fifty feet above its bow, dropping my wing
to get a better view.

But where is the crew? There's no sign of life on deck. Can all
the men be out in dories? I climb higher as I circle. No, there
aren't any dories. I can see for miles, and the ocean's not rough
enough to hide one. Are the fishermen frightened by my plane,
swooping down suddenly from the sky? Possibly they never saw
a plane before. *Of course* they never saw one out so far over the
ocean. Maybe they all hid below the decks when they heard the
roar of my engine. Maybe they think I'm some demon from the
sky, like those dragons that decorate ancient mariners' charts. But
if the crews are so out of contact with the modern world that they
hide from the sound of an airplane, they must come from some
isolated coastal village above which airplanes never pass. And the
boats look too small to have ventured far from home. I have
visions of riding the top of a hurricane during the night, with a
hundred-mile-an-hour wind drift. Possibly these vessels are
anchored north of Ireland, or somewhere in the Bay of Biscay.
Then shall I keep on going straight, or turn north, or south?

I fly over to the next boat bobbing up and down on the swells.
Its deck is empty too. But as I drop my wing to circle, a man's
head appears, thrust out through a cabin porthole, motionless,
staring up at me. In the excitement and joy of the moment, in the
rush of ideas passing through my reawakened mind, I decide to
make that head withdraw from the porthole, come out of the
cabin, body and all, and to point toward the Irish coast. No sooner
have I made the decision than I realize its futility. Probably that

fisherman can't speak English. Even if he can, he'll be too startled
to understand my message, and reply. But I'm already turning
into position to dive down past the boat. It won't do any harm to
try. Why deprive myself of that easy satisfaction? Probably if I
fly over it again, the entire crew will come on deck. I've talked to
people before from a plane, flying low with throttled engine, and
received the answer through some simple gesture—a nod or an
outstretched arm.

I glide down within fifty feet of the cabin, close the throttle,
and shout as loudly as I can "WHICH WAY IS IRELAND?"

How extraordinary the silence is with the engine idling! I look
back under the tail, watch the fisherman's face for some sign of
understanding. But an instant later, all my attention is concentrated on the plane. For I realize that I've lost the "feel" of flying.
I shove the throttle open, and watch the air-speed indicator while
I climb and circle. As long as I keep the needle above sixty miles
an hour, there's no danger of stalling. Always before, I've known
instinctively just what condition my plane was in—whether it had
flying speed or whether it was stalling, and how close to the edge
it was riding in between. I didn't have to look at the instruments.
Now, the pressure of the stick no longer imparts its message
clearly to my hand. I can't tell whether air is soft or solid.

When I pass over the boat a third time, the head is still at the
porthole. It hasn't moved or changed expression since it first
appeared. It came as suddenly as the boats themselves. It seems
as lifeless. I didn't notice before how pale it is—or am I now
imagining its paleness? It looks like a severed head in that porthole,
as though a guillotine had dropped behind it. I feel baffled. After
all, a man who dares to show his face would hardly fear to show
his body. There's something unreal about these boats. They're as
weird as the night's temples, as those misty islands of Atlantis, as
the fuselage's phantoms that rode behind my back.

Why don't sailors gather on the decks to watch my plane? Why
don't they pay attention to my circling and shouting? What's the
matter with this strange flight, where dreams become reality, and
reality returns to dreams? But these aren't vessels of cloud and
mist. They're tangible, made of real substance like my plane—sails
furled, ropes coiled neatly on the decks, masts swaying back and
forth with each new swell. Yet the only sign of crew is that single

head, hanging motionless through the cabin porthole. It's like "The Rime of the Ancient Mariner" my mother used to read aloud. These boats remind me of the "painted ship upon a painted ocean".

I want to stay, to circle again and again, until that head removes itself from the porthole and the crews come out on deck. I want to see them standing and waving like normal, living people. I've passed through worlds and ages since my last contact with other men. I've been away, far away, planets and heavens away, until only a thread was left to lead me back to earth and life. I've followed that thread with swinging compasses, through lonely canyons, over pitfalls of sleep, past the lure of enchanted islands, fearing that at any moment it would break. And now I've returned to earth, returned to these boats bobbing on the ocean. I want an earthly greeting. I deserve a warmer welcome back to the fellowship of men.

Shall I fly over to another boat and try again to raise the crew? No, I'm wasting minutes of daylight and miles of fuel. There's nothing but frustration to be had by staying longer. It's best to leave. There's something about this fleet that tries my mind and spirit, and lowers confidence with every circle I make. Islands that turn to fog, I understand. Ships without crews, I do not. And that motionless head at the porthole—it's no phantom, and yet it shows no sign of life. I straighten out the *Spirit of St. Louis* and fly on eastward.

The Twenty-eighth Hour

Is that a cloud on the northeastern horizon, or a strip of low fog—or—*can it possibly be land?* It looks like land, but I don't intend to be tricked by another mirage. Framed between two gray curtains of rain, not more than ten or fifteen miles away, a purplish blue band has hardened from the haze—flat below, like a water-line—curving on top, as though composed of hills or aged mountains.

I'm only sixteen hours out from Newfoundland. I allowed eighteen and a half hours to strike the Irish coast. If that's Ireland, I'm two and a half hours ahead of schedule. Can this be another, clearer image, like the islands of the morning? Is there something strange about it too, like the fishing fleet and that haunting head? Is each new illusion to become more real until reality itself is meaningless? But my mind is clear. I'm no longer half asleep. I'm awake—alert—aware. The temptation is too great. I can't hold my course any longer. The *Spirit of St. Louis* banks over toward the nearest point of land.

I stare at it intently, not daring to believe my eyes, keeping hope in check to avoid another disappointment, watching the shades and contours unfold into a coast line—a coastline coming down from the north—a coast line bending toward the east—a coast line with rugged shores and rolling mountains. It's much too early to strike England, France, or Scotland. It's early to be striking Ireland; but that's the nearest land.

A fjorded coast stands out as I approach. Barren islands guard it. Inland, green fields slope up the sides of warted mountains. This *must* be Ireland. It can be no other place than Ireland. The fields are too green for Scotland; the mountains too high for Brittany or Cornwall.

Now, I'm flying above the foam-lined coast, searching for prominent features to fit the chart on my knees. I've climbed to two thousand feet so I can see the contours of the country better. The mountains are old and rounded; the farms small and stony. Rain-glistened dirt roads wind narrowly through hills and fields. Below me lies a great tapering bay; a long, bouldered island; a village. Yes, there's a place on the chart where it all fits—line of ink on line of shore—Valentia and Dingle Bay, *on the south-western coast of Ireland!*

I can hardly believe it's true. I'm almost exactly on my route, closer than I hoped to come in my wildest dreams back in San Diego. What happened to all those detours of the night around the thunderheads? Where has the swinging compass error gone? The wind above the storm clouds must have blown fiercely on my tail. In edging northward, intuition must have been more accurate than reasoned navigation.

The southern tip of Ireland! On course; over two hours ahead of schedule; the sun still well up in the sky; the weather clearing! I circle again, fearful that I'll wake to find this too a phantom, a mirage fading into mid-Atlantic mist. But there's no question about it; every detail on the chart has its counterpart below; each major feature on the ground has its symbol on the chart. The lines correspond exactly. Nothing in that world of dreams and phantoms was like this. I spiral lower, looking down on the little village. There are boats in the harbor, wagons on the stone-fenced roads. People are running out into the streets, looking up and waving. This is earth again, the earth where I've lived and now will live once more. Here are human beings. Here's a human welcome. Not a single detail is wrong. I've never seen such beauty before—fields so green, people so human, a village so attractive, mountains and rocks so mountainous and rocklike.

*   *   *

I bank steeply around and set my course southeastward, cutting across the bouldered fjords, flying low over the hilltop farms, the rock fences, and the small, green fields of Kerry. Now, I can check the engine—All cylinders hitting on the left switch—All cylinders hitting on the right—And all instrument readings are normal.

Sheep and cattle graze on their sloping pastures. Horse-drawn carts crawl along their shiny roads. People move across walled-in barnyards, through doorways of the primitive stone buildings. It must be a hard place to gain a living from the soil. And it would be worse than New England for a forced landing.

Even the wish to sleep has left, and with it the phantoms and voices. I didn't notice their absence before; but now, as I settle down for the last six hundred miles to Paris, I realize that they remained behind with the fishing fleet. They vanished with that first strange touch of Europe and of man. Since I sighted those specks on the water, I've been as wide awake as though I started the flight this morning after a warm breakfast and a full night's sleep. The thought of floating off in a bed of feathers has lost its attractiveness.

Time is no longer endless, or the horizon destitute of hope. The strain of take-off, storm, and ocean, lies behind. There'll be no second night above the clouds, no more grappling with misty walls of ice. There's only one more island to cross—only the narrow tip of an island. I look at England's outline on my map. And then, within an hour, I'll see the coast of France; and beyond that, Paris and Le Bourget. As Nova Scotia and Newfoundland were stepping-stones from America, Ireland and England are stepping-stones to Europe. Yesterday, each strip of sea I crossed was an advance messenger of the ocean. Today, these islands down below are heralds to a continent.

It's as though a curtain has fallen behind me, shutting off the stagelike unreality of this transatlantic flight. It's been like a theater where the play carries you along in time and place until you forget you're only a spectator. You grow unaware of the walls around you, of the program clasped in your hand, even of your body, its breath, pulse, and being, You live with the actors and the setting, in a different age and place. It's not until the curtain drops that consciousness and body reunite. Then, you turn your back on the stage, step out into the cool night, under the lights of streets, between the displays of store windows. You feel life surging in the crowd around you, life as it was when you entered the theater, hours before. Life is real. It always was real. The stage, of course, was the dream. All that transpired there is now a memory, shut off by the curtain, by the doors of the theater, by the passing minutes of time.

Striking Ireland was like leaving the doors of a theater—phantoms for actors; cloud islands and temples for settings; the ocean behind me, an empty stage. The flight across is already like a dream. I'm over villages and fields, back to land and wakefulness and a type of flying that I know. I'm myself again, in earthly skies and over earthly ground. My hands and feet and eyelids move, and I can think as I desire. That third, controlling element has retired to the background. I'm no longer three existences in one. My mind is able to command, and my body follows out its orders with precision.

Ireland, England, France, Paris! The night at Paris! *This* night at Paris—less than six hours from Now—*France and Paris!* It's like a fairy tale. Yesterday I walked on Roosevelt Field; today I'll walk on Le Bourget.

CHARLES A. LINDBERGH,
The Spirit of St. Louis

Charles Lindbergh and the *Spirit of St Louis* welcomed by huge crowds at Croydon after his successful trans-Atlantic flight.

The tutelage of Ernest K. Gann

Ernest K. Gann has flown every kind of plane since the 1920s, and in addition is one of the outstanding aviation writers of our time. When I met him in New York in 1981 he had just survived a crash landing at his home at Friday Island in the state of Washington, and had gone on from there to Massachusetts to buy himself a small submarine.

He has a unique gift of taking the reader into the cockpit and making him see things through the pilot's eyes. Yes, we say when we have read a Gann story, that is how it must have been.

An outstanding airman and airplane writer:
Ernest K. Gann.

Beattie reaches to the floor beside his seat and takes up the log-book. It is two pieces of metal hinged together and painted a dark blue with the number of the aircraft stencilled on the outside. The forms are inside. It is the uninspiring duty of every co-pilot to complete these forms. Some do so begrudgingly, others approach the task with the grubby exactitude of postal clerks writing a money order. Our pay is calculated from the times recorded in these log-books and the formula for computation is so absurdly involved that a mistake of only a few minutes can result in the loss of several dollars. Therefore, all pilots take an inordinate interest in the time figures whereas, if the flight is routine, they hardly notice those recording engine temperatures, pressures, and fuel consumed.

Beattie turns up the small spotlight behind his head and focuses it on the log-book. He sighs audibly and begins to fill in the vacant squares with symbols and numerals.

I can feel the passengers moving about in the cabin, almost count their individual trips to the washroom in the tail. They have been looking at their watches and know we must soon be on the ground. Their movements come to me through the adjustments required on the stabiliser. I am obliged to move the wheel controlling it frequently, thus, counter-balancing their weight. The stewardess will come forward in a few minutes. Her name is Katherine and she will smell better than we do and she will ask how soon we are going to land. When she is told she will stand for a moment in the darkness between the baggage and mail bins and adjust her girdle. Then she will return to the cabin. Or because Beattie is a bachelor, she may linger without explanation.

I reach into my left-hand shirt pocket and take out a celluloid disc about the size of a small saucer. Actually it is a slide rule, by means of which I can quickly calculate the time required to descend from five thousand feet to approach altitude at New York. I can easily compute the time in my head. The slide rule is merely habit, and a good one, for it is always a reminder that the days of happy guesswork are gone.

Our altitude is still five thousand and fifty feet. The time now—nine-twenty-eight.

Two things displease me. The extra fifty feet above five thousand is sloppy flying and there is too much light in the cockpit.

I glance at Beattie, then ask him to turn down his light. As he complies my eyes return to the flight instruments and my hand caresses the stabiliser wheel. I rotate it forward an inch or so then pull back the two red-topped throttles a like amount. At once a subtle change occurs within the cockpit. The constant muffled roar of our slipstream takes on a more urgent tone. The rate of climb needle sags. The air speed increases to one hundred and eighty and the altimeter starts its slow unwinding. For the moment both Beattie and myself are entirely absorbed in the instruments, for their silent passing of information has a remarkable, nearly hypnotic way of capturing any pilot's eyes. The momentary result is an unblinking stare as if we would question their honesty for the ten thousandth time.

This is as it should be. When, as now, things are going well, our faces are those of men in harmony with the exactness of machinery. We are attentive, yet lulled by the security so gently transmitted from the luminous dials and needles. We are the masters in sure command of all those mechanical contrivances which comprise the unit of this one flying machine. We do not trouble our sense of authority in brooding on those rare enough occasions when we were more the frightened servants than the master; when the machine rebelled with the instruments to rob us of all dignity and make us feel like the sorcerer's apprentice.

The altimeter needle indicates precisely five thousand feet. We have lost only the sloppy fifty feet and I hold the exact five thousand for perhaps thirty seconds while my eyes travel upward to the windshield glass. This trifling hesitation before continuing the descent is not to rest my eyes. It is only because my seat is somewhat too far back. Now my sole desire is to adjust it according to long-established personal taste, thereby innocently deceiving myself that from such a particular position of the seat and from no other can I make a good and proper landing.

I bend down, seeking the lever which controls the fore and aft movements of the seat. Surging my body, I move it forward one notch and hear it click. As I straighten Beattie snaps the metal log-book closed with a gesture of finality.

My hand seeks the stabiliser wheel again. My eyes alternate between the rate of climb needle and the black windshield. A few seconds pass. Beattie is preoccupied with stuffing a pencil into his shirt pocket. He also looks ahead, not in anticipation of seeing anything—facing the windshield is simply the most easy and natural position. There is just enough light within the cockpit faintly to reflect Beattie's image in the glass. Compelled only by his scrupulous regard for personal appearance, he bends forward and starts to adjust his tie. This humble gesture is almost the very last the human body identified as Beattie will ever be called upon to make.

For his next movement is a parting of his lips followed by a horrible inarticulate sucking sound, audible even above the engines. His actual cry of instantaneous shock is still unfinished when my own attention is drawn to the windshield. My every sense is appalled. There is not time-space for true fear to build, but the primeval urges are instantly uncovered. My stunned brain demands a challenging scream yet I am unable to make any sound. My body along with my soul has stopped dead, severed of all vitality within.

My hands freeze on the control wheel. In the blackness ahead there is a sudden hideous apparition; the mass is no more than a thickening of the night but it supports a green wing-tip light and just below it—two flickering tongues of engine exhaust flame.

The whole frightful assembly slides swiftly across our field of vision. It is so close it seems I could reach out and touch it. It is too late for any reaction. Almost before our minds can appreciate its significance, the spectacle is gone from ahead. Beattie, his face pressed against the glass, follows its disappearance off to our right. His whole body swivels quickly with its ghostly progress.

The entire drama begins and ends in two seconds. Beattie and I are sole members of the audience for it is obvious those in the other aeroplane never saw us. Yet except for a miraculous separation of no more than fifty feet they would also be quite dead. Only a new audience on the ground would have heard the explosion. And watched the descent of two bundles of flaming metal.

It is over. The peril was instantly there and then almost as instantly, not there. We peeped behind the curtain, saw what some dead men have seen, and survived with it engraved forever on our memories.

Now we are not even afraid. That will come when there is time for contemplation. I have not moved nor is there even a quickening in my breathing.

Slowly Beattie turns in his seat and our eyes meet. A smile touches the corner of his mouth, but it is a melancholy smile and for the moment it seems the perfect comment on what has been our utter helplessness. Those fifty additional sloppy feet held only a few minutes previously, so insignificant then—are now revealed as the pinion of our lives. To have maintained those fifty feet one second more would have matched our altitude exactly with the stranger. Then who chose the moment to descend? Why, just then? It was certainly not our own premeditated decision.

I pick up the microphone slowly, my movements now devoid of flourish.

"New York from Flight Five . . ."

"Go ahead, Flight Five."

"Have you any reported traffic?" I want desperately to accuse him—any handy victim will do until I can vent my fury on Air Traffic Control. Yet even as I wait I realise they cannot be aware of every outlaw ship in the sky. The reply is a foregone conclusion or we should have been warned.

"No reported traffic . . . Five."

"Okay. Five."

I replace the microphone carefully and fumble in my pants pocket for a cigarette. When I bring it out the package is squashed. They are always squashed, which they would not be if I would ever learn to carry them elsewhere. In such poor thoughts my mind seeks momentary refuge, convincing itself, or trying to, that what I have just seen really was not seen. I should much prefer the innocence of our passengers who almost performed the interesting feat of instantly perishing whilst in the act of combing their hair or dabbing a drop of perfume behind an ear.

Since the choked, half-born sounds which were more plaintive than defiant, Beattie and I have not made any audible exchange. Lighting my cigarette with a hand that has no true cause to be so steady, I prospect through several things I might say to my companion in fortune.

Tradition calls for me to be outwardly calm and collected which is not overly difficult, doubtless because the actual exposure to imminent death was of such short duration. Peace within is not so easily re-established. That one-second difference, its selection, the reason for it, must haunt the rest of my living days whatever their number. Years may pass before I will relive that instant, but it must come to me again and again, always jeering at logic, always mysterious and incomprehensible. Why should that second of time have been given to Beattie and myself and to our eleven passengers whoever they might be, and to Katherine, the stewardess? I can only assume that the occupants of the outlaw plane were not deliberately bent upon a combination of suicide and mass murder. They, too, were spared by a particle of time.

And then, what of the uneasiness Beattie and I had both known before the near catastrophe? There had been no basis for it, yet it would not be denied. Strangely, now that the moment has passed, the feeling no longer persists.

To my personal God I mutter two words of gratitude. My thank you is given almust begrudgingly for it is still extremely difficult to appreciate our salvation. I can only think that the moment was an evil one, and so long as the issue does not constitute a mere reprieve, then I am content to believe it must be good.

After a decent time, as if he is reluctant to break the silence between us, Beattie asks for a cigarette.

"I didn't know you smoked."

"I don't. I just think I might like to try one . . . now."

ERNEST K. GANN,
Fate is the Hunter

The Trail-Blazers

1. Cobham and the death of Elliott

The most successful of the early British pioneers was Alan (later
Sir Alan) Cobham. During the 1920s and 1930s his successful
trips to Rangoon, Australia and the Cape made his name a
household word. As a boy I remember vividly reading in the
newspapers of the extraordinary event that befell him and his
engineer Elliott near Basra on the 1926 trip to Australia.

At Baghdad Elliott had many old friends in the Air
Force—curiously, several school pals—and they all seemed so keen
and interested in the flight that there were at least half a dozen
on the seaplane, giving a hand either at filling up or cleaning the
plugs, or any job that might assist Elliott. I shall always have
distinct memories of sitting on board the gun-boat feeling very
sorry for myself, wondering whether I ought to go back to bed or
whether I ought to fly on. At last I decided that I should be all
right if I could once get in the air, although only a few moments
before I had almost made up my mind to take another day's rest.
Once in the air we were soon heading down the Tigris towards
Bushire in the Persian Gulf, which was our next stop, five hundred
miles away.

While we were cruising along I came to the conclusion that
one of the great problems of the new age of world aviation would
be that of fortifying the human being against the sudden changes
of temperature and atmosphere. For example, if we are to fly, as
it is anticipated, within the next few years from England to India
in a matter of four days, then something must be done to protect
the passenger against the sudden change of temperature. For
instance, a person might leave London on a cold April morning
with a temperature somewhere in the fifties, and after a flight of
about three days in moderately cool air at a fair altitude, find
himself descending at Basra into a temperate of 100° in the shade
or even more. This state of affairs would naturally be a big tax
even on a robust constitution, and it might be fatal to a weakling.
So here is a problem for our doctors, to find some means of

fortifying the human system against such violent changes. Of course for the next few years air routes will be sufficiently slow to make the change of temperature fairly gradual, so that the would-be traveller of to-day need have no fears in this direction.

After we had crossed over again from the Tigris to the Euphrates and had flown about one hundred and fifty miles I noticed we were getting into a sand-storm region, and a little later we were forced to descend from a comfortable altitude, lower and lower, owing to the thickening sand-storm, until we were flying but a few feet above the river bank, in order to find our way in the blinding dust. From my experience I know that these sand-storms rise to a great altitude, and even if one could fly above them it would be impossible to see the ground beneath and equally impossible to find one's way over a more or less trackless desert. Moreover on a compass course the risk in arriving at one's destination at a high altitude with a thick dust storm raging beneath would be great, for it would be a decided adventure to come down through the blinding dust and find one's exact whereabouts. Therefore rather than take any of these risks we flew low and followed the bank of the river, and as we were in a seaplane fitted with floats we carried on with a feeling of absolute safety, with the knowledge that we could land on the water of the river at a moment's notice should the dust ever become so thick that there was not sufficient visibility for us to carry on.

At last this state of affairs occurred and, spotting a native police hut on the bank of the river, I landed on the water near by, quietly turned our machine and gently beached her on the mud bank. When the propeller stopped, Elliott hopped ashore, taking with him the anchor which he planted deep in the soft earth inland, well away from the bank, remarking as he did so that he thought this was real sound, practical aviation. At the time I was feeling none too energetic and a little worried and depressed at having the original schedule of our flight so changed. Of course we were gathering fresh information and it was all new experience, which was what we were really out for, but even so I could hardly satisfy my anxieties with these observations. Elliott was very cheerful, and soon we had found shelter from the dust and heat in the big mud police hut where the natives had very kindly taken our mosquito nets and rigged them up over rough beds for us to lie on. Then at 9 a.m. in the morning we found ourselves under our nets endeavouring to sleep.

Before settling down I had sent a native off on horseback to the nearest telegraph station so that our whereabouts could be notified to the R.A.F. Head-quarters at Baghdad. I suppose we must have rested for about an hour when the native police brought us delicious hot tea, Russian style, and after that another fellow brought us a huge melon with ample sugar, much to the delight of Elliott! And so we remained with these kindly folk until about 1.30 or so in the afternoon, when the dust storm lifted a little and I thought we might have another shot at reaching Basra instead of Bushire that day.

All went well for about the first half-hour of our flight, but as we were nearing the beginning of the great swamp area above Basra we ran into another dust storm, and so we continued to fly low. The River Euphrates enters the Hammar Lakes just above the town of Suke Shuyuk when it gradually becomes a mere channel through a vast inundated area. As long as one has a definite horizon or some distinct feature such as a river bank upon which to focus one's gaze it is not a difficult matter to fly in even very bad visibility. It must be remembered that whereas it is a comparatively simple matter for a motor car to go at forty miles an hour along a road with a five or six hundred yard visibility, it is a vastly different thing to pilot an aircraft at one hundred miles an hour with the same visibility and an indefinite horizon.

For these reasons I was worried about flying over the open swamp of the lake, because the muddy brown waters merged into the brown dust-laden atmosphere and I felt it would be difficult to distinguish which was water and which was air. When a pilot is enveloped in thick fog and has no horizon whatever, he very quickly loses his equilibrium and cannot make his own level; in fact he loses all sense of where the ground is, or which is top and which is bottom. The same conditions exist in a blinding sand-storm as in a fog, and therefore I felt that if I lost my horizon as a result of the water merging into the sand-storm I might find myself in a very awkward predicament. However, fortunately there were rushes and weeds drifting on the lake which were sufficient for me to distinguish its surface, and this gave me a horizon to work on.

Soon we left the town of Suke Shuyuk behind us, and as we went on I was determined that no matter what direction I might be taking I would follow the somewhat irregular definite coast line of rush swamp rather than go out on a direct course over the open water. And so, flying at about fifty feet above the reeds, I made a zig-zag course along the somewhat indefinite edge of the lake. I was making for its southern shore where I knew we should meet hard earth and thus have something distinct to see, and although at times I seemed to be flying back on my tracks, I kept on, knowing that eventually we should come out to the hard desert again.

Gradually the swamp area began to give way to the irregular sandy coast-line, and I was just congratulating myself that we should soon be out of our worst difficulties and flying at an altitude of not more than forty feet in order to get the maximum visibility ahead, when suddenly there was a violent explosion which appeared to come from the cabin. Instantly I shouted through the connecting window to Elliott asking him what had happened and if we were on fire, for my first thought was that possibly one of our rocket-pistol cartridges had exploded, and as the rocket burns for many seconds with an intense flame it would certainly set the machine on fire. Elliott shouted back in a very feeble voice that a petrol pipe had burst, but it was difficult to hear him and as I was unable to shut my engine off and glide owing to our very low altitude, I tore a sheet of paper off my writing-pad and handed it through the window to him. Presently a message came back to the effect that the petrol pipe which leads from the reserve tank in the cabin to the supply tank on the top wing had burst a few inches from the point where it was joined to the cabin tank, and that he was hit in the arm very badly and was "bleeding a pot of blood". As he handed the message through to me I noticed how terribly pale he looked and I knew that he must be very seriously wounded.

Immediately I was confronted with the problem of whether to land and endeavour to render first aid, or whether I had better carry on. I looked beneath me and there was nothing but the dirty brown shallow waters of the great swamp. The heat was terrific and I reflected that even if I did land without the aid of a second man I should most certainly have to drift on the water and run the risk of beaching the machine on a mud bank; and worse still, having rendered what aid I could to Elliott, I should have to start up the machine again single-handed—no easy matter when both engine and atmosphere are very hot. Furthermore there would be the difficulty of leaping into my cockpit and taking control of the machine again after the engine had started. Then again I thought, "Elliott is bleeding and I might be able to stop it," and yet again I argued that if he were very badly hit he would need a doctor's attention, and to run the risk of trouble through landing in the swamp in a dust-storm, many miles away from any habitation or help, and of being unable to restart—having rendered first aid—seemed wrong. Therefore I made the decision that the only thing to do was to fly on and try to make Basra as quickly as possible, and perhaps this decision was confirmed when a few seconds later I hit up the definite southern desert coast-line of the Hammar Lake, then headed eastwards as hard as I could go to Basra, where I knew there would be every possible assistance and a hospital.

It was 110° in the shade that day and flying low at fifty feet with the throttle wide open did not make for a pleasant trip. The heat was overpowering; gradually my oil temperature rose, and, considering that my engine was air-cooled, it was going to be a severe test. I estimated that we must be nearly a hundred miles from Basra and I was hoping to land on the river there in about forty minutes, so that it might be possible to get medical assistance in under the hour. Our old bus did about a hundred and twenty-five miles an hour full out, and at this speed we hurtled along, skimming over the bank of the lake mile after mile, while all the time I was wishing I could go still faster. It was an enormous relief when the weather began to clear and the dust storm abated, and when within about thirty miles of Basra itself we came out into brilliant sunshine I was able to climb to a more convenient height.

At last the great port of Mesopotamia came into view and I could see the broad river littered with a mass of shipping. The next problem was to know where and how to land. It must be remembered that when one is floating on the water with a seaplane, as long as the engine is running the craft is moving forward and the moment the engine stops, unless there is no current and no wind, the seaplane is drifting either with the wind or with the current.

Now I could see that there would be a strong current running at Basra so I knew that once I had landed I would have to beach the machine on the bank forthwith because, owing to the fact that when taxying there is not enough speed to create sufficient draught to cool the engine, we should very quickly over-heat and run the risk of our engine seizing up. As we passed over the palm groves, to my dismay I discovered that the river had an embankment on each side, or piles, or shipping, or some obstruction or other for miles on either bank and there seemed not a spot with an open mud beach upon which I could run our floats. At last I spied a little mud bank next to a small creek and decided that I must get down on to the water and make that bank. Fortunately there was a clearing of the small craft at that moment on the water beneath and we were able to land quite well, and then I taxied as quickly as possible towards our refuge. It was difficult to steer the machine against the current but, knowing what was at stake, I could not be too particular about damaging our floats, and so at a fair pace I taxied up towards the mud bank, then slowed down and, just as I was about to drift broadside, opened up full throttle and ran the floats high up on the mud. Luckily the mud was soft and we came gently to rest high and dry. So I shut off the engine and got to the cabin as quickly as I possibly could. As soon as I opened the lid I discovered poor Elliott in a terrible state, sitting huddled up on his seat in the corner at the back of the cabin. It was about four o'clock in the afternoon and the heat was terrible; I noticed that he was having great difficulty in breathing. He told me feebly that he was sure he had got a hole in his side and that he was breathing through that hole.

Natives had gathered round, and perhaps the sudden landing of the machine had scared them, for they were most stupid and would render me no aid whatever. However, by sheer force I lugged one up on to the floats and made him stand up and help me lift Elliott down. It was an awful job raising him out of his seat, for I felt that I must inevitably hurt him. At the same time I did not want him to exert himself at all although he was so willing, despite his agonies, to assist in lightening his own weight as I lifted him out. Elliott had always been incredibly methodical with his duties, specially in the matter of engine maintenance, and I shall never forget that while I had him in my arms and was struggling with the assistance of the native to step down from the lower wing on to the floats, he said to me, "Turn the oil off," (it was a job that always had to be done immediately the engine stopped), and feebly tried to push down the lever which was close by.

As soon as we were off the floats we laid him gently down on the bank and endeavoured to prop his head up with some cushions out of the machine. I had a quick look at his arm and the wound in his side and could see that, apart from temporarily plugging the wounds with cotton wool, I could do nothing. During the flight I had been able to hand him my brandy flask, but after a time he had become too weak to lift it to his lips and so I was now able to give him another drink and then set to work immediately to get help. I wanted a stretcher or bed on which he might be carried, but all the stupid natives did was to run away. Not one would go in search of a doctor; they simply shut their doors in my face when I asked for help. However, at last I got one fellow to go over to the B.O.C. bungalow and warn them that we had a man who must go to hospital, and then I tried again to make some sort of improvised stretcher on which we could lift Elliott. I felt like murdering every fool I came in contact with, but fortunately at this juncture two launches arrived with white men on board who had evidently seen our landing. Very quickly the situation was explained to them, whereupon they rushed to the nearest native hut, walked in, took the first rush-made bed and converted it into a stretcher. On this we lifted Elliott and a few moments later, having left someone to guard the machine, we were speeding down the river towards the B.O.C. bungalow.

Going out of the open air into the bungalow at Basra was like going out of a very hot room into the night air in England, for inside its thick walls the air was cool and we soon had Elliott lying on soft cushions with two electric fans going full out above him. Then came another interminable wait until the doctors arrived, and although they were tearing in cars full out they had to come a long distance. To me it seemed that they would never come and that they did not realise the gravity of the case, for I suppose by this time I was suffering a certain amount of reaction after a

somewhat trying day. A little later Elliott's wounds were temporarily dressed and he was taken away to hospital. I remember
Elliott saying that he could not understand how the petrol pipe
had burst. In the meantime I went back to the machine and we
towed her down the river and up into the backwaters of the Royal
Air Force inland water-transport dock and there moored her.

During dinner I endeavoured to explain to the Commanding
Officer how it had all occurred, and the engineers present maintained that it was impossible for the petrol pipe to burst, for the
simple reason that it was open at both ends and that it was not
a pressure pipe, for the petrol was simply lifted by the pump to
the top tank. They were convinced that there was no earthly
reason why it should burst and even having done so, why it should
do so much damage. I went to bed that night with the news that
Elliott was doing quite well, but still wondering why it had all
happened.

The next morning at breakfast the engineer-officer asked me
if I had seen any natives about when I was flying over the swamp
and I replied that we could see nothing at all for the blinding
dust-storm. He then told me that natives were there right enough
and that they had shot at us; that it was not the petrol pipe that
had caused the damage but a bullet which had entered our
machine, pierced the petrol pipe and hit Elliott, and to prove this
he took me down to our seaplane and sure enough there was a hole
through the cabin side, and the despatch box from the Foreign
Office to the Governor-General of Australia which lay against the
cabin wall had a hole right through it.

Then I planned it all out. The explosion that I had heard had
been the firing of the gun, for we were flying so low that the sound
of the explosion and the bullet arrived simultaneously. The shot
had been fired evidently by an Arab who had pointed his gun at
the approaching machine and had fired up at an angle of about
45 degrees. The bullet must have passed between our two floats
and just missed the edge of the plane and a couple of flying wires.
It then pierced at a slanting angle the wall of the cabin, passed
straight through the petrol pipe inside the cabin and then on
through Elliott's arm, shattering the bone, on again into his side
passing through both lobes of the left lung until it finally buried
itself under his right arm-pit.

Head-quarters asked me to show them on the map the exact spot where this had occurred, but owing to the prevailing sand-storm it had been impossible to read a map. We therefore decided that the only way in which we could trace the culprit would be to fly back over our tracks, tracing back in an aeroplane the course we had come until I recognised the actual spot where the tragedy had occurred. And so it came about that I journeyed out to the Air Force aerodrome at Shiba with the object of taking off at dawn the next morning in an Air Force machine.

At this stage I was so depressed that I literally had no heart to go on with the flight. I had been to see Elliott, who was in a very weak condition and told me I should have to go on with the job without him, but I assured him I would wait until he got better. The doctors seemed happier now they knew it was a bullet, for they said they could easily extract it and that although Elliott was dangerously ill, there was no reason why he should not pull through. With these thoughts in my mind I spent the late evening with Squadron-Leader Stoddart at Shiba. It was only two short years before that Elliott and I had visited Shiba together on our flight to Rangoon and back, and many of the personnel on the aerodrome were still with the 84th Squadron. We were just about to turn in to bed, in view of our early start on the morrow, when a telephone call came through for me. I found it was a message from the hospital. The connection was very bad and I could hardly distinguish the message, but when I thought I understood what the man at the other end was saying I became nervous and called Stoddart to function for me. So armed with pencil and paper Stoddart repeated clearly sentence for sentence—"Tell Cobham that his engineer Elliott had a sudden relapse and died at 11.15 to-night."

Crowds on Westminster Bridge cheer Alan Cobham as he returns from his record-breaking seaplane flight to Australia and back, October 1926.

Alan Cobham after alighting on the Thames.

Alan Cobham replies to the speech of welcome by the
Government on the Terrace of the House of Commons.

For a moment I was stunned and could not realise it all; and
I made Stoddart ring up again to confirm the news. When I found
that it was indeed true I felt that surely now I must give up the
flight. I felt I could not go on with it, for this was the culminating
point of a depression which had existed almost from the start of
the journey. In this state of mind I turned into bed and that is
about all I did do, for after interminable wakeful hours the dawn
broke at about four o'clock and Stoddart came in to tell me that
the machines were being run up and that we were ready to take
off in search of the scene of the tragedy. There is rarely much
wind in the early morning at this time of year and it is therefore
the best period of the day for flying, for as the morning progresses
and the sun rises the wind springs up and if it is very strong

dust-storms develop such as we had been caught out in on the previous day.

There were about four machines in the flight and I went up as passenger with Stoddart, directing him back over the course we had flown the previous day. After just over an hour's flying we came near the place where I had heard the explosion, and in a few minutes I estimated the approximate spot where I thought it had occurred. To make doubly sure we went on beyond until I recognised familiar land-marks we had passed over before we had been fired at, and thus by coming back over our tracks again I was able to locate within a few hundred yards the spot whence the bullet had come. We then flew off to the temporary landing ground at Nasiriya where by previous arrangement we were met by the Political Officer residing in that region. He got aboard one of the other machines and followed us back to the place I had already located, and I fired pistol rockets at the ground to show him the approximate spot. Near by was an Arab shepherds' encampment, and we flew very low endeavouring to have a look at these people and, as Stoddart said, "To try and draw the—devils' fire." When I hinted at risk, Stoddard reminded me that ever since 1914, he had never been hit and that his luck was not likely to fail him now! We dived and skimmed over their heads within a few feet, but they were not having any, and not so much as a rifle was raised.

So we reluctantly turned back towards Khamisiyah, a village a few miles away, and there ascertained what tribe was encamped at the place I had identified. With this information we went straight back to the landing ground at Nasiriya and lost no time in getting to the town. The Political Officer was soon informed that the chief of that particular tribe happened that morning to be visiting the town, and within half an hour he had been found and detained in the local gaol pending investigations. From then onwards the investigations progressed which led to the ultimate identification and confession of the Arab who had commited the crime.

SIR ALAN COBHAM,
Australia and Back

THE PIONEER

They go among the wandering stars,
And the grey gathered clouds divide
Before the broad-winged shining cars
Whereon the new knight-errants ride;
Distance, and time, and ancient fears
Have been forgot:
Storm and the sea, the old barriers,
    Control them not.

Because he wallowed foolishly,
They swing across black skies or blue.
Because he fought and failed, they fly.
Because he dreamed, their dream is true.
Doubtless, in spheres we do not know,
Whither he went,
His patient, valiant spirit, now
    Is well content.

He never sailed the open sky—
No such proud wings as theirs he had:
And he had e'en such bravery,
But he was called a fool, and mad—
Though the flesh failed, the spirit knew
And vainly tried.
Few heeded when he lived, and few
    Knew when he died.

NEIL EAST,
from *A Talent of Silver*

2. Amy Johnson makes an unexpected landing

The first two women pilots to catch the public imagination were the American Amelia Earheart and the English girl Amy Johnson. Both eventually lost their lives while flying, Amelia Earheart in the Pacific, Amy Johnson in the English Channel.

The incident related here took place during Amy Johnson's spectacular solo flight to Australia in 1930.

At dawn next morning, the fourth day of her flight, she left for Baghdad, nearly five hundred miles across the desert. She was wearing her Sidcot suit as usual, for she did not anticipate how unbearable the heat would be later in the day. And although she knew that such things as dust storms occurred in this part of the world, she was unprepared for the very frightening experience ahead of her. "All went well until I was almost within sight of Baghdad. The heat was terrific and I was flying at 7,000 feet to avoid the worst of the heat and the bumps. The air was very hazy and visibility poor. Immediately ahead of me appeared a much thicker haze than any I had already encountered and I began to wonder whether it would be too thick for me to see through. Suddenly my machine gave a terrific lurch, the nose dipped, and *Jason* and I dropped a couple of thousand feet. The drop was so sudden and far that the propeller stopped for a few agonising moments, and I was terror-stricken at this unexpected happening ... The machine dropped again with a sickening feeling as though I were in a lift with the machinery broken ... again the engine choked and stopped and again picked up, only just in time for still a further dive downwards. In less time than it takes to tell I had dropped to within a few feet from the ground, and was helplessly being blown hither and thither at the mercy of some force I could not understand. ... Sand and dust covered my goggles, my eyes smarted, and I couldn't control the machine sufficiently to keep it straight. ... I had never been so frightened in my life ... All at once I felt my wheels touch ground although I could see nothing ... I throttled down the engine and tried to steer into wind. The machine swayed and bumped and every second I expected to see it turn over or run into some obstacle. To my untold relief it finally came to rest and I switched off the engine and jumped out as

Amy Johnson in 1930.

quickly as I could, hindered as I was by my parachute . . . I pulled
the machine round to face into the wind. The force of the wind
started to push it backwards, and I hastily pulled out my luggage
from the front cockpit to put behind the wheels. My next job was
to try to cover up the engine to keep the dust and sand out of the
carburettor, but . . . as fast as I tied down one side of my canvas
cover and raced round . . . to tie down the other side, the first side
would be torn from its fastenings. It must have been about half
an hour before I had finally managed to get the cover fastened on.

Then I climbed on the top of the engine and tied my handkerchief over the air-vent hole in the petrol tank ... I couldn't see a yard in any direction and had no idea where I was or how far from civilization. Turning my back to the wind, I sat down on *Jason*'s tail to try to keep it down, and settled myself to wait for some lull in the storm. Once I heard dogs barking and my terror broke out afresh as I had heard that these desert dogs wouldn't hesitate to attack and tear their victims in pieces. I therefore pulled out my small revolver and waited ...

"After three hours the wind began to abate and soon I could see quite a distance ahead. In terror lest I should miss the opportunity, I raced round collecting my luggage and uncovering the engine, tools falling on the sand in my haste and getting covered up at once. ... The engine started at the first swing of the propeller, and feeling devoutly thankful for this piece of good luck ... I opened up and took off, going in the direction in which I thought Baghdad would be. If I had gone in the wrong direction I should have headed into hundreds of miles of desert ...

"Within a short time I was in sight of Baghdad."

CONSTANCE BABINGTON SMITH,
Amy Johnson

Short-snorters

Many DC-4s are still flying the humbler aerial tasks in various parts of the world, and a unique device guarantees their memory will long survive even after the last of the breed goes to scrap. Tucked away in closets and attics of former DC-4 crewmen are countless rolls of paper money. Some are as long as fifteen feet and are composed of the standard currency bills of many lands taped end to end. Known as "short-snorters" for reasons which still remain obscure, these rolls contain as many signatures as their far-roving owner could obtain. They were a caprice of World War II, most popular just when the C-54s were in their prime, and as such represent a montage of people involved in their operation. While most "short-snorter" rolls bear only the signatures of various Kilroys who dropped back into obscurity once they returned to civilian life, the more dedicated collected a composite list of scribblings which in their special way tell of great events and the personages involved. Perhaps with an eye to history they asked for and were obliged with the marks of Eisenhower, on the way to Casablanca; Bradley, Patton, and Clark returning to state-side triumphs; Franklin Delano Roosevelt en route to Yalta; Douglas MacArthur bound for Tokyo; Secretary of State Hull to Moscow; Churchill to Ottawa; General George Marshall around the world; Marlene Dietrich to North Africa; Martha Raye and Bob Hope bound almost anywhere American fighting men were stationed.

The large majority of those signatures were rendered in or about one of the great aircraft of all time.

ERNEST K. GANN,
The Flying Circus

On the beak of an Ancient Pelican

My heart had long been scorched with envy, for other men were lofting to regions I could never achieve. It was the year of the Geminis, of plans for the moon, of supersonic transport design, of fighters slashing thrice the speed of sound. Like most people I had no choice but to remain an observer, a grubby role for one who has flown with eagles. Perhaps that is why I instantly agreed when Freddie called and asked, "How would you like to fly a DC-3 from San Francisco to Apia?"

If there is anyone who does not know where Apia is, then it is in Western Samoa, which is very far over the South Pacific horizon.

It had been nineteen years since I had flown a DC-3. Where now was my hard won wisdom? There was the belief I had always held that a wise man never tries to go back?

And yet . . . Apia, a siren whispered the name. An author named Robert Louis Stevenson is buried in Apia and if he could make it in a sailing craft, certainly I should be grateful for a DC-3. The analogy would be abused, I knew, by well-meaning, jet-minded friends.

"A *DC-3?* It's four thousand over-water miles to Samoa!" A preliminary measuring reminded me it was *four thousand, three hundred and fifty miles.*

"You'll go crazy! It will take you thirteen hours just to Honolulu . . ." *My specially designed pessimistic computer insisted it would take longer.*

"A jet takes only four hours plus. Stay home and write books. No one ever drowned writing and making a fortune."

But how much had they lived?

"What happens if one engine quits?"

According to my recollection most DC-3s eventually arrived at their destination if they carried enough fuel. In my private manual I firmly believed the only time there was too much fuel aboard any aircraft was if it was on fire. As for single engine emergencies, I had enough familiarity with the proper mixture of fright, sweat, and faith to remain convinced "it can't happen to me."

"All DC-3s are ancient. What about metal fatigue? If you take a tin can and bend it a million times . . . well?"

Well? Never having flown with the handicap of an engineering degree, I had never worried about such things. But I would bend as gently as possible.

Freddie, while masquerading as just another Pan American pilot, was, as everyone knew, the uninaugurated president of the Pacific Ocean. On the telephone he had advised, "The father of our country will be your navigator."

I was pleased because *this* George Washington was a stocky, alert, New Zealander, at the moment Operations' Manager-Chief Pilot-all around-high chieftain of Polynesian Airlines. And he smiled easily. This infant airline had been flying a route pioneered by Captain Cook, rechecked by William Bligh, and publicized by Somerset Maugham and James Michener. With a single borrowed DC-3, Polynesian Airlines had been serving Apia in Western Samoa, Pango Pango in American Samoa, flying thence to Atitaki and Rarotonga, or westbound to Tongatapu and Fiji. Now, after two years of operation Polynesian had taken an important step. Business was so good they had resolved to buy an airplane they could call their own. Following sound advice they had bought a DC-3.

Freddie said, "John Best will be Flight Engineer. He can also do some of the flying when you want a stretch."

Best was also a New Zealander. Though still in his early twenties he approached genius as an aircraft mechanic. It was he who had nursed Polynesia's single rented DC-3 so tenderly, soothing its brow against all weariness. Many people believed the line operated four airplanes.

"And who," I asked Freddie, "will be the copilot?"

"Copilots for ferry flights are hard to come by . . . you can sort of switch around."

Freddie is easily given to sweeping statements when bothersome details threaten his multitudinous affairs. He is a man who likes to launch projects. If allowed he will plan your coming week, month, year, or life.

"Freddie," I said patiently, "George Washington is going to be very busy navigating and when he is not actually holding octant in hand he should be catching a few minutes sleep. John

Best should be checking fuel consumption and a lot of other things. Without even knowing what the winds will be, it will certainly take us fourteen hours or so just to make Honolulu. That is a long time for these bifocaled eyes to be staring at instruments. There should be a copilot, someone—"

"What about Dodie? She could double as stewardess."

I swallowed thoughtfully. Dodie was my girl Friday secretary. It was true that she was taking flying lessons and was almost ready for her private license, but when she signed on for her job, the fringe benefits did not include a possible voyage in a life raft. Personally, I would feel much safer a thousand miles from the nearest land in a DC-3 than on any freeway, but Dodie's decision to go might hinge on loyalty. I remembered only too well that ferry flights were never the same as routine passenger flights. There would be the usual makeshift arrangement of extra fuel tanks installed for one flight only, and of course a subsequent weight overload. Yet the ferry flights I knew about had arrived at their destinations in good grace . . . almost always.

"I'll ask her."

Thus it was that the fourth member of our crew was a girl named Dodie. Do not offer adventure to a certain kind of female unless you want them to accept.

The San Francisco night is unusually soft, and a near full moon is rising across the Bay. It is Friday the thirteenth, which may have accounted for three lucky takeoffs and landings I had executed during my afternoon reunion with a DC-3. After nineteen years . . . there she stands quite as resolute as ever, a bit paunchy-looking perhaps with the new type landing gear doors, but otherwise the blood sister of those I had flown regularly from New York to Cleveland and Chicago in 1939, to California in 1940, and across the Atlantic to Greenland and Iceland when there were no radios to guide us because the towers for constructing same were our cargos.

Below the cockpit window I notice her christened name—*Savaii*, the name of the second island of the two which constitute the new nation of Western Samoa. John Best has painted the red and blue national flag on her tail.

Beyond *Savaii* is the enormous San Francisco airport. Jets keen their elephantine way along the runways, others sigh down one after another for their landings, still others blast their hot breaths against the night with power we had never dreamed of only a few years ago. I watch them soar towards the moon.

The contrast seems almost too much for the *Savaii*. The brilliant hangar light is cruel to her, the new paint becomes the pitiful striving of an old harridan trying to look her best at a relative's wake. There is something sheepish about her. And why not? In a few moments I will guide this anachronism along taxiways five times wider than she requires. The takeoff runway is so long that even with an overload *Savaii* should be able to make an ascension from one end, fly momentarily, and land at the other end with room to spare.

John Best comes to my side. "We are ready."

"All tanks topped off and checked?"

"Personally . . ."

After a few minutes we are taxiing slowly towards a moon path on San Francisco Bay.

George Washington calls the control tower and I try to persuade myself his New Zealand accent is to blame for the patronizing tone in the controller's voice. The tone changes to consolation when he recites our airways clearance to Honolulu. Beneath the obligatory technical mish-mash he seems to be saying, ". . . now, not to worry. But are your life jackets handy?" The coward within me is momentarily resurrected, then dies one of his ten thousand deaths.

When we run up the two engines and check the magnetos we sound like vacationists playing with their outboards on a quiet lake. Just behind us, crouched like a prehistoric monster, is an American Airlines jet. I must know the pilots, or at least the captain. Long ago, beyond the swiftly closing mists of aviation time, we must have flown over the same routes as comrades, in DC-3s which really *were* brand new and glistening, and of which we were extremely proud. And it is very possible the rest of the captain's crew have never flown an airplane with a propeller on it.

I am reasonably sure what they are saying on the flight deck of the American 707 while they contain their impatience with this obstructive gnat, "Some people have it tough . . . flying a beat-up old DC-3 to Honolulu."

Lo, how the mighty have fallen.

Moments later *Savaii* demonstrates that however humble, she is far from beat-up and is not about to join the fallen. In spite of the overload she soars from the runway like a frightened sea gull. As altitude and airspeed mount I yell triumphantly, "We are in orbit!" The night allows me the deception of playing astronaut. And those who have been there have told me there is no more "G" sensation transmitted to their backsides by a Saturn 5 at blastoff than a pair of Pratt and Whitneys. And during the launch at least, I have a better view of the stars from a DC-3.

Four minutes later the shadowed land slips from beneath us and we are over the darker ocean. It is, as the gooney bird flies, 2,091 miles to Honolulu. The tower bade us farewell with a hint of good riddance, and George Washington has switched to the en route radio frequency.

As I ease *Savaii* upward, four thousand memories assail me, for I have as many hours in DC-3s. In cramped cocoons nearly identical to this one, I had frozen in the arctic and melted in the tropics. I had been sublimely content in autumn evenings above the shores of Lake Erie and awed by the aeronautical cruelties lurking in Catskill thunderstorms. Living so many hours in these noisy little cavities, I had belly-laughed over inconsequentials, dreamed ambitions never to be satisfied, scribbled naive notes for books I would never write, made lifelong friends, and wept for some who were slain. In these drafty little cubicles of aluminum lined with green leather I had known shame, lust, triumph, and near despair. And I had learned humility.

It is little wonder that after an absence of nineteen years I have absolutely no difficulty reaching for every control, absorbing the information offered by every instrument, or responding to the tolerant flight demands of a DC-3. These things, all of them, are engraved in my mind forever. Like the prisoner of Zenda, I know my cell.

We are supposed to report our arrival over "Briney", a radial intersection twenty-two miles offshore. We have not troubled to inform Air Traffic Control that we lack the electronic gear for such an exact fix. They would not understand our reasoning or our temporary reliance on dead reckoning. Yet air traffic controllers, like all the rest of us, are comfortable with the familiar. For years they have been clearing jets to "Briney" and no matter what their computers tell them they obviously cannot believe the near static target on their radar screens. Are we a balloon? How can we be so lackadaisical in reaching "Briney"?

They call three times to ask when we estimate arrival. When George Washington gives them an educated guess they wait only a few minutes before calling again. Wouldn't any self-respecting flying machine long ago have passed "Briney"? In contrast to the old blips swimming quickly about their screens we are apparently stuck in the celestial mud.

"They won't believe me!" George Washington's eyes are hurt. I wonder what would happen if I should pick up my own microphone and scold them for insulting his name.

To the controller's relief we eventually decide we are arrived at "Briney". He is rid of us. We have also struggled to 6,000 feet. The moon peers benignly over my left shoulder as I level *Savaii* and ease the engines into long-range cruising power. Far above us moves the modern world of flight. Here, with our two engines snoring like contended pigs we slide along smoothly enough. Anachronism be damned! The top-gallants and royals are set. The breeze is drawing fine. Sail on!

Soon we are free of our radar fetters, and George Washington retires to his small navigating table situated just behind my seat. A curtain between us shields his light from the cockpit, but where it should button against the curving side of the fuselage there is a separation. The buttons are missing and so a narrow band of reflected light is created on my side window. As if observing him on a miniature television screen I can watch George Washington settle down to work at his flight log and chart. He opens a book of tables and scribbles with his pencil. He wets his lips several times and frowns. He is making computations concerning the stars and planets which will be our beacons during the balance of the night. Suddenly, I am sorry for those who no longer use the heavens to guide their way.

You there, aloft in your jets so high above us! Are you content with the magic of your Inertial Navigation System? Do those impersonal, ultra-efficient, cold green numbers flicking across the panels of your obsequious machine now seem to match the beauty of the stars we use in our subterranean world? If so, I fear you are lost men bound to genuflect before an electronic marvel and I do not envy you.

Now for us, there is only the firmament, the vast ocean, and ourselves.

I am reluctant to turn on the automatic pilot, wishing to prolong this very special, rather sensuous experience, the return to an old and willing love. *Savaii* responds to my slightest touch . . . a change of altitude twenty feet . . . a few degrees off course . . . ah. Beyond the windshield is *Savaii*'s broad snout. The moon outlines it clearly now and it droops down to a line of fluff balls, innocent little clouds marching along the black line of the sea.

For a time I seem to be alone with *Savaii*, staring at the fluorescent instruments exactly as I had done through so many long nights, almost hypnotized by their somnolent gentle motions, slipping pleasantly into that unique trance peculiar to night flying, that strange mixture of alertness and lethargy which somehow magically adds up to inner peace.

How many nights had I sat in just this way? During the Korean War it seemed we carved a track through these same skies; so many times did we pass back and forth with our cargos of fresh men out, and torn men home. And before that there was a steamship company which employed me to fly their first attempts to leave the surface for the air. But those flights were made in much bigger four-engined airplanes, so heavily manned and relatively sumptuous there were two bunks for resting when we pleased.

Dodie is standing in the moonlight beside me. I pretend to be working instead of luxuriating. She blinks at the rows of instruments.

"Coffee . . . tea . . . or milk?" Her nasal tone is part of our agreement. I had said that she could come if she rehearsed the stewardesses' chant to perfection.

"No thanks. Sit down and fly."

She needs a hundred-mile cross country for her private license. Though flying *Savaii* will not satisfy the FAA it will at least make a startling entry in her logbook. I take my hands and feet away from the controls. *Savaii* wavers momentarily, then settles obediently back to business. In the moonlight I watch Dodie's knuckles turning white. It will pass. *Savaii* is far larger and heavier than the little plane's she knows. She will soon relax.

John Best has come forward. He scratches at the curly locks of his hair and I wonder if all New Zealanders are curly-headed since George Washington's hair is much the same.

"Are you ready to go on the fuselage tanks?"

"Wait. Let's burn off the auxiliaries another fifteen minutes."

"Right."

"Did you like the United States?"

"Yes . . ."

I wonder at a strange lack of enthusiasm in his voice.

"You wouldn't care to migrate . . . become a citizen?"

"No, thank you, skipper." Cold and flat. Too bad. John Best is the kind of young man we need.

Midnight. The cockpit has been like a miniature stage upon which our limited dramatis personae appear, speak their few lines in the subdued light, then exit into the darkness from whence they came.

Dodie has gone back to the cabin to tinker with the buffet. The heater is not working properly. John Best has turned four fuel valves so that now *Savaii*'s engines are sucking life from the long metal tanks which are lashed in the area normally occupied by passenger seats. Each tank holds four hundred gallons and passage between them is barely possible.

Two hours ago George Washington came forward to announce that his first star fix placed us in central China. Then he chuckled and pounded on the side of his head.

"I not only mixed up my Greenwich time, but was looking in the south latitude tables instead of north."

Later he returned with a second fix which was as near perfect as man could ask.

George Washington is a good navigator. Now, reflected in my side window, I can see him winding his octant. There had been so many nights over the North Atlantic when I had performed the same manipulations although our octants were not nearly so fancy. In these same type airplanes, we had done our own navigating. While the copilot flew the airplane I would go back to the cabin, climbing over bodies and cargo with octant in hand. If lucky I could catch a significant star through one of the cabin windows or

the narrow skylight above the toilet. Sometimes it was necessary
to signal the copilot for a turn to the right or left and thus reveal
a certain star. It was a clumsy arrangement and our "fixes", if
they could be dignified with the title, were heavily dependent on
imagination. And hope. But we made it to Labrador and Greenland
and Iceland as we would make it this night to the island of Oahu.
In the intervening years the only apparent change is the addition
of an astrodome through which George Washington observes the
identical stars.

Dawn. It comes slowly for we are bound away from it and
even our leisurely pace delays our pursuit by the sun. We are
weaving between towering cumulus which would be dwarfed to
toadstools by high-flying jets but appear as formidable bastions to
us. We pass in dreamlike sequence from one to another and around
the next. We are a butterfly seeking its way through a forest.

George Washington is patiently trying to transmit a position
report on the radio. He holds his flight log in one hand and the
microphone in the other while he reads off the long list of numbers
which describe our whereabouts, our future whereabouts, comment
on the weather, and our fuel endurance. It is a frustrating business
which must be attempted every hour. Listening to my own headset
as we strive for the most elementary communication with our
fellow men, I am disillusioned. As it was long ago. In an emergency
we would be more dependent on God and Pratt and Whitney than
electronics for our survival. In the midst of fantastic progress,
aviation has neglected its Achilles heel. I cannot detect how en
route long-range radio communications have made the slightest
improvement in the past fifteen years.

Now the moon rides ahead of us. Against the pale sky of a new
day it looks a fake, like something the property man forgot to
take down. The stars have taken their leave so George Washington
has retreated to the cabin for a well earned rest. He will resume
his duties when the sun is high enough to offer a good shot. I have
also rested, slumbering like a child while John Best twisted the
knobs on the automatic pilot. And now it is his turn to close his
eyes.

Dodie brings me tea, apologizing for its cool temperature.
"The buffet is *cassé*."
I tell her it is too early in the morning for such corny rhymes.

G

She has also brought a sandwich of salami and cheese and while I munch at it and watch the glorious dawn, Dodie flies *Savaii*.

I glance down at the ocean and appreciate how the depths of the clouds are still wrapped in gloom. Yet a moment later, still munching, I see the left wing tip twinkle with the first touch of sun. Here is great contentment. All is as it should be in my aerial world.

Thirteen hours and fifty-three minutes after taking off from San Francisco, *Savaii*'s tires kiss the runway at Honolulu. And again we have offended the normal order of things. The control tower, speaking its annoyed mind, confesses it knows not what to do with us. We wait, orphaned in the middle of the vast airport while great jets scream past. Who are we who dare bring ancient history into the hectic morning business of a great airport? Go away, flying Dutchman! There is no longer any appropriate nest for an aged DC-3.

Finally we are directed to a lonely tin hangar, itself an anachronism. A man from the State of Hawaii arrives in a yellow truck to collect $29 for the landing fee.

Twelve hours later we are airborne again, bound for Apia. And on this second night, climbing in the humid Hawaiian sky, I am suddenly possessed with the fancy that this whole flight is a dream. I will awaken any instant and this candy-floss airplane will vanish. My hands now caressing the controls will grasp only air. Or perhaps, as the lights of Honolulu sink into the depths, *Savaii* will become a submarine with this unbelieving Captain Nemo trying to fit his anachronistic craft into reasonable harmony with the instructions rattling in my earphones.

Earphones? Anachronism upon anachronism. These heavy pre-World War II types always made me feel like a yoked ox.

Honolulu Departure Control has us on their radar screen. The controller himself is loquacious with local gossip. ". . . you have traffic at two o'clock."

We peer at the night and see a great nothing. Even the stars are obscured by a cloud level we have yet to reach.

"Traffic, slow moving . . . at ten o'clock . . . two miles."

There. The blinking lights of an aircraft off to our left. He slips swiftly overhead and is gone. In earlier days we might have been innocent of his presence.

The controller asks if we have "VOR" equipment.

"Negative."

I hope he will reply, "How quaint . . ." but there is only silence.

The omission of VOR in *Savaii* is deliberate. Of what use would such sophistication be when the simple islands of the South Seas have no stations to transmit the necessary signals? Our next radio navigational aid will be a plain old-fashioned, nondirectional beacon located on Canton Island, over 1,600 miles of ocean and sky to the southeast. There is nothing in between. Now the situation is the same as our departure from San Francisco. Lacking the sophisticated electronic aid of VOR equipment we cannot depart the busy Honolulu area with sufficient exactitude to please Air Traffic Control. We are quite capable of wandering off on our own, but such carefree license was for leather-jacketed country bumpkins—not for the now in aviation.

"I will vector you on course", the controller announces. "Turn right to one eight five degrees."

I oblige. Big Brother is watching us. He can see aircraft we cannot see so it is wiser to let him escort us toward the great outdoors. Where we are bound the entire sky will more certainly be ours.

"Turn left to one seven zero degrees. You are now forty miles southeast of Koko Head . . . good night."

Thank you and good night, dear Big Brother. You cannot imagine how silly it feels flopping around in your radar controlled world on the beak of this ancient pelican. We are not pressurized so we can open the side windows when we please and toss our gum out or the wrapping of a sandwich or anything else which is messy and displeases us. We can open the window and stick out our noses and sniff at the moist lukewarm air, or peer down at the black sea, or enjoy an unadulterated view of the heavens. This, Big Brother, is something you cannot do in a jet.

Midnight again. At this time last night we were far to the east of Honolulu in regions heavily traveled by sea and air; here with our chances of seeing another aircraft or any ship on the sea infinitesimal, I rediscover a wonderful loneliness. Once, the New Bedford whalers sailed this area, and long before the incredible migration of Polynesian peoples followed this same general line in reverse until they came upon the Hawaiian Islands. And during

World War II the skies were busy. But now . . . nothing. Our first flights across the North Atlantic had been much the same. We were entirely self-reliant, a condition which sweetens all loneliness. We worried about many things, but not about collision.

We are cruising at 6,000 feet again. The stage moon has been hung for another performance, this time shoved around until it is perched on *Savaii*'s nose. The cumulus buildups which normally surround the Hawaiian land masses have been left behind. Below there is only the sea shimmering in the moonlight with here and there lost dumplings of vapor looking for a parent.

It is dark in the passageway which leads aft from the cockpit. George Washington is standing on a ten gallon oil drum taking his first fix of the night. The octant hangs from the center of the star-studded astrodome and seems to be a projection of George Washington's body.

John Best has switched to the cabin-ferry tanks and is standing beside me. His youthful face is intent on the fuel pressure gauges. He wants to be certain there is no air lock in the ferry system. In this vigilance he has my hearty endorsement.

"She seems to be feeding fine, skipper."

"Yes . . ."

John Best reaches for the booster pump switches and flips them off one at a time. The pressure needles sag and then revive. He turns back into the blackness and soon Dodie arrives to sing the coffee-tea-or-milk song. There is a look in her eyes which has nothing to do with refreshment.

"You really came up here to fly, didn't you?"

"I confess . . ."

"Take over, Mrs. Mitty. The sky is all yours."

For a time I sit half-dreaming in the square of moonlight framed by the windshield. And as inspired by so many similar nights I find myself marveling at fortune's inexplicable arrangements. During those easily memorable times when I flew open cockpit Wacos, Birds, Ryans, Stearmans, and anything else I could beg or borrow, how could I have envisioned these circumstances? Below is an ocean with the nearest land already hundreds of miles away. On my right is a young lady flying a heavy twin-engined aircraft better than I had hitherto thought she might do. Yes, perhaps I should stow my male chauvinist helmet and goggles away forever and admit there are no longer any great physical demands upon a pilot. At least it was some consolation to realize "they" have not so far automated the weather.

Or man's resistance to fright—as I would later be reminded.

Hours later it is my turn to rest in the cabin. I lie down on our makeshift bunk and discover the belt of Orion framed in the nearest window. There is Rigel on the right; Betelgeuse on the left, and farther out in left field is Procyon twinkling as brightly as I have ever seen it. Here, near the tail, the engines' muffled drone is soothing and mixed with the hissings of countless drafts spewing from as many small openings in the fuselage. It is true non-supercharged fresh air and I breathe deeply of it. Who could not sleep here with the tail swinging so gently back and forth as if some long gone aviator would rock me in the cradle of his heights?

Just before dawn I make my way forward between the fuel tanks and pause by George Washington's tiny cubicle. He has crossed the last of three small lines and holds the tip of his pencil upon it.

"I doubt if I'll have another fix until mid-morning. We are coming up on the intertropical front now and I should suppose we'll do a bit of bouncing about."

We have passed the equator and are in a region once known to sailing ship men as the Doldrums.

"Why don't you get some sleep?"

"I rather think I shall. I'm tired of bucking the bloody radio. Nandi is guarding us now."

Nandi is in Fiji, a long way over the horizon—like 2,000 miles.

I move forward to the darkened cockpit and tap John Best on the shoulder. He surrenders his seat with a smile.

"Just in time. There's some fire up ahead."

During my absence the moon has rolled from the left side of *Savaii*'s nose to the right. Presently it occupies a lozenge-shaped clear space in the sky and illuminates a long wall of cumulus which extends much higher than *Savaii* could ever climb. Occasionally the fat and bulbus tumors, charged with their interior lightening, flicker brilliantly. Then they become quiescent for a while and soon, as if commanded by an energy-hungry Wotan, commence flashing again.

I watch the show from my front-row balcony seat. It appears to be no more of a threat than any other intertropical front I have ever seen, which if reviews were given for spectacle would place it considerably below a line of Appalachian thunderstorms and far down the honors list from the permanent thunderstorm front which lies off the west coast of Africa. There I had played audience to extravaganzas so visually terrifying I had wanted to crawl under my seat and hide, yet once a part of the performance I discovered they invariably had more bravado than bite. But this?

I remember a night when I had been overly casual about entering a line of thunderheads assembled over the Irish Sea and in two minutes found myself praying audibly for immediate salvation. Obviously my airplane would not survive. I resolved then and there that I would never trust a line of cumulus no matter how flabby their appearance.

Dodie, now awakened, joins me in the cockpit while I guide *Savaii* along winding cloud streets pressed on both sides by gigantic ramparts. Occasionally we reach a dead end and plunge into cloud. Then rain hisses at the windshields, *Savaii* is rudely jostled, and I ask Dodie to pull on a bit of carburetor heat. But these sessions are brief, not at all ugly, and soon we are gliding along another street. There are times when it is necessary to change course as much as twenty degrees to avoid the larger anvil-headed cumulus which really might be grisly. I always compensate a like number of degrees in the opposite direction lest George Washington have complaint that his carefully plotted course has been fouled. Our extra wanderings will not consume more than ten minutes. Why trade this much peace for that much war?

After an hour or so, when the dawn light has overpowered the moon's, we pass beyond the front. Now there are strange rills of curiosity passing through each of us, for soon there must be something to see. There? No . . . it is too early. Another ten minutes . . . maybe fifteen.

There!

Canton Island is an ill-defined bronze blob on the sea horizon which appears to have been dropped from the cloud stretching above it. All of *Savaii*'s crew are gathered in the cockpit for their first sight of land since the night before. The intervening time has been like a passage from another life.

Very abruptly we are brought back to our immediate existence.

For suddenly there is a violent spasm of shudderings and regurgitations from both engines.

Our human responses are immediate. Dodie's hands try to squeeze juice out of the plastic control wheel. George Washington, ever the cool one, purses his lips and frowns. John Best disappears into the cabin.

With the speed of a d'Artagnan I turn on both main fuel tanks and hit the booster switches. When the engines settle back into their usual sonorous melody and my heart slides back down and off my tongue, I find it difficult to believe a former helmet and goggle man could have moved so fast.

John Best returns to the cockpit wearing the frown of a man betrayed.

"I don't understand it. The cabin tanks were still reading thirty gallons on my measuring stick."

"Do you abide by Murphy's law in New Zealand?"

"Ah? . . . Yes."

"When the plumbing system was installed someone bent a pipe up when it should have been bent down, or vice versa."

"It must be."

Fright, being merely a spark of fear, is much more quickly extinguished. Having swallowed my heart I affect a nonchalance suitable to the occasion. For lack of other gestures to fix the image I calmly call Canton and give our identification and destination.

At once I regret having opened the liaison. For the man who resides somewhere on that lonely atoll asks, "Are you landing Canton?" There is an unmistakable plaintiveness in his voice—a yearning.

"Negative."

From the atoll there is only the silence of disappointment. Then hopefully, should we change our minds, the voice recites the surface wind and altimeter.

"Thank you . . . so long." Even a little DC-3 has managed to pass over Canton Island.

Once we leave Canton it seems we have already arrived, although Samoa lies almost seven hundred nautical miles beyond. Yet it is close enough to rouse the homing instinct in half our crew. George Washington goes about his navigating with increasing zest instead of succumbing to the natural wilting which marks the very last part of most long flights. He keeps trying to tell Nandi our estimated arrival time in Apia, though he might as well holler down a barrel which is exactly what both he and the Nandi station operator sound like.

I turn to chide him. "You've been homesick."

"Of course."

John Best is also becoming increasingly restless. There is no room to pace, but he makes innumerable trips from the cabin to the cockpit. He will stand beside me for minutes, looking over the nose, scanning the horizon although he knows very well it will be hours before any land will appear. He borrows my pocket computer so he can calculate our true airspeed.

"One hundred and sixty knots true . . ." Not quite true because his heart has added a knot for hope and perhaps two more knots for anticipation and his heart has hinted to his eyes that if he leans far enough to one side when he reads the airspeed indicator it will appear to read faster than if he looks directly at it.

Now suddenly, in a frenzy of activity, everyone is taking pictures of each other and of the sky which is now dulled by a high overcast and certainly the least photogenic sky since we left San Francisco. I put it down to a mutual urge to disperse minutes, something to do while the faithful engines drone on, something to keep hands occupied while time segments drag between arithmetical fact and desire.

In contrast I become morose and find myself behaving like a sentimental fool. In spite of a certain weariness I do not really want this anachronistic flight to end. I touch the elevator trim tab in a way that should be reserved for a woman, then catch myself pretending to wipe at a spot of grease. I know it will be a very long time before I will fly a DC-3 again.

Faleolo is the airport for Western Samoa, located a long twenty-two miles from Apia. It is one of the world's fast vanishing grass airports, which makes it a sensuous pleasure to land any airplane.

It is a strip of green confined by the sea on one side and ranks of coconut palms on the other. George Washington had given our arrival time hours before. He had predicted 1:35. It is 1:35.

I point to the brooding island, most of which is shrouded in gray, soggy-looking clouds.

"You lied, George Washington. We will not be on the ground until thirty-eight."

Three minutes. Three minutes deviation in a flight that had commenced over 4,000 miles away.

I call for the landing gear to be lowered. George Washington recites the litany of the cockpit check list, and after fifteen hours in the sky we slide down through the warmth to the grass.

There are many people waiting to greet us. They place welcoming leis around our necks and admire *Savaii* as if she were the sleekest supersonic transport.

Walking away from *Savaii* I paused to look back at her. And I saw beyond the people clustered all around her, volubly expressing their wonder. Suddenly I knew my long nourished envy of astronauts had been eased. For had our aerial voyage been beyond the moon, I thought, our sense of detachment would have been much the same. Now I knew there had been no true measurement of the distance from our fellow earthlings. *Savaii*, a phantom from the past, had been our space ship carrying us above reality and in her we had made a reluctant reentry. Thus may the useful life of a thing be prolonged and that of some men temporarily exalted.

ERNEST K. GANN,
The Flying Circus

PASSENGERS

A trip to Paris (1)

When he (my father) left, he made me a present of ten pounds to travel back to Italy "in comfort", and I spent it on an aeroplane ticket to Paris, and chose a front seat beside the observer. The air service was still very young. They dressed me in sheepskins and (as it was hard to move at all, so wrapped up) lifted me across some part of the engine to the little double seat in front with all open except for a wind-screen before it. The observer sat down beside me, but there was never a thought of strapping in: when I noticed that the rush of the engine had lifted me on to my feet, and that the observer beside me was holding on to the screen in a determined way, I did so too. I have never enjoyed an air journey so much. The observer shouted out names of towns below, but they were blown away before they reached me; one could put one's head out from the screen a second, and feel as it were the rush of the world through space. When we reached Le Bourget, there was no place reserved to change in, and I was apparently expected to drive into Paris in my dishevelled state: I explained to the Customs official that this was impossible: a mirror must be found. "It is only reasonable," said the French Customs. A mirror *was* found, and placed on the bench among the luggage . . . and I am probably the originator of the first thought for female comfort that ever crossed the mind of an air-line. Very soon afterwards, a lunatic shot the pilot of a London–Paris aeroplane from my little front seat, and it was forbidden to passengers.

FREYA STARK,
Traveller's Prelude

A trip to Paris (2)

However, I did succeed in getting away from England, and that
was all I really cared about. In February 1929 almost every cause
was present which can contribute to human discomfort. London
was lifeless and numb, seeming to take its temper from Westminster, where the Government, conscious of failure, was dragging
out the weeks of its last session. Talking films were just being
introduced, and had set back by twenty years the one vital art of
the century. There was not even a good murder case. And besides
this it was intolerably cold. The best seller of the preceding months
had been Mrs. Woolf's *Orlando*, and it seemed almost as though
Nature were setting out to win some celestial Hawthornden Prize
by imitation of that celebrated description of the Great Frost.
People shrank, in those days, from the icy contact of a cocktail
glass, like the Duchess of Malfi from the dead hand, and crept
stiff as automata from their draughty taxis into the nearest tube
railway station, where they stood, pressed together for warmth,
coughing and sneezing among the evening papers. Intense cold
seems peculiarly insupportable in a great city, where one's converse
with the seasons is wholly capricious and unrelated to the natural
processes of germination and decay.

So I packed up all my clothes and two or three very solemn
books, such as Spengler's *Decline of the West*, and a great many
drawing materials, for two of the many quite unfulfilled resolutions
which I made about this trip were that I was going to do some
serious reading and drawing. Then I got into an aeroplane and
went to Paris.

I had been up before. During what proved to be my last term
at Oxford, an ex-officer of the R.A.F. appeared in Port Meadow
with a very dissolute-looking Avro biplane, and advertised passenger flights for seven and sixpence or fifteen shillings for "stunt-
ing". On a very serene summer evening I went for a "stunt" flight.
It was a memorable experience. Some of the movements merely
make one feel dizzy, but "looping the loop" develops in the mind
clearly articulated intellectual doubts of all preconceived habits
of mind about matter and movement. There used to be a very

terrifying thing at Wembley called the Great Racer. "Looping the
loop" is that thing prolonged to its logical extreme. There were
moments on the Great Racer, when the car was in full flight,
during which one's nerves reached the highest point of excitement,
trembling between ordinary healthy terror and mad panic. Just
at that zenith of emotion the car always slackened in speed or
changed its direction, so that a few seconds of comparative calm
were interspersed between the successive crises. In "looping", the
aeroplane shoots steeply upwards until the sensation becomes
unendurable and one knows that in another moment it will turn
completely over. Then it keeps on shooting up and does turn
completely over. One looks down into an unfathomable abyss of
sky, while over one's head a great umbrella of fields and houses
have suddenly opened. Then one shuts one's eyes. My companion
on this occasion was a large-hearted and reckless man; he was
President of the Union, logical, matter-of-fact in disposition,
inclined towards beer and Ye Olde Merrie Englande, with a
marked suspicion and hostility towards modern invention. He had
come with me in order to assure himself that it was really all
nonsense about things heavier than air being able to fly. He sat
behind me throughout, muttering, "Oh, my God, oh, Christ, oh,
my God." On the way back he scarcely spoke, and two days later,
without a word to anyone, he was received into the Roman Church.
It is interesting to note that, during this aeroplane's brief visit to
Oxford, three cases of conversion occurred in precisely similar
circumstances. I will not say that this aeronaut was directly
employed by Campion House, but certainly, when a little later,
he came down in flames, the Jesuits lost a good ally, and to some
people it seemed as if the Protestant God has asserted supremacy
in a fine Old Testament manner.

My flight to Paris was not at all like this. It was disagreeable
but quite unexciting. I was taken with one other passenger in a
charabanc from the London office to Croydon. The ticket seemed
very cheap until they weighed my luggage and got me to understand how much there was to pay. Then I wished I was going by
train. The other passenger was a smartly dressed woman of early
middle age; she had only a small attaché case with her. We got
into conversation in the charabanc. She said she made this journey
on business every week. She was in business in Paris. When you

All

smart

people

fly

in

these

days

Shot. Wilshaw

She is wearing this travelling suit in one of the smart new autumn tweeds 5½ gns · and her friend's coat is in corduroy velour. · 8½ gns · from

FENWICK
of Bond Street
(Corner of Brook St.)
Ladies' Tailors   Tel.: Mayfair 4314

... and they are just off to Paris by the mid-day 'Silver Wing' air liner — as all smart people do in these days

IMPERIAL
AIRWAYS
Airway Terminus
Victoria Station, S.W.1 Tel.: Victoria 2211 (Day & Night)

Models posing as smart people in a joint advertisement by
Fenwick of Bond Street and Imperial Airways.

were very busy with business it saved time to fly. I suppose business women never get bored with the idea of their being business women. It is an adventure all the time.

The charabanc took us to a large station with a waiting-room and ticket office, a buffet and a passport officer and a bookstall. It was rather a surprise to leave this building and find a grass field and a huge aeroplane. The business woman and I climbed up a ladder into the aeroplane. It was not the newest sort because they are more expensive. Low wicker arm-chairs were arranged on each side of a narrow gangway. At the back was a funny little lavatory. The floor sloped steeply uphill when the machine was on the ground. The windows were small and filled with sliding panes of glass. These, I discovered when we started, kept opening of their own accord through the vibration. The body of the aeroplane was built over the panes, so that we could not see out very easily.

The pilot and the mechanic got in, and we started our flight. Although, presumably, we were travelling a great deal faster than the old Avro in Port Meadow, there was practically no sensation of speed. We seemed to float along in the gentlest way possible. The only movement of which I was conscious was the sudden dropping into air pockets, and this was sensible to the stomach rather than the eye. The chief discomforts of air travelling were, I discovered, those which had drawn me from London, only intensified very severely—cold and noise. The roar of the propellers was shattering. I followed the advice of the company and put cotton wool in my ears, but even so had a headache for some hours afterwards. The cold is worst about one's feet, which are provided with fur-lined footbags. The things which amused me most were (1) the spectacle of a completely horizontal rain storm, and (2) of the pilot telephoning our positions (it seemed extraordinary that they could hear him at Le Bourget when we could scarcely hear him within a few feet), and (3) the look of frightful scorn on the face of the business woman when, soon after we left Le Touquet, I was sick into the little brown paper bag provided for me. One does not feel nearly as ill being air-sick as sea-sick; it is very much more sudden and decisive, but I was acutely embarrassed about my bag. If we had been over the channel it would have been different, but I could not bring myself to throw it out of the window over the countryside. In the end I put it down the little lavatory. As this opened directly into the void the effect was precisely the same, but my conscience was easier in the matter.

The view was fascinating for the first few minutes we were in the air and after that very dull indeed. It was fun to see houses and motor cars looking so small and neat; everything had the air of having been made very recently, it was all so clean and bright. But after a very short time one tires of this aspect of scenery. I think it is significant that a tower or a high hill are all the eminence one needs for observing natural beauties. All one gains from this effortless ascent is a large scale map. Nature, on an elusive principle, seems usually to provide its own view-points where they are most desirable. The Citadel at Cairo, or Canoni Point at Corfu, or the top of the mountain road above Catarro, lose nothing at all of their supremacy from the knowledge that we can now always go higher if we want to, but, on the contrary, seem rather to gain by their peculiar fitness and adequacy. There was one sight, however, which was unforgettable—that of Paris lying in a pool of stagnant smoke, looking, except for the Eiffel Tower, very much like High Wycombe indefinitely extended. After the exaggerated cleanliness and sparkle of the preceding country, this exaggerated sombreness and squalor, called up (particularly to me, who had lately been sick) all the hatred and weariness which the modern megalopolitan sometimes feels towards his own civilisation.

Then we saw below us the aerodrome of Le Bourget, marked out as though for some game. The aeroplane went far beyond it, and only the obvious calmness of the business woman, who closed with a snap the little notebook which she had been filling with sums during the journey, reassured me that we were not being misled. Then we turned round, banking over and descending rapidly, till it seemed as though our wing must catch on the top of the hangars; then a slight bumping and a feeling of buoyancy proclaimed that we were on the ground; we ran forward more slowly and came to rest in front of the station. Here our passports and luggage were examined and we were transferred to a chara-banc, which presently deposited us and our luggage in the middle of Paris at the very inconvenient hour when everyone had just finished his luncheon.

EVELYN WAUGH,
Labels

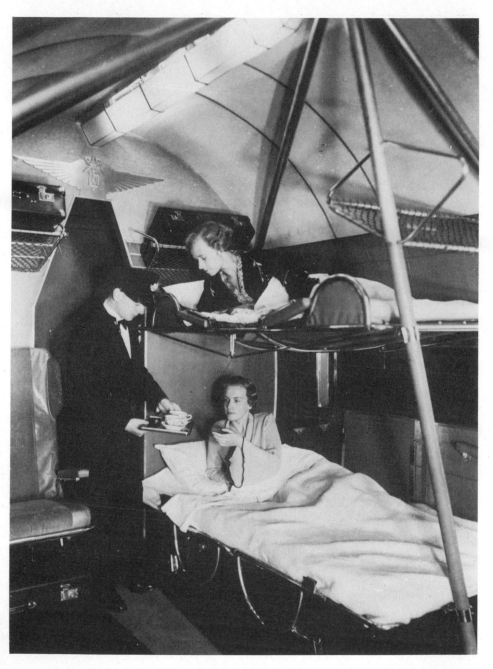

Early morning tea for overnight passengers on the KLM
route to the Far East.

Joyriding

1. In Texas

The U.S. astronauts may have got man a lot farther toward the moon, but they didn't risk their lives the way I did.

One day early in the 1920s a flying machine, as they were then called, circled the water tower several times in our town in West Texas and then headed for the cow pasture at the edge of town and landed. The entire township, all 262 of them, gathered there as instantly as a mule can run.

The aviator was waiting beside the flying machine, a tall, slim young man with a little pencil moustache. He wore one of those tight, soft-leather helmets, and he had goggles pushed up above his eyes. In his leatherjacket, his lace-legged, moleskin boot pants, and his English boots, he seemed to a twelve-year-old to be a man of infinite dash, making the rest of us look like clodhoppers. A real devil, obviously. As soon as the fathers had spotted him, they made their daughters go back and sit in the car.

The aviator made a little speech. He said that for two dollars he was offering one and all the chance to ride in this flying machine, the marvel of the ages.

He didn't exactly get an enthusiastic response. Most of the men frowned at the flying machine and fingered their money and decided that buying rides in a flying machine was a foolish frivolity. But I had two dollars, barely, and a great temptation.

As I remember that plane, I shudder. It was an old spruce and cloth biplane. The cloth on the wings and the fuselage had been sewn in a hundred places, and a few slits had been patched with tire tape.

The wings were kind of loose, too; but at the time, that didn't bother me. I thought they were supposed to flap. Anyhow, I didn't see any danger in going up. After all, I had fallen off the top of Charlie Dycus's commission barn without any ill effects.

Just as the aviator seemed to be getting dispirited in his sales pitch, I stepped forward and presented my two dollars—a dollar bill, a quarter, a few nickels and dimes, and quite a few pennies.

The aviator kept a poker face, but it seemed to me his eyes were grinning as he boosted me up into the front seat.

I remember hearing, as I was climbing aboard, a neighbor woman yelling at me, "Your daddy will hear about this."

The plane had a rotary motor. I think they called it a Wright Whirlwind. The aviator started it by flipping the propeller, and as the plane started forward, he ran around to the side and mounted into the cockpit as you would mount a horse. I remember thinking wildly that he would miss it, and I would be up in the air without any way to get down. He didn't.

We had quite a flight, and he did something that I think used to be called an Immelmann. It would have been better if I hadn't been eating the peanuts. I couldn't stand up very well when we got down.

The aviator handed me back the dollar bill.

"Keep it, sport," he said. "I'd give you the whole two dollars back, but I'd hate to have to count the rest of it."

Sure enough, my dad heard about this, and I heard about it plenty from him. In the words of our town, I had completely blowed the wages of a week's weed-cutting on something as silly as shooting at the moon.

PAUL CRUME,
The World of Paul Crume

2. In general

There can be no doubt that, in all countries where there was a supply of war-time pilots and planes, joy-riding did a great deal to prepare the public for scheduled services. Its main service, perhaps, was to convey the idea that flying was basically safe, since during the war the emphasis of newspapers and magazines had always been on the perils of flying and on the heroism of the men who flew. There was a certain irony in the situation, however, since the great majority of the joy-riders belonged to the lower-income groups while the early passengers on scheduled flights and charters came from much further up the social scale. The workers, in other words, proved that flying was safe, and enjoyed themselves in the process.

KENNETH HUDSON,
Air Travel: a social history

BACK FROM AUSTRALIA

Cocooned in Time, at this inhuman height,
   The packaged food tastes neutrally of clay.
   We never seem to catch the running day
But travel on in everlasting night
With all the chic accoutrements of flight:
   Lotions and essences in neat array
   And yet another plastic cup and tray.
"Thank you *so* much. Oh no, I'm quite all right."

At home in Cornwall hurrying autumn skies
   Leave Bray Hill barren, Stepper jutting bare,
   And hold the moon above the sea-wet sand.
The very last of late September dies
   In frosty silence and the hills declare
    How vast the sky is, looked at from the land.

JOHN BETJEMAN,
A Nip in the Air

Imperial Airways Afternoon Tea-Flight over London. Cars took the passengers from Haymarket to Croydon, where they embarked in a Silver Wing Argosy. The fare was two guineas. Through the window, Nelson's Column and Trafalgar Square.

3. Tea over London

You would welcome a new and delightful experience? Then book your seat at once for an Afternoon Tea Flight over London in one of Imperial Airways' multi-engined luxury air liners! The same type as used on the Continental and Empire Services.

A dainty tea will be served to you in your comfortable armchair in the air liner while London unrolls like a map before you. Every familiar landmark is there—yet looking quite different and new from your eagle's viewpoint.

There is the familiar traffic—but crawling antwise and oddly. Here is the Tower. There is your own street! Look, Buckingham Palace! The Thames snakelike from Chelsea to its mouth. Wonderful! Fascinating beyond all describing.

Try it for the sheer pleasure of the trip and also because there is no finer way of accustoming yourself to air travel, which is so much the quickest and most comfortable means of going to the Continent and the Empire that you will use it on every possible occasion when once you have experienced the joys of flight.

*Imperial Airways
advertisement, 1933*

Passengers in the U.K.

The early passengers expected and received very little in the way of comfort or amenities. On the London-Paris service, after the first few months, they were taken from city-centre to city-centre. They registered at the office of the company, or of an agent, and were then driven to the aerodrome in a hire-car. Luggage was carried to and from the aircraft by mechanics, whom it was forbidden to tip. There was a 40 lb weight-limit for baggage, but it was not strictly enforced. The habit of weighing the passengers themselves was introduced during the mid-1920. The weighing machine at the office counter had its face politely turned inwards, so that only the clerk on duty could see it. The maximum weight allowance was for a passenger and his baggage together, so that a small, thin man could take a lot more luggage than a large, fat man. The name of one's next-of-kin was included with the facts about one's weight. The distribution of weight in the plane was almost as important as the total weight itself. If weather conditions were difficult, the airport authorities would work out the plane's centre of gravity and ask some of the passengers to move to other seats during take-off. The pilot shepherded his own passengers through the Customs on arrival and he was personally responsible for them until they and their baggage had been cleared.

KENNETH HUDSON,
Air Travel: a social history

Passengers in the U.S. (1)

Aerial royalty or not, life with and aboard the trimotored Fords was far from ideal. For American passengers there was little comparison between the cold box lunches tossed into their laps by the copilot, and the soup-to-nuts-on-a-white-tablecloth cuisine offered by equivalent British and European aircraft.

Ford passenger cabins were always too hot or too cold and the decibel level assured them a top place among the word's noisiest aircraft. Immediately on boarding, passengers were offered chewing gum which would allegedly ease the pressure changes on their eardrums during climb and descent, but it was just as much to encourage a cud-chewing state of nerves. They were also offered cotton which wise passengers stuffed in their ears so they would be able to hear ordinary conversation once they were again on the ground. Wise pilots employed cotton for the same purpose, and many who scoffed at such precaution had trouble meeting the hearing requirements on their physicals for years after their service in Fords was done.

In the first Fords there were no seat belts. Only hand grips were provided to stablize passengers, and summertime flying could become a purgatory. While they bounced around in low-altitude turbulence the passengers muttered about "air pockets" and a high percentage became airsick. Even with a few windows open the cabin atmosphere developed a sourness which only time and scrubbing could remove.

If the passengers retreated to the lavatory they found little comfort at any season. In winter the expedition became a trial-by-refrigeration since the toilet consisted of an ordinary seat with cover. Once the cover was raised for whatever purpose there was revealed a bombardier's direct view of the passing landscape several thousand feet below, and the chill factor in the compartment instantly discouraged any loitering.

The long transcontinental trips were best endured by confirmed masochists, although over the western part of the United States there was often one redeeming feature. It was a rare occasion when all a Ford's seats were occupied, and a word to a sympathetic pilot or copilot could alleviate matters. Frequent passenger Will Rogers was among the first to discover how the backs of the newer-type Ford seats could be lowered flat enough to meet the one just behind and so create a passable bunk. In addition to their mandatory list of maps, flashlights, and mail pistols, many pilots carried a small wrench to make the seat adjustment.

ERNEST K. GANN,
The Flying Circus

Passengers in the U.S. (2)

On 30th November 1962, an Eastern Air Lines DC-7B was nearing Idlewild, New York, inward bound from Charlotte, North Carolina. It was told on approach that the conditions were one mile visibility, with ground fog. The weather was, in fact, far worse, the visibility being not one mile but nearly zero. The pilot tried to pull out, but hit the ground 500 feet to the left of the runway. Twenty-five people died in the crash.

Much worse, however, was to come. It concerned a TWA flight engineer named Miller, a man with fifteen years' service with the company. On 3rd October 1962, Miller staged an exhibition at the George Washington Inn, in Washington DC, of certain photographs he had taken, for the benefit of a number of Congressmen and other interested persons. The exhibition had come about in this way. The Washington columnist, Jack Anderson, reported in his paper that pictures had been taken by a flight engineer of pilots "snoozing at the controls, reading newspapers and cavorting with stewardesses in flight". Reading this, the Federal Aviation Administration wrote to the President of the Flight Engineers' Union for further information. Not exactly trusting the FAA, the Union stalled.

Engineer Miller was on sick leave at the time and judged it prudent to retire to the Sierra mountains of California. He was, however, eventually persuaded to make the journey to Washington, with his photographs. Once there, he told a sub-committee of Congress that in 1956, the year in which the American Airline Pilots' Association voted that all flight-deck crew on jet aircraft should be qualified pilots, he had become concerned at the increasing number of mid-air collisions, and felt that most of them were caused by what he called "care-safety laxity" in the cockpit. So he decided to produce documentation.

He bought "a real cheap camera" and fixed it to the rear wall of the cockpit, with an extension control which allowed him to sit in his usual place behind the pilots and photograph their activities with the help of an infra-red flash bulb. In four years he took more than 300 photographs, of which 298 turned out to be clear enough to identify the pilots. Somewhat reluctantly he explained what a number of these photographs showed. The instruments contained in the pictures indicated that the pilot let the aircraft drift off altitude 400, 500 or even 600 feet for thirty minutes to an hour at a time, instead of disengaging the autopilot and flying the plane back to its correct cruising altitude. This, not unnaturally, made Miller nervous, because he knew that, with East-West traffic separated by only 1000 feet and altimeters incorrect by as much as 500 feet, a pilot who allowed his aircraft to drift 500 feet off its assigned level was asking for a mid-air collision. Miller showed the Congress sub-committee numerous photographs of pilots and co-pilots sleeping or reading or absent from their seats. One picture showed a stewardess sitting on a captain's lap and Miller comments, "I've heard many times a request, almost a demand, that a girl get on his lap, and, since the girls are under his command, this puts them in a very difficult position."

He also produced a picture of a donkey wandering about a plane in flight. The animal had been brought on board by a party of convention drunks, whom the pilot referred to, according to Miller, as "just a bunch of good Joes". "The good Joes," he said, "turned the donkey loose in the cabin, while they destroyed the furnishings." While the aircraft was landing, the donkey fell against the door leading to the cockpit and was prevented from catapulting into it only by Miller's foot holding the door partly closed.

Miller was not suggesting, of course, that on every flight operated by an American airline there was a donkey or its equivalent roaming around in the cabin, nor that captains spent most of their time asleep on duty or dallying with stewardesses in the cockpit. His revelations, which the sub-committee had to accept, were merely George Johnson's star piece of evidence in his attempt to show that the public's trust in the airlines was not always well placed and that up-to-date equipment, so far from contributing to the safety of passengers, might well lead to their deaths, because it permitted air crew to be doing what they should not have been doing. From the beginning, the airlines had devoted a lot of time, money and effort to telling the public what selfless, responsible men pilots were, and any cracks in this particular façade were not likely to be good for business.

KENNETH HUDSON AND JULIAN PETTIFER,
Diamonds in the Sky

AT 30,000 FEET

A fleck of silver against the darkening blue
The hollow cylinder rockets under the sky's dome,
Unavailingly pursued by the thunder of its sound
Until that final scarlet reverberation;
Like the telegraphed words burning meaninglessly
Upon the slip of yellow paper, and the explosion
Of grief within the mind, this fire and thunder
Do not quite coincide:
The eyes of the watcher see the disaster
Before its voice awakens in the ear.

Nothing that has meaning descends again to earth;
The lighted runway waits vainly
To feel the screeching tyres;
Customs official will not search this baggage
That downward flakes in dust on silent fields;
Hands cannot clasp, nor lips press
What is now blown weightlessly about the sky.

There was a moment when they drowsed
Deep in luxurious chairs;
Read magazines, wrote letters;
When stewardesses served coffee and liqueurs,

And dirty dishes were neatly stacked
In the bright kitchen.

No other moment followed;
Time stopped. There was nothing . . .

No doubt there is a meaning to this event;
But not the one that can be read
On the white face of the farmer
In mid-furrow gazing upward from his plough,
Nor in the burned minds of those who wait
At the airport barrier.

BERNARD GILHOOLY,
New Poems

Charladies cleaning the windows of a Junkers F13
belonging to Lufthansa.

Waiting on airfields

Waiting on airfields is an activity of which I believe my experience is well above the average. When I hear world travellers talking proudly about the number of flying hours they have done I am not greatly impressed. It is the non-flying hours that take it out of you, the elastic and incalculable hours between your ETD and the time you actually take off. The peculiar blend of boredom with anxiety, of false hopes with unnecessary fears, which characterize these periods is a stern test of character. Sometimes, of course, the traveller is told how much delay there will be, and why, and then only a little straightforward patience is called for. But very often there is an element of uncertainty strong enough to make him doubt whether he will fly that day at all, whether in the evening he may not have to return to the hotel he was so glad to quit or to the host whose hospitality he suspects he has already over-strained. Among connoisseurs of non-flying hours there are two sharply-divided schools of thought; those who hold that it is worse when the aircraft is actually on the airfield but is unable to take off for the time being, and those who find this situation easier to support than one in which the aircraft is not visible, being still (supposedly) on its way.

After all these years I am still not quite sure to which school I belong. If the aircraft is actually present—immobile indeed, but glossy and reassuring in appearance—it is generally grounded by an unfavourable weather report, by a mechanical breakdown or—in wartime or in some Oriental countries—by the non-arrival of an important passenger; and at first it seems to us that these causes of delay are bound to be transient. The weather (which looks perfectly good to us) will surely improve; and if there really is a bad patch farther along our route, cannot they fly over it or round it, nowadays? As for that trouble with the port engine, or whatever it is, the devoted mechanics are already at work on it and everyone seems full of hope that it will be remedied ere long. But gradually, as we wait, the omens become less and less encouraging. The sky clouds over, and some vile fellow says that if you

get bad weather in this part of the world it generally lasts for a
week. The cowling on the port engine is replaced and we gather
our belongings hopefully together, one inexperienced traveller even
knocking out his pipe; but when they rev her up, although to us
the roar sounds perfectly satisfactory, the crew shake their heads
and the cowling comes off again. In the end the great silver
machine, whose air of being poised for flight once seemed encouraging, becomes a hateful spectacle, a symbol of futility and
disillusionment.

When it has not yet arrived, we at least escape being tantalized
by its presence; but are we really any better off? If after two hours,
or three, or four, it has not arrived, is there any real reason to

A BOAC publicity picture of what to expect in the lower
deck cocktail lounge of a Stratocruiser.

suppose that it will ever arrive at all? Anything may have happened to it. At the distant sound of engines our spirits rise, we feel that we are practically airborne already; but the plane, if it lands, turns out to belong to some other service, and we resume our moody vigil with the worst possible grace. The stubble on our chins, the breakfast which was bolted hastily in the dawn and makes us feel dyspeptic, remind us of how early we were dragged from that state of oblivion which we now crave on mental as well as physical grounds. We long to deface the posters in the waiting-room which extol the celerity, the comfort, the almost Elysian delights of travel by air. We long, above all, to do what we came here to do: to fly.

PETER FLEMING,
With the Guards to Mexico

Love at a great height

In 1958, the late Kenneth Tynan flew to New York to discuss with the editor of the *New Yorker*, William Shawn, the possibilities of his becoming the magazine's drama critic—a post he subsequently held for the next two years.

Nothing I experienced during my two-year engagement, however, gave me a greater sense of fulfilment than a curious event that took place immediately after my first meeting with Mr. Shawn. I drove back to the airport feeling thoroughly exalted and deeply regretting that I was alone. The Tudor poet Samuel Daniel said that when Bolingbroke entered London in triumph, he "did feel his blood within salute his state". I felt much the same as I boarded the plane. The first-class compartment was almost empty. I was placed alongside a pretty, dark-haired girl, guessably in her mid-twenties, who occupied the window seat. I longed to introduce myself and celebrate my new appointment with her; but it was a

H

Hugh Hefner, President of Playboy Enterprises, and his
girlfriend Barbara Benton on the circular bed of his private
all-black D.C. 9, *The Big Bunny*.

night flight, which means a truncated sleep; and the girl soon
covered herself with a blanket, turned towards the window and
switched off the light.

   I had half a bottle of champagne inside me, and it occurred
to me that I would very much like to make love to her. I delicately
removed the detachable chair-arm that stood between us, and
obtained two blankets from the luggage rack. Reclining on my
right side, I spread one over myself and the other across the girl.
While doing so, I let my left hand rest lightly on her hip. She did
not stir. After a short pause I let my hand travel down to the hem
of her skirt. Still no reaction: I paused again as the stewardess

passed by with a tray full of tinkling drinks. Now for stage three.
I explored the area beneath the skirt, encountering first the glossy
tingle of nylon and then, further up, warm flesh. (This was before
the great counter-revolution against gropers took place, impris-
oning women from the waist down in the impregnable puritanism
of tights.) As my fingers moved higher, I came up against the
armadillo-like casing of a girdle. Acknowledging defeat, I withdraw
my hand.

   Suddenly the girl sat bolt upright, seized her handbag and
sprang to her feet. I uttered a silent scream, like Helene Weigel
in *Mother Courage*, and froze. She pushed her way past me and
marched off down the aisle, obviously to report me to the stewardess. I could see the headlines: "Indecent Assault on Plane:
Critic Charged", perhaps even: "Girl Goosed Over Gander". Should
I deny everything, or claim that she had started it? As I wondered,

The Big Bunny awaiting take-off.

sweating, which course to take, I heard soft footsteps and then her voice: "Excuse me"—the first words she had uttered. She slid back into her seat, arranged the blankets as before, and adopted exactly the same posture. I counted to twenty before replacing my hand on her flank. Somehow the tactile sensation was different. Tumescence crept back as I realised what the difference was. This unprecedented darling had removed her girdle: that was why she had taken her handbag to the loo. Less slowly now, I raised her skirt. No obstacle remained: and by moving against her in what is known as the spoon position, I was able to achieve an enchanting, slow-motion climax.

For an hour or so we slept, awakening in the pink-grey dawn over Shannon. We breakfasted in silence until I asked whether she would like my orange juice, which she declined with a smile. I discovered that she was on her way back to the Middle East, where her father worked for the American Embassy. I told her about my new job, and she made appropriate noises of congratulation. At London Airport I offered her a lift in my taxi, which she accepted. When I dropped her at the smart hotel she had named, I invited this paragon of cool to dine with me that evening.

"It's very kind of you," she said, "but I have to be up at dawn to catch a plane to Beirut." I swore she would be back at the hotel by midnight, but this smiling, still knickerless hypocrite would not budge. "And in any case," she said as she turned towards the revolving door, "my parents don't like me to go out with people I haven't been introduced to." I looked deep into her eyes and found there no trace of irony. She was not mocking me: she was utterly sincere. She had expunged from her consciousness all that had passed between us on the jet. We shook hands, and that was the last I saw of her.

Thus I sealed and commemorated the date of my accession to the staff of the *New Yorker*. I have never since been able to separate the joy of getting the job from the joy of getting the girl. Within the space of 24 hours, my private life and my professional life had each scaled a new peak. I'm still not sure which pinnacle gave me a more durable glow of satisfaction.

KENNETH TYNAN,
from *PUNCH* 16 April 1975

NIGHT FLIGHT, OVER OCEAN

Sweet fish tinned in the innocence of sleep,
we passengers parallel navigate
the firmament's subconscious-colored deep,
streaming aligned toward a landlocked gate.
Schooled (in customs, in foreign coin), from
      zone
to zone we slip, each clutching at the prize
(a camera, a seduction) torn from some lone
shore lost in our brain like the backs of our
      eyes.
Nationless, nowhere, we dream the ocean
we motionless plummet above, our roaring
discreet as a stewardess padding, stray yen
or shillings jingling in the sky of our snoring.
Incipient, we stir; we burgeon, blank
dim swimmers borne toward the touchdown
spank.

JOHN UPDIKE,
Tossing and Turning

President Kennedy returns to Washington

Goaded by a mighty tailwind, the Presidential aircraft hurtled eastward at a velocity approaching the speed of sound. Beyond the airport Jim Swindal had looked down on a flat tan-and-green plain criss-crossed by parallelograms of cyclone fences and highways, a tract blank as a plate. Ahead lay a navy blue blob of water and, in the distance, a crinkling of mountains. The pilot radioed Andrews Air Force Base his estimated time of arrival—"2305Z": Air Force "Zulu Time"—Greenwich Mean Time. It would be 6.05 p.m. in Washington when they breasted Andrews. In the old propeller-driven flying boxcars Jim had shuttled over the Hump against the Japanese the thirteen-hundred-mile flight would have taken at least five hours, but in the great flagship he could make it in scarcely more than two.

He reset his watch; 3 p.m. in Texas (2100 Zulu) was 4 p.m. in Washington. Then, spitting flame, Angel climbed steeply. Swindal's rate of ascent leaped from 600 feet a minute to 4,000: he was burning a gallon of fuel every second. The colonel was cleared to 29,000 feet. He was determined to go as high as he could, however, higher than anyone had ever taken President Kennedy, and reaching out he spun his small black trim-tab wheel clockwise, rising another 12,000 feet before levelling off. At this tremendous altitude, nearly eight miles straight up, the sky overhead was naked and serene. Its tranquillity was deceptive. Andrews was relaying reports of tornadoes below—he leaned over and saw black combers of wind-swept scud freckled with hurrying rain—and behind him a cold front was moving in from Arizona. Already wild squalls were lashing the Panhandle. At Love Field the temperature was plunging, and the western sky was livid. Kennedy weather had left Dallas with him.

Instinctively Swindal ticked off the landmarks which he knew lay under the churning clouds: the scribbly banks of the Mississippi, the tartans of Memphis and Nashville. He was glad he couldn't see them. He wanted to flee every familiar cairn, and his instruments seemed to offer a way to improve upon nature. He poured on the oil, riding the tailwind. He soared, and by his very celerity he hastened the end of illusion. There could be no escape, nor even a healing lacuna under the sun, for he was going the wrong way, racing away from it.

At 535 mph, night approaches swiftly. Less than forty-five minutes after their departure shadows began to thicken over eastern Arkansas. In the southern sky he saw a waif of a moon, a day and a half off the quarter, hanging ghostlike near the meridian. At the outset he thought of the darkness as a blessing. Returning this way it would be best to land in gloom. The inkier Washington was, the better. But as the light failed, the crescendo of the day hit him harder and harder. He and John Kennedy had been exactly the same age. John and Jacqueline Kennedy, he reflected, had been "the best we as a country had to offer". He had brought the President to Texas in exuberant spirits, at the height of his remarkable powers; and now he was ferrying him back in a box. Swindal slumped in his harness. Since boyhood he had been in love with aeroplanes. He had progressed to flight school, to MATS, to the post of personal pilot for the Secretary of the Air Force, and then to this, the ultimate accolade. Now the spell was broken. The passion of his life had been spent. Henceforth flying would be commuting, like driving a bus. His deracination deepened as the sky deepened until, over Tennessee, he "felt that the world had ended". Behind him (as he thought of it then) were the President, the First Lady, the Vice-President, and Mrs. Johnson. No aircraft commander had ever been charged with so grave a responsibility, yet he wondered whether he could make it to Andrews. He was near collapse. "It became," in his words, "a struggle to continue."

His co-pilot was, if anything, in worse shape. Lieutenant Colonel Lewis Hanson was normally a buoyant young New Englander. His mother-in-law lived in Dallas; she had been recovering from a stroke, and he had decided to call on her during the motorcade. When she had greeted him with the cry, "Kennedy's been killed!" he had thought she had lost her reason. Then, after turning on her television set, he had begun to doubt his own. Back at the airport he had become obsessed with the desire to leave Texas immediately—at any moment he had expected the fuselage to be raked by machine-gun fire—and twice during the wait for

Sarah Hughes he had started the engines on his own. Now, as Swindal manipulated the controls, Hanson mechanically fingered his headset, pinpointing 26000's rapidly changing position for Andrews. The fliers didn't speak to one another. Roy Kellerman came up briefly and sat in the jump seat. The three men started to speculate about motives behind the assassination and gave up. The fliers didn't trust their voices. They fell silent again, and Roy quietly crawled back.

The magenta twilight turned to olive gloaming and became dusk. The last thin rays of sunlight glimmered and were succeeded by early evening. The colonels looked out upon the overarching sky. There was a lot to see. In the last ten days of autumn the firmament is brilliant. Saturn dogged the moon. Jupiter lay over the Carolinas, the Big Dipper beyond Chicago. Arturus was setting redly behind Kansas; Cassiopeia and the great square of Pegasus twinkled overhead. But the brightest light in the bruise-blue canopy was Capella. Always a star of the first magnitude, it seemed dazzling tonight, and as the Presidential plane rocketed towards West Virginia it rose majestically a thousand miles to the north-east, over Boston.

*   *   *

Mrs. Kennedy, in Moyers' words, "chose to stay with the body". In her own words she sat looking at "that long, long coffin".

She sat on the aisle seat, closest to the body; Ken O'Donnell brooded beside her. After the hasty reconstruction of the tail compartment to accommodate the casket, those were the only two seats left. Godfrey, Larry, and Dave stood throughout the flight, and the visitors from the staff cabin would stand among them, shifting this way and that to avoid jostling one another. Afterwards an incorrect report was circulated that some of them sat on the casket. They never touched it. Mary Gallagher felt a pervasive desire to kiss it, but knowing that would upset Mrs. Kennedy she turned away. Like everyone there, Mary's first thought was to spare the widow, to help and serve her. There was about them an air of consecration; they couldn't even bring themselves to lean over her. When Larry O'Brien first spoke to her, he knelt, and the others followed his example. Approaching Andrews, O'Donnell rose and knelt, too.

This was an entirely new relationship. The day had gone for ever when the polls dismissed the President's wife as Jackie the Socialite. And she herself was a new Jackie, transformed by her vow that the full impact of the loss should be indelibly etched upon the national conscience. She declined Moyers' invitation because she had no need of the bedroom. Remembering the strangeness of the fresh clothes that had been laid out there, she reflected that during her three years in the White House she had learned much about Lyndon Johnson. Their rapport had been excellent, but a great deal depended upon what the press was told when they landed. She sent for Kilduff and said, "You make sure, Mac—you go and tell them that I came back here and sat with Jack." Kilduff bowed his head. He mumbled, "I will."

The new Jackie contrasted so sharply with the First Lady they had known that even the inner circle of Kennedy intimates was slow to grasp the extent of the *volte-face*. For as long as they could remember she had been quiet and retiring; she had dodged limelight, and when she did appear in public she was the apotheosis of the well-groomed alumna of Miss Chapin's, Miss Porter's, and Vassar. Stoughton had read O'Donnell's thoughts correctly; Ken was furious about the release of the oath pictures, fearful that they would show the stains on her. The feeling that something must be done about her appearance had become universal. In the stateroom the Johnsons and Rufe Youngblood were concerned about it, but so were the standees in the tail cabin. "Why not change?" Godfrey asked her. She shook her head vigorously. Kilduff saw the rust-red blood caked under the bracelet on her left wrist and recoiled. Mary's first thought, on arriving from the front of the plane, was to fetch a warm washcloth and soap. Speaking in hushed tones, she consulted Godfrey, Clifton, and Clint Hill about it until O'Donnell came over and said, "Don't do anything. Let her stay the way she is." Ken now grasped her purpose. Finally she broke her silence and spelled it out to Dr. Burkley. Kneeling, the physician indicated her ghastly skirt with a trembling hand. "Another dress?" he suggested diffidently. "*No*," she whispered fiercely. "Let them see what they've done."

The last man to realize that she really meant it was Kilduff.

He thought long about how they could off-load the coffin at Andrews without pictures being taken. His solution was to open the galley door on the starboard side, opposite the usual exit. That way the great mass of the fuselage would mask both the coffin and the widow; photographers and television cameramen would see nothing. He proposed the plan. She vetoed it. "We'll go out the regular way," she said. "I want them to see what they have done."

*   *   *

Slumped in his co-pilot's seat, Hanson continued to radio position reports ahead as Air Force One climbed yet higher into the starlit night. The names on his flight chart read like an atlas of small-town America—Rockwall, Hope, Carthage, Stuttgart, Henderson, Hartsville, Paintsville, Louisa, Gassaway, Clendenin. The Presidential plane was passing above half the country, and on the map the route from Love Field looked like a dark blue curving scar. Unlike the passengers, who hadn't the faintest notion of where they were, he had to know 26000's precise location on the arc that swung up through eastern Texas, Arkansas, Tennessee, Kentucky, West Virginia, and Virginia, towards Washington and Andrews, in Maryland, although like Swindal—like everyone else aboard—the co-pilot gave no thought to the land eight miles down.

But the people below were thinking of them, and only of them. Beneath Angel's swept-back wings the United States was in the throes of an unprecedented emotional convulsion. As Air Force One climbed over the border states, pivoting slightly north of Murfreesboro for a three-hundred-mile leg which would carry it directly towards Cape Cod before Swindal swung right for the capital, approximately 110 million Americans knew it was aloft and would reach its destination at about 6.05 p.m. Its exact route, of course, was secret. This was an elementary security precaution. Even on normal trips the pilot's long zigs and zags were clandestine. The directions were the subject of highly classified messages to key Air Force officers. On this flight the plane lacked the customary ground network of local Secret Service agents, stationed in unmarked automobiles to confirm its passage overhead with detection gear. Angel's sole contact was Acrobat, which was monitoring the co-pilot with exceptional care and listening intently on other frequencies for reports of "unidentified, unfriendly" aircraft on the radar screening the south-eastern quadrant of the country. If the assassination of Kennedy were the first blow in a Soviet or Sino-Cuban machination, the airborne Presidential aircraft would be a prime target for a second blow. Air Force One, its backup, and the Cabinet plane not only were unarmed; all three lacked escorts. The U.S. Government was exceedingly vulnerable. The Pentagon had placed every Air Force base along 26000's route on stand-by, ready to scramble jet fighters; pilots were actually belted in and ready to go.

*   *   *

Front Royal, Manassas, Falls Church . . .

Over Dulles International Airport Jim Swindal knifed down through a thin overcast, and for the first time since leaving East Texas he saw land. The lights of metropolitan Washington loomed ahead; beyond lay Upper Marlboro and the dark reaches of the Chesapeake Bay. Crossing the Potomac, he lost altitude rapidly. The Tidal Basin became visible from the cockpit, then the massive square dome of the National Archives and, beneath the No. 1 engine pod, Capitol Hill. Swindal eased out his flaps and dive brakes and lowered his landing gear. The pilot's head was still throbbing, but he knew this would be the last time he would take the President down. He wanted it to be right.

Bolling, St. Elizabeths Hospital. They were gliding in over rural Maryland: Oxon Run, Silver Hill, Suitland, Morningside . . .

Lyndon Johnson was in the Presidential bedroom, shaving, combing his hair, and changing his shirt again. In the staff cabin corridor Clint Hill approached Roy Kellerman and said, "She wants to see you." Back in the tail compartment Dave Powers told Roy, "Mrs. Kennedy wants you agents who were with the President to carry him off, and she wants Greer to drive." Knowing how the chauffeur was suffering, Kellerman was struck by the thoughtfulness of the gesture. Mrs. Kennedy herself was speaking to Evelyn Lincoln, Mary Gallagher, Muggsy O'Leary, and George Thomas, who had also been summoned. "I want you near the coffin," she said to each, and to Godfrey McHugh she said, "I want his friends to carry him down." Ted Clifton came back to tell Ken O'Donnell, "The Army is prepared to take the coffin off." O'Donnell replied shortly, "We'll take it off.'

Lyndon Johnson being sworn in as President of the United States in the cabin of Air Force One after the assassination in Dallas of President Kennedy.

Ken passed the word in the staff area that Mrs. Kennedy wished to have those who had been closest to her husband accompany him upon debarkation. But there was a second President aboard, and it does seem clear that everyone had priority over the new Chief Executive, including stewards. Fifteen people were wedged into the tiny corridor. Kilduff saw that the President was left standing there in the stateroom.

The acting press secretary was humiliated. Later in the evening his embarrassment increased. At the EOB he discovered that Johnson continued to be annoyed and that he held Kilduff responsible. The new President was still brooding over the incident the following afternoon. After presiding over the Cabinet for the first time he confided to one of its members that he had "real problems with the family." According to this Secretary's notes, set down later that same day:

"He said that when the plane came in ... [they] paid no attention to him whatsoever, that they took the body off the plane, put it in the car, took Mrs. Kennedy along and departed, and only then did he leave the plane without any attention directed or any courtesy toward him, then the President of the United States. But he said he just turned the other cheek ... he said, what can I do, I do not want to get into a fight with the family and the aura of Kennedy is important to all of us."

"Let's remember the happy things, not the sad things," Jacqueline Kennedy said to Clint Hill as they taxied towards the MATS terminal. Colonel Swindal's landing had been a triumph. None of his passengers had known when they touched the ground. The crowd waiting by the chain fence had realized that arrival was imminent because they heard the whining jets. They couldn't see its silhouette, however; the klieg lights blinded them. At 6.03 p.m. these were abruptly cut off. The reason was commonplace. The pilot had to see his way. The effect was nevertheless dramatic: under the dim fragment of November moon the plane looked like a great grey phantom slowly creeping upon them from a quarter-mile away. The couldn't even hear it any more, because the Colonel had switched off three of his pods, and the fourth was drowned out by the warm-ups of two of the wasplike helicopters. Closer and close the huge ghost crawled until Swindal, looking down, could identify two of the waiting men. Robert McNamara was facing him, looking peculiarly tall. Robert Kennedy had just left the sanctuary of his truck and was posed in a tense half-crouch, to spring aboard.

Swindal paused momentarily for the croucher. The eyes of the crowd were on the rear hatch, the President's. A ramp had been readied for the front entrance, and the Attorney General vaulted on it, unseen; he was pumping up the steps while it was still being rolled into place. Leaping in, he darted through the communications shack, the staff cabin, and the stateroom. Liz Carpenter, recognizing his gaunt features, reached out to pat his shoulder. He didn't notice her or the Johnsons—next day the President observed to one of his advisers that Kennedy hadn't spoken to him—because he was intent on reaching one person. "I want to see Jackie," Liz heard him mumble. In the tail compartment he slid behind and then beside Mrs. Kennedy. "Hi, Jackie," he said quietly, putting an arm around her. "I'm here." Those around them started: his voice was exactly like his brother's. "Oh, Bobby," she breathed, and she thought how like Bobby this was; he was always there when you needed him.

The aircraft glided forward once again and parked. Outside the floodlights went up. Swindal and Hanson scooted down the ramp, stationed themselves under the port wing, and faced the rear door, saluting stiffly. The ponderous yellow lift was wheeled up. The door swung open, Larry O'Brien's round face peered out. The officials below saw the haggard profile of the Attorney General and were astonished; they hadn't known he had been in Dallas. He was holding the widow's fingers; her purse was dangling from her other hand. Presently they saw the stains on her. And then in the next moment Kellerman, Greer, O'Leary, Hill, and Landis manhandled the casket into place in front of the two Kennedys. The light fell full upon it, it glinted uglily. Theodore H. White yearned for "a cry, a sob, a wail, any human sound". Earl Warren saw "that brave girl, with her husband's blood on her, and there was nothing I could do, nothing, *nothing*". Taz Shepard saw the skirt; he looked up into her haunted eyes and felt a stone in his chest. Ted Reardon prayed to himself, *Jesus, Mary, and Joseph, I wish I hadn't come*. Yet all these were unspoken monologues. There wasn't a single voice. Speechless, they were incapable of taking their eyes off the dark red-bronze coffin. All afternoon they had been thinking about it; now it was here. And that made it irrevocable. Now they knew, now it was true.

WILLIAM MANCHESTER,
The Death of a President

The man from Liberia

There were six of us in the plane from Robertsfield to Lisbon, and six Pan Am stewardesses, so it looked like a nice flight. I had three seats to myself, and another man took the three seats on the opposite side of the aisle. He was a small middle-aged man with a balding head and spectacles and a sharp foxy little face. He looked as if he might have a bit of a temper.

They gave us lunch after take-off, and then I read for an hour. Yet all the time I was aware of Foxy's presence. He hardly touched his lunch, and I lost count of the number of cans of beer and menthol cigarettes he had since the bar opened. Although he had been given a glass for his beer he seemed to prefer drinking it from the can. He just sat by the window, swilling down the beer and puffing at the cigarettes. He looked as though he had something on his mind.

I put down my book and glanced in his direction at the very moment he was doing the same to me.

"Care to have a drink with me?" he said.

I moved to the seat beside him, and the stewardess brought another can of beer and a glass of brandy. Foxy took the cigarette-packet from the tray and flicked a cigarette towards me. I said I didn't smoke. He took one himself and said, "Been in Liberia long?"

"Two weeks," I said. "And you?"

"Five months. Boy, am I glad to be getting out!"

"What were you doing?"

"United States Seabees. You heard of them?"

"They're the naval construction corps, aren't they?"

"Right. I'm a Petty Officer Instructor. There was a group of us sent there to teach Liberians about mechanics. Or I should say to *try* to teach Liberians about mechanics. They're unteachable."

"Really?"

"Sure. We were stationed way out in the boondocks, about a hundred miles from Monrovia, near a place called Foya."

"I know."

"Yeah? Well, there were thirteen of us, and we lived in these Quonset huts, and gave these guys lessons. I'd say to them: 'In an internal combustion engine there are four strokes to make up the cycle. The first is the intake stroke, the second is the compression stroke, the third is the power stroke, and the fourth is the exhaust stroke.' Well, I'd go through it all with these guys and then I'd say to the first man, 'What is the first stroke?', and you know what he'd say? *The crank shaft!* Christ? I must have gone over that routine at least twenty-eight times." He took a pull of his cigarette and said, "I don't know how I'd *describe* Liberians if anyone asked me. It would take a week. They gave us some books to read about the place before we went there. One of them was by this fellow John Gunther. I don't recall the name of it, but I thought he was exaggerating. Turned out he was *under*-exaggerating. That's a fact."

"In what way?"

"Liberians are about one remove from the monkeys. I'm telling you. I've seen things no white person has ever seen. One night I saw a boy of nine initiated into manhood. He came into this hut, all wet and with nothing on, and this old man who was sitting there picked him up and put him over his knee and cut his shoulders and chest with this sharp steel knife. You should have seen the blood that came out. *Christ*, the blood! And when he was through with that, he turned him over and circumcized him. The boy didn't make a sound. I don't think he had anything to deaden it, but he didn't make a sound.

"Then they used to get drunk regular on this cane-juice. God, does that stuff drive them out of their minds! Cane-juice is a kind of ruin. I'd say it was around 180 per cent proof. You can put a match to cane-juice. You won't see it burn, but you can't put your hand over the top of it. The area gets smaller and smaller and then it's all burnt up and there's nothing there."

"Did you ever try it?"

"God, no! I don't drink nothing that don't come out of a can or bottle or hasn't got a label on it that I can read. I don't believe in that home-made stuff."

"Did you ever get down to Monrovia?"

"Not too often. About once a month we'd make a trip there

and walk around and do the night-clubs. The women there are dead though. They're like logs."

"So I've heard."

"I used to spend my leisure time on the Ham Radio. I'm a great Ham enthusiast. There was a guy in some A.I.D. educational outfit at Foya, and he didn't live too far from the camp. He was a Ham enthusiast too. I'd go over there week-ends, and we'd have a great time. We used to call up people all over the world . . . Japan, Korea, Australia. That was great."

He looked out of the window and said, "Christ, we're a long ways up." Then he stubbed out his cigarette and said, "You on a business trip?"

"No, I'm a writer," I said.

He looked at me with sudden interest, as if I was a new arrival at the zoo. He pulled out another cigarette and said, "Anyone tell you about Careysburg?"

"You mean the V.O.A. place?" I said.

"No, I don't mean the V.O.A. place. I mean the area around."

"No" I said. "I don't think anyone mentioned that."

"It would interest you, being a writer. Boy, that's quite a place! You don't want to break down there at night."

"Why?"

"People just disappear."

"White people?"

"No, blacks."

"What happens to them?"

"Nobody knows. But ask any Liberian about Careysburg, and he'll tell you the same thing."

"What do *you* think happens to them?"

He took a puff at his cigarette, looked me hard in the face and said, "I think they get eaten."

I ordered another round of drinks, and when they had come, Foxy said, "I haven't told you why I'm going back to the States."

"No."

"As a writer it might interest you. I'm in disgrace. I'm being *sent* back."

"What for?"

He took a long pull and said, "You don't know my name and

I don't know yours, and we're not ever likely to meet again, so I'll tell you.

"I got up this training programme for the Liberians I was telling you about, and the shop steward liked it and I liked it and everybody liked it. It was a good programme. But after a few months, living up there in the jungle got to be quite a strain. There was the heat and the insects and the general lack of utilities. And to add to that, there was this balls-up about our papers, so for two months we didn't get paid. And that wasn't any good, because we had to pay for our food and there were other expenses.

"It was all the fault of this new officer. He was twenty-three years old and about the most prejudiced and obstinate man I've ever met. He insulted at least ten Liberians within a week of getting there. He just didn't know how to talk to people. One of the Liberians said to me, 'I went to the States for my education. I got kicked around there because I was a black man. But I don't expect to get kicked around here. This is a black country.'

"So at the end of the week, when we hadn't been paid for two months, I went to this officer and I said, 'Will you fix up these papers over the week-end and send them off to base?' And he said he would, and I went over to Foya and spent the week-end on the Ham radio with this guy I was telling you about. I came back on the Monday and went into the office and the first thing I saw was the papers, which were still lying on the desk and hadn't been touched. So I went into the little cubicle this officer had, and I said to him, 'You haven't done the papers?', and he just sat there on his ass and said, 'No, I haven't gotten around to it yet.'

"So then I blew my top. That's all there was to it. I called him about every name in the book. I know I shouldn't have done it, but I guess I couldn't help myself. A man can only take so much. So he waited until I'd finished and then he said, 'O.K., pack your bags, you're going home.' Well that really loused me up, because I'd worked out a good training programme, and the only reason I'd volunteered for Liberia was to do a good job and help people."

"What happens now?" I said.

"Right now I have to go to Providence, Rhode Island, which is where my base is. The plane I'm booked in goes to Boston, which is only thirty-eight miles away, but this officer has routed my luggage through New York, so I guess I'll have to go there first, and then back to Providence. He fouled that up like he fouled everything else."

"What happens when you get to Providence?"

"I'm going to ask for a court martial because I want the whole situation looked into. I want them to hear my side of the story, not being paid and everything, and what sort of guy this officer is. I've been seventeen years in the Navy, and I've only got another three to go, so I don't want this to mess me up. I'm afraid it may mess me up a little. I know I shouldn't have said what I did. But I guess I was mad at the time. If I'd been a dog I'd have bitten that officer."

"Do you think you will get a court martial?"

"Yeah, I guess so," said Foxy. He pulled out another cigarette, and said, "See, one of the commanders at the base is a very good friend of mine. He's a fellow that knows me well, and that I wouldn't do anything stupid unless I had good reason to. I've already told him what happened."

"You've written to him?"

"No, I haven't written to him. I called him up on the Ham radio."

"Is he a Ham enthusiast too?"

"No, but there's a friend of mine in Providence who is, and I called him up and said I'd like to speak to this commander, and so he got hold of him and I spoke to him the following night."

I mulled it over for a bit, and the more I did, the more curious it seemed. "In the British Navy," I said, "it would be very unusual for a petty officer to call up a commander in this sort of way."

Foxy said, "Yeah, I guess it is kind of unusual." He paused for a moment and said, "See, this commander and I are very close. We have a special kind of relationship." He glanced at me in an odd way and the thought flashed through my mind they might be a couple of queers. Foxy said, "I don't know why I'm telling you this, but this commander is a very good friend of my wife's. He sees a lot of her while I'm away, takes her out in my automobile and things like that, which is very nice for her and O.K. by me." He gave me another quick glance and said, "They're real close, if you understand what I mean."

I nodded. "He's a good friend," said Foxy, "and he'll want to help me all he can."

"Yes," I said, "I can see that."

Foxy turned towards the window and looked down. "Christ!" he said, "that must be the S*ahair*a down there."

LUDOVIC KENNEDY,
Very Lovely People

———◆———

Professor Swallow and Professor Zapp

The passengers who feature in this next contribution are the creation of
the novelist David Lodge.

High, high above the North Pole, on the first day of 1969, two professors of English Literature approached each other at a combined velocity of 1200 miles per hour. They were protected from the thin, cold air by the pressurized cabins of two Boeing 707s, and from the risk of collision by the prudent arrangement of the international air corridors. Although they had never met, the two men were known to each other by name. They were, in fact, in process of exchanging posts for the next six months, and in an age of more leisurely transportation the intersection of their respective routes might have been marked by some interesting human gesture: had they waved, for example, from the decks of two ocean liners crossing in mid-Atlantic, each man simultaneously focusing a telescope, by chance, on the other, with his free hand; or, more plausibly, a little mime of mutual appraisal might have been played out through the windows of two railway compartments halted side by side at the same station somewhere in Hampshire or the Mid-West, the more self-conscious party relieved to feel himself, at last, moving off, only to discover that it is the other man's train that is moving first . . . However, it was not to be. Since the two men were in airplanes, and one was bored and the other frightened of looking out of the window—since, in any case, the planes were too distant from each other to be mutually visible with the naked eye—the crossing of their paths at the still point of the turning world passed unremarked by anyone other than the narrator of this duplex chronicle.

"Duplex", as well as having the general meaning of "twofold", applies in the jargon of electrical telegraphy to "systems in which messages are sent simultaneously in opposite directions" (*OED*). Imagine, if you will, that each of these two professors of English Literature (both, as it happens, aged forty) is connected to his native land, place of employment and domestic hearth by an infinitely elastic umbilical cord of emotions, attitudes and values—a cord which stretches and stretches almost to the point of invisibility, but never quite to breaking-point, as he hurtles through the air at 600 miles per hour. Imagine further that, as they pass each other above the polar ice-cap, the pilots of their respective Boeings, in defiance of regulations and technical feasibility, begin to execute a series of playful aerobatics—criss-crossing, diving, soaring and looping, like a pair of mating blue-birds, so as thoroughly to entangle the aforesaid umbilical cords, before proceeding soberly on their way in the approved manner. It follows that when the two men alight in each other's territory, and go about their business and pleasure, whatever vibrations are passed back by one to his native habitat will be felt by the other, and vice versa, and thus return to the transmitter subtly modified by the response of the other party—may, indeed, return to him along the other party's cord of communication, which is, after all, anchored in the place where he has just arrived; so that before long the whole system is twanging with vibrations travelling backwards and forwards between Prof. A and Prof. B, now along this line, now along that, sometimes beginning on one line and terminating on another. It would not be surprising, in other words, if two men changing places for six months should exert a reciprocal influence on each other's destinies, and actually mirror each other's experience in certain respects, notwithstanding all the differences that exist between the two environments, and between the characters of the two men and their respective attitudes towards the whole enterprise.

One of these differences we can take in at a glance from our privileged narrative altitude (higher than that of any jet). It is obvious, from his stiff, upright posture, and fulsome gratitude to the stewardess serving him a glass of orange juice, that Philip Swallow, flying westward, is unaccustomed to air travel; while to Morris Zapp, slouched in the seat of his eastbound aircraft, chewing a dead cigar (a hostess has made him extinguish it) and glowering at the meagre portion of ice dissolving in his plastic tumbler of bourbon, the experience of long-distance air travel is tediously familiar.

Philip Swallow has, in fact, flown before; but so seldom, and at such long intervals, that on each occasion he suffers the same trauma, an alternating current of fear and reassurance that charges and relaxes his system in a persistent and exhausting rhythm. While he is on the ground, preparing for his journey, he thinks of flying with exhilaration—soaring up, up and away into the blue empyrean, cradled in aircraft that seem, from a distance, effortlessly at home in that element, as though sculpted from the sky itself. This confidence begins to fade a little when he arrives at the airport and winces at the shrill screaming of jet engines. In the sky the planes look very small. On the runways they look very big. Therefore close up they should look even bigger—but in fact they don't. His own plane, for instance, just outside the window of the assembly lounge, doesn't look quite big enough for all the people who are going to get into it. This impression is confirmed when he passes through the tunnel into the cabin of the aircraft, a cramped tube full of writhing limbs. But when he, and the other passengers, are seated, well-being returns. The seats are so remarkably comfortable that one feels quite content to stay put, but it is reassuring that the aisle is free should one wish to walk up it. There is soothing music playing. The lighting is restful. A stewardess offers him the morning paper. His baggage is safely stowed away in the plane somewhere, or if it is not, that isn't his fault, which is the main thing. Flying is, after all, the only way to travel.

But as the plane taxis to the runway, he makes the mistake of looking out of the window at the wings bouncing gently up and down. The panels and rivets are almost painfully visible, the painted markings weathered, there are streaks of soot on the engine cowlings. It is borne in upon him that he is, after all, entrusting his life to a machine, the work of human hands, fallible and subject to decay. And so it goes on, even after the plane has climbed safely into the sky: periods of confidence and pleasure punctuated by spasms of panic and emptiness.

The sang-froid of his fellow passengers is a constant source of wonderment to him, and he observes their deportment carefully. Flying for Philip Swallow is essentially a dramatic performance, and he approaches it like a game amateur actor determined to hold his own in the company of word-perfect professionals. To speak the truth, he approaches most of life's challenges in the same spirit. He is a mimetic man: unconfident, eager to please, infinitely suggestible.

It would be natural, but incorrect, to assume that Morris Zapp has suffered no such qualms on his flight. A seasoned veteran of the domestic airways, having flown over most of the states in the Union in his time, bound for conferences, lecture dates and assignations, it has not escaped his notice that airplanes occasionally crash. Being innately mistrustful of the universe and its guiding spirit, which he sometimes refers to as Improvidence ("How can you attribute *that*," he will ask, gesturing at the star-spangled night sky over the Pacific, "to something called Providence? Just look at the *waste*!"), he seldom enters an aircraft without wondering with one part of his busy brain whether he is about to feature in Air Disaster of the Week on the nation's TV networks. Normally such morbid thoughts visit him only at the beginning and end of a flight, for he has read somewhere that eighty per cent of all aircraft accidents occur at either take-off or landing—a statistic that did not surprise him, having been stacked on many occasions for an hour or more over Esseph airport, fifty planes circling in the air, fifty more taking off at ninety-second intervals, the whole juggling act controlled by a computer, so that it only needed a fuse to blow and the sky would look like airplane competition had finally broken out into open war, the companies hiring retired kamikaze pilots to destroy each other's hardware in the sky. TWA's Boeings ramming Pan Am's, American Airlines' DC 8s busting United's right out of their Friendly Skies (hah!), rival shuttle services colliding head-on, the clouds raining down wings, fuselages, engines, passengers, chemical toilets, hostesses, menu cards and plastic cultery (Morris Zapp had an apocalyptic imagination on occasion, as who has not in America these days?) in a definitive act of industrial pollution.

By taking the non-stop polar flight to London, in preference to the two-stage journey via New York, Zapp reckons that he has reduced his chances of being caught in such an Armageddon by fifty per cent. But weighing against this comforting thought is the fact that he is travelling on a charter flight, and chartered aircraft (he has also read) are several times more likely to crash than planes on scheduled flights, being, he infers, machines long past their prime, bought as scrap from the big airlines by cheapjack operators and sold again and again to even cheaper jacks (this plane, for instance, belonged to a company called Orbis; the phoney Latin name inspired no confidence and he wouldn't mind betting that an ultra-violet photograph would reveal a palimpsest of fourteen different airline insignia under its fresh paint flown by pilots long gone over the hill, alcoholics and schizoids, shaky-fingered victims of emergency landings, ice-storms and hijackings by crazy Arabs and homesick Cubans wielding sticks of dynamite and dime-store pistols. Furthermore, this is his first flight over water (yes, Morris Zapp has never before left the protection of the North American landmass, a proud record unique among the faculty of his university) and he cannot swim. The unfamiliar ritual of instruction, at the commencement of the flight, in the use of inflatable lifejackets, unsettled him. That canvas and rubber contraption was a fetishist's dream, but he had as much chance of getting into it in an emergency as into the girdle of the hostess giving the demonstration. Furthermore, exploratory gropings failed to locate a lifejacket where it was supposed to be, under his seat. Only his reluctance to strike an undignified pose before a blonde with outsize spectacles in the next seat had dissuaded him from getting down on hands and knees to make a thorough check. He contented himself with allowing his long, gorilla-like arms to hang loosely over the edge of his seat, fingers brushing the underside unobtrusively in the style used for parking gum or nosepickings. Once, at full stretch, he found something that felt promising, but it proved to be one of his neighbour's legs, and was indignantly withdrawn. He turned towards her, not to apologize (Morris Zapp never apologized) but to give her the famous Zapp Stare, guaranteed to stop any human creature, from University Presidents to Black Panthers, dead in his tracks at a range of twenty yards, only to be confronted with an impenetrable curtain of blonde hair.

Eventually he abandons the quest for the life-jacket, reflecting that the sea under his ass at the moment is frozen solid anyway, not that that is a reassuring thought. No, this is not the happiest of flights for Morris J. Zapp ("Jehovah", he would murmur out of the side of his mouth to girls who enquired about his middle name, it never failed; all women longed to be screwed by a god, it was the source of all religion—"Just look at the myths, Leda and the Swan, Isis and Osiris, Mary and the Holy Ghost"—thus spake Zapp in his graduate seminar, pinning a brace of restive nuns to their seats with the Stare). There is something funny, he tells himself, about this plane—not just the implausible Latin name of the airline, the missing lifejacket, the billions of tons of ice beneath him and the minuscule cube melting in the bourbon before him—something else there is, something he hasn't figured out yet.

No virgin spinster, Philip Swallow, a father of three and husband of one, but on this occasion he journeys alone. And a rare treat it is, this absence of dependents—one which, though he is ashamed to admit it, would make him lightsome were his destination Outer Mongolia. Now, for example, the stewardess lays before him a meal of ambiguous designation (could be lunch, could be dinner, who knows or cares four miles above the turning globe) but tempting: smoked salmon, chicken and rice, peach parfait, all neatly compartmentalized on a plastic tray, cheese and biscuits wrapped in cellophane, disposable cutlery, personal salt cellar and pepperpot in dolls'-house scale. He eats everything slowly and with appreciation, accepts a second cup of coffee and opens a pack of opulently long duty-free cigarettes. Nothing else happens. He is not required to cut up anyone else's chicken, or to guarantee the edibility of smoked salmon; no neighbouring trays spring suddenly into the air or slide resonantly to the floor; his coffee-cup is not dashed from his lips, to deposit its scalding contents in his crotch; his suit collects no souvenirs of the meal by way of buttered biscuit crumbs, smears of peach parfait and dribbles of mayonnaise. This, he reflects, must be what weightlessness is like in space, or the lowered gravity of moonwalks—an unwonted sensation of buoyancy and freedom, a sudden reduction of the effort customarily required by ordinary physical tasks. And it is not just for today, but for six whole months, that it will last. He hugs the thought to himself with guilty glee. Guilty, because he cannot entirely absolve himself of the charge of having deserted Hilary, perhaps even at this moment presiding grimly over the rugged table-manners of the three young Swallows.

*   *   *

Philip stubs out his cigarette, and lights another. Pipes are not permitted in the aircraft.

He checks his watch. Less than halfway to go now. There is a communal stirring in the cabin. He looks round attentively, anxious not to miss a cue. People are putting on the little plastic headphones that were lying, in transparent envelopes on each seat when they boarded the plane. At the front of the tourist compartment a stewardess is fiddling with a piece of tubular apparatus. How delightful, they are going to have a film, or rather, *movie*. There is an extra charge: Philip pays it gladly. A withered old lady across the aisle shows him how to plug in his headphones which are, he discovers, already providing aural entertainment on three channels: Bartok, Muzak, and some children's twaddle. Culturally conditioned to choose the Bartok, he switches, after a few minutes to the Muzak, a cool, rippling rendition of, what is it, "These Foolish Things" . . .?

Meanwhile, back in the other Boeing, Morris Zapp has just discovered what it is that's bugging him about his flight. The realization is a delayed consequence of walking the length of the aircraft to the toilet, and strikes him, like a slow-burn gag in a movie-comedy, just as he is concluding his business there. On his way back he verifies his suspicion, covertly scrutinizing every row of seats until he reaches his own at the front of the aircraft. He sinks down heavily and, as is his wont when thinking hard, crosses his legs and plays a complex percussion solo with his fingernails on the sole of his right shoe.

Every passenger on the plane except himself is a woman.
What is he supposed to make of that? The odds against such

a ratio turning up by chance must be astronomical. Improvidence at work again. What kind of a chance is he going to stand if there's an emergency, women and children first, himself a hundred and fifty-sixth in the line for the lifeboats?

"Pardon me."

It's the bespectacled blonde in the next seat. She holds a magazine open on her lap, index finger pressed to the page as if marking her place.

"May I ask your opinion on a question of etiquette?"

He grins, squinting at the magazine. "Don't tell me *Ramparts* is running an etiquette column?"

"If a lady sees a man with his fly open, should she tell him?"

"Definitely."

"Your fly's open, mister," says the girl, and recommences reading her copy of *Ramparts*, holding it up to screen her face as Morris hastily adjusts his dress.

"Say," he continues conversationally (for Morris Zapp does not believe in allowing socially disadvantageous situation to cool and set), "Say, have you noticed anything funny about this plane?"

"Funny?"

"About the passengers."

The magazine is lowered, the swollen spectacles turned slowly in his direction. "Only you, I guess."

"You figured it out too!" he exclaims. "It only just struck me. Right between the eyes. While I was in the john . . . That's why . . . Thanks for telling me, by the way." He gestures towards his crotch.

"Be my guest," says the girl. "How come you're on this charter anyway?"

"One of my students sold me her ticket."

"Now all is clear," says the girl. "I figured you couldn't be needing an abortion."

BOINNNNNNNGGGGGGGGGG! The penny drops thunderously inside Morris Zapp's head. He steals a glance over the back of his seat. A hundred and fifty-five women ranked in various attitudes—some sleeping, some knitting, some staring out of the windows, all (it strikes him now) unnaturally silent, self-absorbed, depressed. Some eyes meet his, and he flinches from their murderous glint. He turns back queasily to the blonde, gestures weakly over his shoulder with his thumb, whispers hoarsely, "You mean all those women . . .?"

She nods.

"Holy mackerel!" (Zapp, his stock of blasphemy and obscenity threadbare from everyday use, tends to fall back on such quaintly genteel oaths in moments of great stress.)

"Pardon my asking," says the blonde, "but I'm curious. Did you buy the whole package—round trip, surgeon's fee, five days nursing with private room and exursion to Stratford-upon-Avon?"

"What has Stratford-upon-Avon got to do with it, for Chrissake?"

"It's supposed to give you a lift afterwards. You get to see a play."

"*All's Well That Ends Well*?" he snaps back, quick as a flash. But the jest conceals a deep unease. Of course he has heard of these package tours operating from States where legal abortions are difficult to obtain, and taking advantage of Britain's permissive new law. In casual conversation he would have shrugged it off as a simple instance of the law of supply and demand, perhaps with a quip about the limeys finally licking their balance of payments problem. No prude, no reactionary, Morris Zapp. He has gone down on many a poll as favouring the repeal of Euphoria's abortion laws (likewise its laws against fornication, masturbation, adultery, sodomy, fellatio, cunnilingus and sexual congress in which the female adopts the superior position: Euphoria had been first settled by a peculiarly narrow-minded Puritanical sect whose taboos retained a fossilized existence in the State legal code, one that rigorously enforced would have entailed the incarceration of ninety per cent of its present citizens). But it is a different matter to find oneself trapped in an airplane with a hundred and fifty-five women actually drawing the wages of sin. The thought of their one hundred and fifty-five doomed stowaways sends cold shivers roller-coasting down his curved spine, and a sudden vibration in the aircraft, as it runs into the turbulence recently experienced by Philip Swallow, leaves him quaking with fear.

DAVID LODGE,
Changing Places

FLIGHT 539

The same March sun that polishes St. Paul's
brightens the arches of my rack of toast.
I am flying, after breakfast, to North America.
I crack my egg with an egg-spoon; it is almost

time. I yank at straps, count money and check out,
saluted by a doorman with a calfskin face
who carries one fawn glove and wears the other.
I'm glum but genial; he's aloof. He knows his place,

and clearly indicates I should know mine.
London that shone at my descent with brass
militia, geraniums, throngs of happy subjects
acting naturally, now lets me pass

as though I'd packed up and left yesterday.
"Never hinder a traveller," it says, "never detain
a guest." Its thin smile reaches to the airport.
I am not happy until I see my plane,

grasshopper-still, in fog that crowds like sleep
outside the waiting room. There is a "slight delay".
I buy five-fifths of White Horse and a Penguin
Classic that I should have read and, squared away,

slump in a wicker chair. Nothing happens
for hours. I watch a covey of white nuns who gaily
chirp toward their oblivion in Africa,
a delegation handing roses to a smart Israeli

who weeps and smiles, important in blue serge.
Do they know, I wonder, just where they belong?
My passport photo, smirking, looks me in the eye.
Loudspeakers call my number: I must go along

with all my flight companions to Gate 9.
Two by two, bell-wethered by a china doll,
we file out, mount the ramp, take one last look around,
and find our seats to music piped through a wall

of leatherette. We have all done this before; we're bored
and terrified. Full tilt, our backbones braced
by gravity, we run wide open, lift,
punch through a wadding cloud and, clear at last,

track a bent circle over dunes and troughs
riding a blue elliptic toward the Hebrides.
The monitory lights go off, we drop our belts
and sit, heads back, alike as effigies.

Five hours that I fattened on in coming over
drop off at once. I know the time, but what time is it?
I light a cigarette off Scotland and crush the butt
some eighty miles at sea. The pilot says it

's cold in Boston, that turbulence off Newfoundland
won't reach us since we're six miles up and will soon
go up to seven. I scan the dome of the known world,
trying to imagine what I see. I'd like some one

to talk to. So would the man behind me.
We stand, stretch out, yawning like old familiars,
Unembarrassed, going home. He's been
in Asia Minor where, he says, "our" failures

are conspicuous. Pleased to worry this old bone,
we share our guilt like men of the same kidney.
Then, bumped apart, we sink through clouds which,
we are told almost at once, are over Sydney,

Nova Scotia. We shake hands and, separately, sit down,
having just parted forever. The coast line filters through—
a ragged lace of ice on the North Shore. Then it's
Nahant, Revere Beach smudged with drifts of snow

that look left over from an age of ice.
Levelling, we come down fast and, drifting slightly
(a gull goes by like wreckage from a blast)
in a fan of sun, are thumped to earth as lightly

as an apple from a bough. Is it still two o'clock?
I'm stretched among northern lights! I'm lost on
a reef surrounded by dim bubbles! "Ladies and gentlemen,"
the stewardess says, "we have landed in Boston".

JOHN MALCOLM BRINNIN,
Poetry Chicago

A trip with Prince Philip

He was flying me over Mexico, and I was up front watching him
at the controls. "That's Maya country," he went on with barely
a break, looking down on the inhospitable brown hills. Maya
country? I should have brushed up more.

But time had been short. To see him fly was something I
wanted, but had thought in terms of a quick flip from Luton to
Southend. "Well, come to Mexico," he said. He was going on
Wednesday. We rolled in a Rolls to Heathrow, no roads cleared,
because he hates that. Take-off to the second. He loves that, and
was pleased with the Ottawa (I think) headline: Philip Flies in on
the Dot.

We were strolling along the beach in Florida, outside some sort
of VIP hutments at Patrick Air Force Base, having lodged the
night there for an imminent tour of Cape Canaveral, and he did
not care for an armed escort strolling warily behind.

"They just don't want you shot, sir." A snort. "If it hadn't
been for all the security, Kennedy wouldn't have been shot." I
never worked that one out.

But that was later. Andovers of the Queen's Flight being
strictly short-haul jobs that have to keep stopping for petrol, it

The Flying Duke. Prince Philip at the controls of the
Australian built Victa Airtourer.

took us five days to Mexico City. According to my geography we
should have begun by crossing the Atlantic.

We made off in the wrong direction, but I did not say anything.
Fuelled at Stornoway, Keflavik ("You have to come in here with
one wing scraping the rock," my pilot said), and Sondrestrom,
Greenland, for the first night stop.

To come, Goose, Ottawa, Florida, Yucatan and Maya country.
We should part in Mexico. He would be trundling on to Santa
Barbara, Vancouver, Fiji, Tonga, New Zealand, Australia (official,
from Vancouver joining the Queen).

The NASA men, besides displaying proud moon rocks and
whipping us to the dizzy peak of Apollo 13 awaiting launch, and

tactfully restraining him from climbing into the de-germed capsule (but he saw sense in that), mounted a great show of films, slides, lectures on the bewilderments of space. They did not bewilder him.

Some lecturers, less than concise, had their sentences finished for them. They could answer most of his questions: "But supposing there's a telemetry failure . . . What's the burning sequence . . . Aren't the HF frequencies pre-selected . . . Is it a passive dish?"

A week before, in London, I had been with him to something different, a drug-addiction rehabilitation centre. The questions were equally on the ball, though the first, I remember, on the presentation of a pale inmate, was easy and direct: "How did you get hooked?"

They gave us an informal dinner for six at Patrick, wide-ranging talk, top space brass. Suddenly a general shot up and proposed the health of the Queen, with a well-rehearsed list of her titles and dignities. Startling. An expectant pause for the guest of honour's response.

"Well, thanks very much," he said. "Go on with what you were saying about continental drift."

*   *   *

He had been the focal point of a bigger and more elaborate dinner at Sondrestrom, staged by the Danes and Americans based there to look after the DEW line. It began at 2.45 a.m. by our London stomachs.

He was buoyant, made the best speech of the evening, barely touched the wine, finally said to me, "Do you feel like tottering off?" One advantage of royalty, it only has to stand up and the party's over.

He could have had this in mind, among other things, when once I gasped at his rushing life and he said, "There are compensations."

He came into my adjoining room, laughing, while I was still fumbling for the right end of my pyjamas. The no smoking notice over his bed had a warning: Violators Will be Prosecuted; he wanted to see if I had got one, too. I had, but was too tired to have isolated the double entendre.

J

He had also brought me the draft of an article for some Council of Europe publication. Would I look it over? He had written it (after nine hours' flying) in the short interval before dinner, which might otherwise have been wasted. The energy is numbing. Seen at close quarters it drains one's own. Next day in the Andover I returned the draft with some diffident amendments. He adopted them with thanks.

This was back in the cabin. He pilots so long as it is interesting—take-off, put-downs, tricky weather. Just to sit up front with nothing to do is boring. That is what his R.A.F. co-pilot is for. So we talked of everything under the sun. Or he did. Including the sun; which eventually would fail to pierce the pollution, and that would be the end of the world. His mind darts about. Quite a tirade against form-filling and petty officialdom, youth was right to want to change things . . .

It was nonsense to say we kept royal ceremonial because the tourists liked it, we should keep it because we liked it. Tower blocks, human happiness, the motor car, Richard Nixon, the blue whale, mental deficiency, the melting of the ice-cap.

Did I know (open a bottle) that true Liebfraumilch should be spelt Liebfrauenmilch, and came only from the vineyard slopes around Cologne cathedral?

My eyes may have closed. "How about a stretch-out?" Getting up to lower some sort of bed for me from the cabin wall.

He does not stretch out much. Or did not then. Now 10 years on? I should not think so. There are only so many minutes in an hour, a year, a life. They demand full employment.

Too much of this, perhaps, about the Mexico trip. It is just that, despite red carpets and motorcades at all arrivals, he was in effect off duty. In the air they can not get at you. Well, I did. But that had been his whole idea. I found out more about him, though never all, than in any of the routine interviews.

BASIL BOOTHROYD,
from *The Times*

Basil Boothroyd was Prince Philip's official biographer

Coast to coast

East Coast blanked out from North Carolina right up to the Canadian border; a half-continent under a pat of fog; nothing visible but the extreme tip of the Empire State Building; planes grounded. Fog, the airman's common cold; all the resources of science are squeaking and gibbering under it; lights blink unseen, radar echoes quiver and ping; the gigantic aircraft lumber round the ramps and aprons like death's-head moths in cold weather; money leaks away. We, the privileged, sit in a sort of underground air-raid shelter, racked by public-address systems and blasts of furious air conditioning. Evening drags into night. Everything is astonishly dirty, and time itself is stale. We sit.

Most passengers drift away, to go by train, or try a night's sleep in the airport hotel. But I am going too far to get there any way but by jet. Tomorrow I give the first of three lectures in Los Angeles, on the other side of America. Here it is midnight, or past midnight, or feels like midnight. I am late already, and must go by what flight I can. I cannot telegraph anyone, even though I shall land at the wrong airport.

A loudspeaker honks and burbles. Incredibly, and for the next hour, we have take-off and landing limits. Our plane is getting through; and sure enough, presently it bumbles out of the fog from the runway. I go with our group to Gate Nine, shudder into a freezing night with a dull grey roof. The jet crawls toward us, howling and whistling which keeps it only just under control. For a moment or two, it faces us—no, is end-on to us; for here there is no touch of human, or animal, or insect, no face—only four holes that scream like nothing else in creation. Then it huddles round and is still. Doors open and two streams of passengers ooze out. Their faces are haggard. They ignore the night that has caught up with them. They stagger, or walk with the stiff gait of stage sleep-walkers. One or two look stunned, as if they know it is midnight more or less but cannot remember if it is today or tomorrow midnight and why or what. Strange vehicles flashing all over with red lights come out of the darkness, not for the passengers, but to tend the jet. They crouch under the wings and the front end, attach themselves by tubes while all their lights flash, and lights on the jet flash, and the engines sink from a wail to a moan—a note, one might think, of resignation, as if the machine now recognises that it is caught and will have to do the whole thing over again. But for half an hour they feed it well, while it sucks or they blow, and we stand, imprisoned by the freezing cold and our own need to be somewhere else. Jet travel is a great convenience.

Then we are in, fastening safety belts, and I peer out of the window with a naiveté which seems to increase as I grow older; and a succession of blue lights flicks by faster and faster; and there is an eternity of acceleration at an angle of forty-five degrees, while the whistling holes under the wings seem no longer angry but godlike—see what we can do! Look, no hands! The "No Smoking, Fasten Your Safety Belts" notice disappears. Cupping my hands round my face, squinting sideways and down, I can make out that there is a white pat of fog slipping by beneath us, and over it a few stationary stars. An air hostess demonstrates the use of the oxygen masks.

Comfort, warmth flowing back into rigid hands, comparative silence, stillness except for an occasional nudge as the plane pierces a furlong of turbulence; I try to think of what our airspeed means: it remains nothing but arithmetic. The interior of the plane is like a very superior bus. Am thawed and relaxed. They say that this is not the latest mark of jet—do jets come any faster or bigger or plusher?

Glasses tinkle. Air Hostess brings round drinks—not what happens in a bus. Select Bourbon. (Always live off the country as far as possible). I also secrete the TWA swizzlestick as a memento. Do not cross America often this way. Another Bourbon. That makes the two obligatory drinks before an American dinner. Am cheerful now—but second drink did not contain swizzlestick and wonder if I am detected? Air Hostess approaches for the third time and I cower—but no. She is English and recognises a fellow-countryman. Speaks Kensingtonian, which sounds odd at this place and altitude. (Note to intending immigrants. Kensingtonian despised in a man. Gets him called a pouf. Do not know exactly what this term means, but cannot think it complimentary.

On the other hand, Kensingtonian in a girl widely approved of, Americans think it cute.)

Peripeteia! English Air Hostess has read my books and seen me on English telly! I instantly acquire overwhelming status. Feel utterly happy and distinguished in a nice, diffident, English sort of way. Neighbour put away his briefcase—we all have brief-cases—then talks to me. Is physicist, naturally. Tells me about jets sucking air in at one end and blowing result of combustion out at the other. Encourage him, from a pure sense of joie de vivre. Rash, this, very. Tells me about navigation lights, navigation, fluids, including the sea, acceleration—Bourbon now dying down. Make my way forward to lavatory in diffident but distinguished manner, watched by all the unhappy briefcases who haven't been on telly, or haven't been noticed there by an Air Hostess. Lavatory wonderful, buttons everywhere. Push the lot, just to tell grand-children. Tiny, ultimate fraction of our airstream is scooped in somewhere and directed to blow a jet vertically up out of the pan. Could balance celluloid balls on it and shoot them down with a rifle, as at fairs.

Return to seat and physicist continues course. American Air Hostess comes and talks. More status. Physicist goes to sleep. English Air Hostess comes and talks about London, Paris, Rome, Athens. American Air Hostess counters with Hawaii and Japan. Slight loss of status. I would like to go to sleep. Body here, can see it sitting in the seat. Soul still leaving Atlantic Coast. Time? AHs have got on to books. It's the beard, I think. Beard down there on the deck, just beard. Beard in jet v. distinguished Bourbon quite dead. Return to lavatory for a bit of peace in less distinguished manner. Jet still playing and cannot be bothered to push all the buttons. Return. Physicist says "Di!" very loudly in his sleep. Die? Diana? Diathermy? AHs wander away. Nod. Have instant vision of Ann with sweeper on carpet. She switches it off, switches off all the sweepers in the world, they fade, whining—am started awake—oh my God, my God! "No Smoking—Fasten Your Safety Belts"—briefcases stirring like sea-life under returning tide.

Am awake, dammit, or rather body is awake; soul two thousand miles behind, passing through Nashville, Tennessee, shall never be whole again, body mouldering in the jet, soul marching on

towards Denver. Time? Bump, rumble, rumble, lights, lights! Los
Angeles. Time? Enter Belshazzar's Hall. Body finds hall moving
slowly, but they can't fool body. Body knows the movement is the
world turning to catch up. More halls, enough for whole dynasties
of Belshazzars.

Soul will enjoy this when it catches up. More halls, MENE,
MENE. Briefcases have vanished. Tunnels, fountains, lights, music,
palms, light, more halls—they would have to put MENE, MENE out
by roneograph, or use the public-address system. "A MESSAGE FOR
MR. BELSHAZZAR!" Am delirious, I think. Find broom supporting
man in centre of hundredth hall. Body asks broom politely. "Which
way is out, Bud?" Brooms answers politely, "Don't arst me, Bud,
we just built it."

WILLIAM GOLDING,
Flying Westward

(London—Chicago)

After the horrors of Heathrow
A calmness settles in.
A window seat, an ambient glow,
A tonic-weakened gin.

The pale grey wings, the pale blue sky,
The tiny sun's sharp shine,
The engines' drone, or rather sigh;
A single calm design.

Those great wings flex to altering air.
Ten thousand feet below
We watch the endless miles of glare,
Like slightly lumpy dough.

Below that white all's grey and given,
The wrong side of the sky.
Reality's down in that dim
Old formicary? Why?

What though through years, the same old way,
That world spins on its hub?
The mayfly's simple summer day
Beats lifetimes as a grub!

A geologic fault, this flight:
Those debts, that former wife,
Make some moraine down out of sight,
Old debris of a life.

(Only one figure, far and clear
Looks upward from that trough:
A face still visible from here
—The girl who saw him off.)

The huge machine's apart, alone.
The yielding hours go by.
We form a culture of our own
Inhabiting the sky.

Too short? Yet every art replies,
Preferring for its praise
To Egypt's smouldering centuries
The brief Athenian blaze . . .

That flame-point sun, a blue-set jewel,
Blazed blurredly as it went.
Our arguments run out of fuel.
We dip for our descent.

We drift down from pure white and blue
To what awaits us there
In customs shed and passport queue
—The horrors of O'Hare.

ROBERT CONQUEST,
Forays

An occupational hazard of modern air travel.
Holidaymakers stranded at Heathrow during the 1978
French Air Traffic Controllers' strike.

Whatever next?

Farewelling an early girl-friend on her PamAm 707 flight back to America, I stood heavy-hearted as the plane took off, not because she was going without me but because she was going instead. The aircraft looked powerful enough to reach the Moon. The wheels came up, the flaps retracted, and you could see the flexible wings take the weight as the plane went spearing up through the heat-wobble. Imagine how it must feel. Alas, imagine was all I could afford. When I left for England the means of transport was a rusty old ship that took five weeks to get there. Then there were two or three years in London when I scarcely earned enough to catch a no. 27 bus. But eventually I found myself getting airborne, not—emphatically not—because I had become rich, but because air travel was expanding to embrace the poor.

The Sixties were the great age of the charter flight. Before the wide-bodies had even been invented, mass air travel was already under way. You could get to Milan, for example, for a very small amount of money if you were a student. The planes were ageing Britannias and even older Douglas DC-7Cs belonging to unknown airlines operating from tin sheds at the wind-swept edges of Gatwick or Luton, and most of your fellow students turned out to be 90-year-old Calabrian peasant women in black clothes carrying plucked chickens. On my first flight I was already petrified when we took off, largely because I had made the mistake of looking out of the window at the moment when the pilot arrived by Jeep. He was wearing an eye-patch, walked with a stiff leg and saluted the aircraft with what appeared to be an aluminium hand. Around his neck the silver brassard of a Polish award for bravery gleamed in the weak sunlight. But in the air I was too busy to be afraid. The ancient dwarf nun in the seat beside me—one of my fellow students—had never flown before in her life except when dreaming of the Last Judgment. Her rosary clattered in her gnarled hands like a football fan's rattle and when the plane tilted to avoid the Matterhorn she sang a brief excerpt from a Donizetti aria before being sick into her plastic carrier bag full of new potatoes. I got the job of holding her hand while the heavily loaded plane crabbed sideways on the wind and hit the runway between the two long lines of gutted old DC-4 which in those days told you that you were landing at Malpensa, Milan's second best airport. At Linate, the first best, we would probably not have been allowed to land even if on fire.

Other early flights were equally hair-raising but somehow I never seemed to mind. There was a way of flying to Paris which involved a long bus-ride from London to a grass-strip airfield terminating at the Kentish cliffs, an even longer bus-ride from the French coast to Paris, and an incredibly short hop across the channel. The airborne sector of the trip was accomplished in a high-wing twin-engined British airliner whose make I will not specify, lest you take fright and cancel if you ever find yourself booked on one of the few surviving examples. No doubt it is a perfectly good aircraft in normal circumstances but with a full load including me it took so long to get off the ground on the British side that one felt one might as well have stayed on the bus. Once again I made the mistake of looking out of the window, this time as the aircraft was pitching and yawing over the bumpy grass and dodging between sheep at full power toward the cliff edge. A rabbit popped out of its hole, looked at me, and overtook us.

But it was worth it just to be enskied, even if that particular flight rose only just far enough over the English Channel to clear the upper-works of Greek oil tankers steaming towards each other. I used to spend all those early flights with my nose squashed against the window. Nowadays I have learned the trick of always asking for an aisle seat, so that if you have a drunken Bulgarian hammer-thrower sitting beside you at least you won't have to climb over him to get to the toilet. But in those days I wanted to see everything happening outside, even when what was happening outside was too close to the inside for comfort. You never knew when there would be a revelation. At night the cities were like jewelled cobwebs on black velvet. Coming back from Venice on a BEA Comet 4 night flight, I was one of the only two passengers aboard and got invited to the flight deck just at the right moment to see the lights of Paris. Stacking around Gatwick in a chartered

Britannia while the pilot negotiated through an interpreter for
permission to land, I saw an old Elizabethan—one of the loveliest
aeroplanes ever made—slip out of the cloud 1,000 ft. below us. I
presume our aircraft waggled its wings out of recognition rather
than surprise. There was always something to look at, even if it
was only a sea of cloud, and the more often you flew the more
were the chances of an epiphany, such as the occasional clear day
over the Alps when there was nothing under you except naked
geology up which girls in dirndls ran yodelling, while the jet
engines worked their continuous invisible miracle of plaiting cold
air into a rope of power.

*   *   *

I finally got a trip on a Boeing 707 at just the time it was
about to go out of style, because the first wide-bodies were already
proving their routes. But it was still a thrill, not least because the
destination was Boston—a long way from Europe. Over mid-
Atlantic a BOAC VC-10 going the other way went past a few miles
to our left on my side of the aircraft, and a mile or so above. The
condensation trail came out of the cobalt blue distance like a spear
of snow. Letting down into Boston, I watched the magic suitcase
of the Boeing wing unpack itself, the flaps jacking out and curving
down to turn the aerofoil into a parasol. It was a long time since
I had bought *Flight* magazine every week and memorised the
contents, but I was still clued-up enough to be aware that the
same wing had held the B-52s up in the sky while they split the
ground of South-East Asia and drove a lot of little children crazy
just with the noise. There is good reason for thinking we are alive
in a particularly shameful stretch of history, the only era in which
the innocent have ever been obliterated on an industrial basis.
But on the airliners and in the airports I found myself unable to
pretend that I did not enjoy living in the twentieth century. You
will find an extermination camp in the seventh book of Thucydides.
People have always destroyed each other on as grand a scale as
the prevailing technology allowed. But powered flight has all
happened within a single lifetime. Last week I had dinner with a
man who remembers crossing the Atlantic on the old Aquitania

in 1906, the year the Wright brothers first flew at Kittyhawk.
Even Leonardo, who could do anything, could only dream of flying.
And here was I, without even a licence to drive a car, riding down
out of the sky into Massachusetts after having crossed the Atlantic
in a few hours. A king of infinite space, I was justifiably annoyed
when the immigration officer sent me back to fill out my form
again because I had not pressed hard enough to ink the carbon
copy.

Then the wide-bodies came in and the age of mass aerial
migration was on for young and old. By those who flew them the
wide-bodies were known as heavies and the name was soon in use
among such non-practising pilots as myself. The DC-10 I found
hard to love at first, especially after one of them crashed near
Paris and killed a lot of people, including someone I knew. The
Tri-Star I found disconcertingly hard to tell apart from the DC-
10, until I learned to remember that the DC-10 was the one with
the third engine half way up its tail. Twenty years earlier I would
have learned a 100 different recognition points but as you get older
other things usurp your attention. There was no difficulty, however,
about spotting which of the three principal heavies was the winner.
Nobody with a proper appreciation of the Boeing 747's looks will
ever call it a Jumbo. The 747 is so suavely proportioned that it
doesn't even look very big except when it happens to taxi past its
ancestor, the 707, whereupon you feel that a mackerel has given
birth to a mako shark.

Loved by pilots for its handling qualities and seemingly infinite
reserves of getaway, the 747 flies like a fighter and at first glance
even looks like one. In fact it looks a lot like the old F-86 Sabre,
with its flight-deck bulge perched right forward like a Sabre's
bubble canopy and the same proud angle to its tail feathers. On
the ground the 747 is perhaps a bit fussy underneath, like a house
being moved around on a lot of roller skates, but when it gets into
the air, cleans itself up, and pours on the 100,000 horsepower of
its turbofans, there is nothing less awkward or lovelier aloft. Unless
you had been told, you would never think of it as having 400
people on board. It looks as if there is only one man in there,
having the time of his life.

*   *   *

The most beautiful piece of aerospace architecture on earth is undoubtedly Narita, which has now replaced Hanada as Tokyo's number one airport. The students did all they could to stop Narita but now that the *fait* is *accompli* it is hard not to be glad. Hanada was a health hazard and Narita is a work of art. The main building is one vast, deceptively simple arrangement of glass and distance, while the runways at night are a ravishing display of emeralds, sapphires and rubies. Heading south from Narita last year in a JAL DC-10, I climbed unharmed through miles of sky which had once been full of screaming danger. Here was where the last great strategic battles between aircraft that the world will ever see were fought out to the bitter end. The Japanese, improvising desperately against time, built fighters that could fly just high and fast enough to knock B-29-*san* down. But as Admiral Yamamoto had realised before Pearl Harbour, the war was lost before it started. High over Saipan, whose defenders once fought all the more savagely for having no chances left, I knew just enough Japanese to ask the hostess for more coffee (*kohi aramas ka?*) and she knew just enough English to ask me if I wanted a hot towel (You rike hot taoaroo?). As cultural contact goes it might not have amounted to a securely united world but it beat having to drop bombs on her.

The airliners haven't shrunk the earth. Going all the way around it still feels like a journey. But they have turned it into one place. Beyond the airport boundaries, each country remains odd enough to satisfy anybody's thirst for strangeness. Meanwhile the airports hint at a peaceful world. My only regret is that I will probably be too old for space. I have done my best to snare a window seat on an early space shuttle but so far they are being niggardly with the tickets. To go up so far that there is no down is still one of my dreams of heaven.

Meanwhile, as always, there is poetry enough in the here and now. All I do for a living is put words beside each other but I have been shown wonders without even asking. With raw egg dropping from chopsticks into my lap I have looked down on the North Pole. In the Persian Gulf at midnight I have seen the oil rigs burning like the damned. Best of all, I have found that every way you fly leads home. Crossing the paralysed red rock ocean of Australia's Dead Heart as the sun comes up, Qantas flight QF2 lets down over Sydney Harbour before the morning glare has burned the pale blue summer mist off the silver water. Over there on the right is my house, the sideboard now full of intact crockery. There is time enough to think about the misery we have caused and how much we have destroyed. For now, look what we have created. Only a few minutes ago we were in the cave. Whatever next?

CLIVE JAMES
from *The Observer*,
10th January 1982

A MISCELLANY OF FLIGHTS

ICARUS

In tedious exile
   now too long detain'd,
Daedalus languish'd
   for his native land;
The sea foreclosed his flight,
   yet thus he said:
"Though earth and water
   in subjection laid,
O cruel Minos, thy dominion be,
We'll go through air;
   for sure the air is free."
Then to new arts
   his cunning thought applies,
And to improve
   the work of nature tries.
A row of quills
   in gradual order placed,
Rise by degrees
   in length from first to last . . .
Along the middle
   runs a twine of flax,
The bottom stems
   are join'd by pliant wax:
Thus, well compact,
   a hollow bending brings
The fine composure into real wings.
His boy, young Icarus,
   that near him stood,
Unthinking of his fate,
   with smiles pursued
The floating feathers . . .

Or with the wax impertinently
  play'd,
And, with his childish tricks,
  the great design delay'd.
The final master-stroke
  at last imposed,
And now the neat machine
  completely closed;
Fitting his pinions on,
  a flight he tries,
And hung, self-balanced,
  in the beaten skies.
Then thus instructs his child:
  "My boy, take care
To wing your course
  along the middle air:
If low, the surges
  wet your flagging plumes;
If high, the sun
  the melting wax consumes . . .
But follow me: let me
  before you lay
Rules for the flight,
  and mark the pathless way."
Then, teaching,
  with a fond concern, his son,
He took the untried wings
  and fix'd them on . . .
When now the boy,
  whose childish thoughts aspire
To loftier aims,
  and make him ramble higher,
Grown wild and wanton,
  more imbolden'd, flies
Far from his guide,
  and soars among the skies.
The softening wax,
  that felt a nearer sun,
Dissolved apace,

The first fatal air crash. Lament for Icarus by Herbert J. Draper.

and soon began to run;
The youth in vain
   his melting pinions shakes,
His feathers gone,
   no longer air he takes;
O! father, father!
   as he strove to cry,
Down to the sea
   he tumbled from on high,
And found his fate;
   yet still subsists by fame
Among those waters
   that retain his name.

OVID,
The Metamorphoses
trans. Samuel Croxall

MUSÉE DES BEAUX ARTS

About suffering they were never wrong,
The Old Masters: how well they understood
Its human position; how it takes place
While someone else is eating or opening a window or just walking
   dully along;
How, when the aged are reverently, passionately waiting
For the miraculous birth, there always must be

Children who did not specially want it to happen, skating
On a pond at the edge of the wood:
They never forgot
That even the dreadful martyrdom must run its course
Anyhow in a corner, some untidy spot
Where the dogs go on with their doggy life and the torturer's horse
Scratches its innocent behind on a tree.

In Breughel's *Icarus*, for instance: how everything turns away
Quite leisurely from the disaster; the ploughman may
Have heard the splash, the forsaken cry,
But for him it was not an important failure; the sun shone
As it had to on the white legs disappearing into the green
Water; and the expensive delicate ship that must have seen
Something amazing, a boy falling out of the sky,
Had somewhere to get to and sailed calmly on.

W. H. AUDEN,
Collected Poems

Parachuting

The first of the many

It is very commonly supposed that the parachute, in anything
like its present form, is a very modern device, and that the art of
successfully using it had not been introduced to the world even so
lately as thirty years ago. Thus, we find it stated in works of that
date dealing with the subject that disastrous consequences almost
necessarily attended the use of the parachute, "the defects of
which had been attempted to be remedied in various ways, but up
to this time without success". A more correct statement, however,
would have been that the art of constructing and using a practic-
able parachute had through many years been lost or forgotten. In
actual fact, it had been adopted with every assurance of complete
success by the year 1785, when Blanchard by its means lowered
dogs and other animals with safety from a balloon. A few years
later he descended himself in a like apparatus from Basle, meeting,
however, with the misadventure of a broken leg.

But we must go much further back for the actual conception
of the parachute, which, we might suppose, may originally have
been suggested by the easy floating motion with which certain
seeds or leaves will descend from lofty trees, or by the mode

adopted by birds of dropping softly to earth with out-stretched wings. M. de la Loubere, in his historical account of Siam, which he visited in 1687–88, speaks of an ingenious athlete who exceedingly diverted the King and his court by leaping from a height and supporting himself in the air by two umbrellas, the handles of which were affixed to his girdle. In 1783, that is, the same year as that in which the balloon was invented, M. le Normand experimented with a like umbrella-shaped contrivance, with a view to its adoption as a fire escape, and he demonstrated the soundness of the principle by descending himself from the windows of a lofty house at Lyons.

It was, however, reserved for M. Jacques Garnerin in 1797 to make the first parachute descent that attracted general attention. Garnerin had previously been detained as a State prisoner in the fortress of Bude, in Hungary, after the battle of Marchiennes in 1793, and during his confinement had pondered on the possibility of effecting his escape by a parachute. His solitary cogitations and calculations resulted, after his release, in the invention and construction of an apparatus which he put to a practical test at Paris before the court of France on October 22nd, 1797. Ascending in a hydrogen balloon to the height of about 2,000 feet, he unhesitatingly cut himself adrift, when for some distance he dropped like a stone. The folds of his apparatus, however, opening suddenly, his fall became instantly checked. The remainder of his descent, though leisurely, occupying, in fact, some twelve minutes, appeared to the spectators to be attended with uncertainty, owing to a swinging motion set up in the car to which he was clinging. But the fact remains that he reached the earth with only slight impact, and entirely without injury.

It appears that Garnerin subsequently made many equally successful parachute descents in France, and during the short peace of 1802 visited London, where he gave an exhibition of his art. From the most reliable accounts of his exploit it would seem that his drop was from a very great height, and that a strong ground wind was blowing at the time, the result of which was that wild, wide oscillations were set up in the car, which narrowly escaped bringing him in contact with the house tops in St. Pancras, and eventually swung him down into a field, not without some unpleasant scratches.

The first parachute descent. Made by André Jacques
Garnerin from a height of about 3000 feet above the Parc
Monceau, Paris, 22 October 1797.

Nor was Garnerin the only successful parachutist at this period. A Polish aeronaut, Jordaki Kuparento, ascended from Warsaw on the 24th of July, 1804, in a hot air balloon, taking up, as was the custom, an attached furnace, which caused the balloon to take fire when at a great height. Kuparento, however, who was alone, had as a precaution provided himself with a parachute, and with this he seems to have found no difficulty in effecting a safe descent to earth.

REV. J. M. BACON,
The Dominion of the Air

The ultimate in air travel: sky-diving.

PARACHUTE

Parachute men say
The first jump
Takes the breath away
Feet in the air disturbs
Till you get used to it

Solid ground
Is now where you left it
As you plunge down
Perhaps head first
As you listen to
Your arteries talking
You learn to sustain hope

Suddenly you are only
Holding an open umbrella
In a windy place
As the warm earth
Reaches out to you
Reassures you
The vibrating interim is over

You try to land
Where green grass yields
And carry your pack
Across the fields

The violent arrival
Puts out the joint
Earth has nowhere to go
You are at the starting point

Jumping across worlds
In condensed time
After the awkward fall
We are always at the starting point.

LENRIE PETERS,
Poems

Gliding

Straight and level

Most of us who glide say that we do so because it stimulates us. What we mean is that it frightens us. The question is, "How much?" If it frightens us too much we no longer enjoy it; if it does not frighten us enough we become bored. Somewhere between the two, we think, lies the special appeal of our sport, and it leaves a fairly wide scope for individual variation.

Ever since I took up gliding I have always been a member of the Straight and Level Club. Aerobatics are only enjoyable to me in their mildest forms. Chandelles are all right, loops are my limit, and anything which disturbs the dust from the cockpit floor is well beyond it. Thus when I arrived to watch the World Gliding Championships at Leszno in Poland in the summer of 1958 I was astonished, as I got down from the taxi which had brought me from the station, to see a two-seater Bocian glider circling at 500 feet over the middle of the aerodrome *upside-down*. It was not until the following day that two of my friends from the Midland Gliding Club told me that they had both been indulging in this doubtful entertainment and one of them—a Pole named Teddy Proll—said that if I wanted to fly during my short four days at Leszno he could arrange it. At this point I thought I made myself clear that although there was nothing I should like to do more than to sample the Polish thermals, there was nothing I wished to do *less* than to fly upside-down. An hour or so later Teddy Proll approached me excitedly and said he had arranged it all and that in a few moments I could have a flight in the two-seater Bocian.

Now this machine was not entirely new to me because a week before I had flown in one at Helsinki and had found it, although not to my way of thinking quite so attractive as an Eagle, nevertheless a perfectly gentlemanly aircraft of high performance and considerable comfort. I therefore looked forward to my flight with lively anticipation and soon afterwards, at the launch point, I was introduced to the charming young man who was to fly with me. He spoke a very few words of English and a very few words of German, and to make quite sure I explained to him at some length in both languages that the limit of my ambition was perhaps an hour of comfortable thermal soaring after which I hoped to return equally comfortably to earth. He seemed an intelligent young man and appeared to understand me perfectly. There was some delay because on the previous landing the air-brakes had become inexplicably jammed. When the seats were removed a screwdriver was found wedged behind the air-brake control. Apparently during inverted flight it had slipped out of a pocket. At least this particular hazard would not come my way. No inverted flight for me!

We were launched by aero-tow with a sixty-foot tow rope—half the length of the tow ropes I was used to. It was of a suitable thickness for towing a motor-car and wholly innocent of any "weak link" arrangement which would be obligatory in England. I found that the climb to 500 metres required all my attention, for the tug—a low-wing monoplane—was terribly close in front of us. To begin with when I flew in the standard position, with the tug's wings just below the horizon I was looking down into the cockpit and could almost read his instruments. I was shortly corrected by my young colleague and told that I must keep all of the tug above the horizon. This I did and was surprised not to fall into his slip-stream, but it turned out to be quite a comfortable position. Nevertheless the short tow rope still required a high degree of concentration. At 500 metres we released in an indifferent thermal and I started to turn. My companion shouted, "No, no! Not yet!" and seized the controls. We flew further into the thermal, which then admittedly improved, and was of such enormous dimensions that the straight period did not carry us through to the other side as it would have done in an English thermal. As we began to gain height I found that my companion was a confirmed "pudding-stirrer"; the control column was in constant motion and as a result (so it seemed) we had quite a rough ride. After a while the thermal grew weaker and I asked if I could fly again. Here I was lucky, for I decided to move over to another thermal underneath a cloud which was just forming and this was so much stronger that we roared up at about 500 feet a minute. And so we wound our way to cloud base (but not into cloud because the turn-and-slip indicator batteries were flat). From 5,000 feet we headed back towards the aerodrome. "Now . . . aerobatic!" said my friend. Could it be that he had misunderstood me? Well, there was no harm in the simple ones. I performed a couple of fairly mild chandelles followed by a loop. "Is very nice," said my friend, "now I show you." He took over the controls and in a second we had half-rolled and were flying upside-down. A number of unfortunate circumstances dominated the next few moments. First I had not taken the elementary precaution of tightening the lower pair of straps. Tightly though my shoulders were held, my midriff was only loosely supported. In order to offset this disadvantage I had found a convenient hand grip for my left hand under the seat. Everything seemed under control although I was hanging rather far away from the seat itself. A few moments later my companion began an inverted turn. At this point the seat, unaccustomed to an "upward" pull of one and a half times my weight, gave way with a splintering crash. This was greeted by a loud guffaw from behind me. I wonder whether you can remember as a child lying belly downwards in your bath? I was in just such a position, only the bath was the perspex canopy. It was at this stage, to my undying shame, that I could no longer withhold a stifled cry for mercy. With a flip back of the stick positive G was restored as we half-looped out. Hastily I tightened the straps, for clearly we had not seen the end of this business. In a few seconds we were involved in two consecutive slow rolls. But with the straps tighter I felt slightly more secure, although my toes were curled around something—perhaps the variometer bottle—which was quite certainly not designed to take the strain now bearing upon it.

The next thing was a half-loop to inverted-flight and at that precise moment we hit the edges of a thermal. "Ah-ha," said my companion and we began to circle upside down. It was only when he started to tighten the turns and we had already gone up fifty metres that I allowed a further expression of dismay to escape my lips. This time, in what I hoped was a firm voice, I followed it with "right way up now, please". A few seconds later a more normal world was restored to me. We were still regrettably high. "Now Immelmann," said my companion, and in quick succession we performed two half-loops, rolling off the top. After what I had already suffered these were, it must be admitted, comparatively mild and I even made so bold as to try one myself, but it was executed at too slow a speed, and my companion demonstrated with two more. As we now approached the lower limit of what in this country would be regarded as aerobatic height I began to breathe again, but my relief was premature. First came two rather charming little flick stall turns, a manoeuvre which only leaves you on the straps for a second or so. It is not unpleasant as a sensation and is quite spectacular in appearance, for the glider seems to cartwheel in the sky. We were now down to 500 feet. Down went the nose yet again. "What now?" I thought. At the edge of the aerodrome our Bocian half-rolled on to its back and we made a run across the whole width of the field upside-down. Oh dear, oh dear! But surely there could not be much more. We half-rolled out, went up into a chandelle, round, out brakes and a spot landing which trickled us up to the hangar door. An enthusiastic Teddy Proll rushed up to take a snapshot and to ask the inevitable question, "Did you enjoy it?"

PETER SCOTT,
The Eye of the Wind

IN A SAILPLANE

Still as a bird
Transfixed in flight
We shiver and flow
Into leagues of light.

Rising and turning
Without a sound
A summer lifts us
Off the ground.

The sky's deep bell
Of glass rings down.
We slip in a sea
That cannot drown.

Hang-gliding.

We kick the wide
Horizon's blues
Like a cluttering hoop
From round our shoes.

This easy 'plane
So quietly speaks,
Like a tree it sighs
In silvery shrieks.

Neatly we soar
Through a roaring cloud:
Its caverns of snow
Are dark and loud.

Into banks of sun
Above the drifts
Of quilted cloud
Our stillness shifts.

Here no curious
Bird comes near.
We float alone
In a snowman's sphere.

Higher than spires
Where breath is rare
We beat the shires
Of racing air.

Up the cliff
Of sheer no-place
We swarm a rope
That swings on space.

Breezed by a star's
Protracted stare
We watch the earth
Drop out of air.

Red stars of light
Burn on the round
Of land: street-constellations
Strew the ground.

Their bridges leap
From town to town:
Into lighted dusk
We circle down.

Still as a bird
Transfixed in flight
We come to nest
In the field of night.

JAMES KIRKUP,
The Prodigal Son

The first American astronaut in space. John Glenn hoists
himself into the Mercury Space Capsule which in 1962 took
him on three orbits of the earth.

Space

1. The voyage of *Friendship 7*

On 20th February 1962 John Glenn's spacecraft *Friendship 7*
was launched from Cape Canaveral on the first manned orbital

space flight. Tom Wolfe's account of his mission conveys dra-
matically and convincingly the atmosphere of the weird world
in which the astronaut operates, night and day succeeding each
other with bewildering rapidity, astride one continent or ocean
one moment, approaching another the next.

He was riding backward, looking back toward the Cape. It must
be tremendous, it must be beautiful—what else could it be? And
yet it didn't look terribly different from what he had seen at
50,000 feet in fighter planes. He had no greater sense of having
left the bonds of earth. The earth was not just a little ball beneath
him. It still filled his field of consciousness. It slid by slowly
underneath him, just the way it did when you were in an airplane
at forty or fifty thousand feet. He had no sense of being a *star
voyager.* He couldn't see any stars at all. He could see the Atlas
booster tumbling behind him and beginning to grow smaller,
because it was in a slightly lower orbit. It just kept tumbling.
There was nothing to stop it. Somehow the sight of this colossal
great tumbling cylinder, which had weighed more than the average
freighter while it was on the ground and which now weighed
nothing and had been discarded like a candy wrapper—somehow
it was more extraordinary than the view of earth. It shouldn't
have been, but it was. The earth looked the way it had looked to
Gus Grissom. Shepard had seen a low-grade black-and-white movie.
Through his window Glenn could see what Grissom saw, the
brilliant blue band at the horizon, a somewhat wider band of
deeper blues leading into the absolutely black dome of the sky.
Most of the earth was covered in clouds. The clouds looked very
bright, set against the blackness of the sky. The capsule was
heading east, over Africa. But, because he was riding backward,
he was looking west. He saw everything after he had passed over
it. He could make out the Canary Islands, but they were partly
obscured by clouds. He could see a long stretch of the African
coast . . . huge dust storms over the African desert . . . but there
was no sense of taking in the whole earth at a glance. The earth
was eight thousand miles in diameter and he was only a hundred
miles above it. He knew what it was going to look like in any case.
He had seen it all in photographs taken from the satellites. It had
all been flashed on the screens for him. Even the view had been

K

simulated. *Yes ... that's the way they said it would look ...*
Awe seemed to be demanded, but how could he express awe
honestly? He had lived it all before the event. How could he
explain that to anybody? The view wasn't the main thing, in any
case. The main thing . . . was *the checklist!* And just try explaining
that! He had to report all his switch and dial readings. He had to
put a special blood-pressure rig on the arm of his pressure suit and
pump it up. (His blood pressure was absolutely normal, 120 over
80—*perfect stuff!*) He had to check the manual attitude-control
system, swing the capsule up and down, side to side, roll to the
right, roll to the left . . . and there was nothing novel about it, not
even in orbit, a hundred miles above the earth. *How could you
explain that!* When he swung the capsule, it felt the same as it did
in a one-g state on earth. He still didn't feel weightless. He merely
felt less cramped, because there were no longer any pressure points
on his body. He was sitting straight up in a chair drifting slowly
and quietly around the earth. Just the hum of his little shop, the
background noises in his head-set, and the occasional spurt of the
hydrogen-peroxide jets.

*   *   *

Forty minutes into the flight, as he neared the Indian Ocean,
off the east coast of Africa, he began sailing into the night. Since
he was traveling east, he was going away from the sun at a speed
of 17,500 miles an hour. But because he was riding backward, he
could see the sun out of the window. It was sinking the way the
moon sinks out of sight as seen on the earth. The edge of the sun
began to touch the edge of the horizon. He couldn't tell what part
of the earth it was. There were clouds everywhere. They created
a haze at the horizon. The brilliant light over the earth began to
dim. It was like turning down a rheostat. It took five or six
minutes. Very slowly the lights were dimming. Then he couldn't
see the sun at all, but there was a tremendous band of orange
light that stretched from one side of the horizon to the other, as
if the sun were a molten liquid that had emptied into a tube along
the horizon. Where there had been a bright-blue band before, there
was now the orange band; and above it a wider dimmer band of
oranges and reds shading off into the blackness of the sky. Then

all the reds and oranges disappeared, and he was on the night side of the earth. The bright-blue band reappeared at the horizon. Above it, stretching up about eight degrees, was what looked like a band of haze, created by the earth's atmosphere. And above that . . . for the first time he could make out the stars. Down below, the clouds picked up a faint light from the moon, which was coming up behind him. Now he was over Australia. He could hear Gordon Cooper's voice. Cooper was serving as the capcom at the tracking station in the town of Muchea, out in the kangaroo boondocks of western Australia. He could hear Cooper's Oklahoma drawl.

"That sure was a short day," said Glenn.

"Say again, *Friendship 7*," said Cooper.

"That was about the shortest day I've ever run into," said Glenn. Somehow that was the sort of thing to say to old Oklahoma Gordo sitting down there in the middle of nowhere.

"Kinda passes rapidly, huh?" said Gordo.

"Yessir," said Glenn.

The clouds began to break up over Australia. He could make out nothing in the darkness except for electric lights. Off to one side he could make out the lights of an entire city, just as you could at 40,000 feet in an airplane, but the concentration of lights was terrific. It was an absolute mass of electric lights, and south of it there was another one, a smaller one. The big mass was the city of Perth and the smaller one was a town called Rockingham. It was midnight in Perth and Rockingham, but practically every living soul in both places had stayed up to turn on every light they had for the American sailing over in the satellite.

"The lights show up very well," said Glenn, "and thank everybody for turning them on, will you?"

"We sure will, John," said Gordo.

And he went sailing on past Australia with the lights of Perth and Rockingham sliding into the distance.

He was over the middle of the Pacific, about halfway between Australia and Mexico, when the sun began to come up behind him. This was just thirty-five minutes after the sun went down. Since he was traveling backward, he couldn't see the sunrise through the window. He had to use the periscope. First he could see the blue band at the horizon becoming brighter and brighter. Then the sun itself began to slide up over the edge. It was a brilliant red—not terribly different from what he had seen at sunrise on earth, except that it was rising faster and its outlines were sharper.

"It's blinding through the scope on clear," said Glenn. "I'm going to the dark filter to watch it come on up."

And then—*needles!* A tremendous layer of them—Air Force communications experiment that went amok ... Thousands of tiny needles gleaming in the sun outside the capsule ... But they couldn't be needles, because they were luminescent—they were like snowflakes—

"This is *Friendship 7*," he said. "I'll try to describe what I'm in here. I am in a big mass of some very small particles that are brilliantly lit up like they're luminescent. I never saw anything like it. They're round, a little. They're coming by the capsule, and they look like little stars. A whole shower of them coming by. They swirl around the capsule and go in front of the window and they're all brilliantly lighted. They probably average maybe seven or eight feet apart, but I can see them all down below me also."

"Roger, *Friendship 7*." This was the capcom on Canton Island out in the Pacific. "Can you hear any impact with the capsule? Over."

"Negative, negative. They're very slow. They're not going away from me more than maybe three or four miles per hour."

They swirled about his capsule like tiny weightless diamonds, little bijoux—no, they were more like fireflies. They had that lazy but erratic motion, and when he focused on one it would seem to be lit up, but the light would go out and he would lose track of it, and then it would light up again. That was like fireflies, too. There used to be thousands of fireflies in the summers, when he was growing up. These things were like fireflies, but they obviously couldn't be any sort of organism ... unless all the astronomers and all the satellite recording mechanisms had been fundamentally wrong ... They were undoubtedly particles of some sort, particles that caught the sunlight at a certain angle. They were beautiful, but were they coming from the capsule? That could mean trouble. They must have been coming from the capsule, because they traveled along with him, in the same trajectory, at the same speed. But wait a minute. Some of them were far off, far below ... there might be an entire field of them ... a minute cosmos ... something never seen before! And yet the capcom on Canton Island didn't seem particularly interested. And then he sailed out of range of Canton and would have to wait to be picked up by the capcom at Guaymas, on the west coast of Mexico. And when the Guaymas capcom picked him up, he didn't seem to know what he was talking about.

"This is *Friendship 7*," said Glenn. "Just as the sun came up, there were some brilliantly lighted particles that looked luminous that were swirling around the capsule. I don't have any in sight right now. I did have a couple just a moment ago, when I made the transmission over to you. Over."

"Roger, *Friendship 7*."

And that was it. "Roger, *Friendship 7*." Silence. They didn't particularly care.

Glenn kept talking about his fireflies. He was fascinated. It was the first true unknown anyone had encountered out here in the cosmos. At the same time he was faintly apprehensive. *Roger, Friendship 7*. The capcom finally asked a polite question or two, about the size of the particles and so on. They obviously were not carried away by this celestial discovery.

*   *   *

Glenn was now over Africa, riding over the dark side of the earth, sailing backward toward Australia. The Indian Ocean capcom said, "We have message from MCC for you to keep your landing-bag switch in off position. Landing-bag switch in off position. Over."

"Roger," said Glenn. "This is *Friendship 7*."

He wanted to ask why. But that was against the code, except in an emergency situation. That fell under the heading of nervous chatter.

Over Australia old Gordo, Gordo Cooper, got on the same subject: "Will you confirm the landing-bag switch is in the off position? Over."

"That is affirmative," said Glenn. "Landing-bag switch is in the center off position."

"You haven't had any banging noises or anything of this type at higher rates?"

"Negative."

"They wanted this answer."

They still didn't say why, and Glenn entered into no nervous chatter. He now had two red lights on the panel. One was the warning light for the automatic fuel supply. All the little amok action of the yaw thrusters had used it up. Well, it was up to the Pilot now . . . to aim the capsule correctly for re-entry . . . The other was a warning about excess cabin water. It built up as a by-product of the oxygen system. Nevertheless, he pressed on with the checklist. He was supposed to exercise by pulling on the bungee cord and then take his blood pressure. The Presbyterian Pilot! He did it without a peep. He was pulling on the bungee and watching the red lights when he began sailing backward into the sunrise again. Two hours and forty-three minutes into the flight, his second sunrise over the Pacific . . . seen from behind through a periscope. But he hardly watched it. He was looking for the fireflies to light up again. The great rheostat came up, the earth lit up, and now there were thousands of them swirling about the capsule. Some of them seemed to be miles away. A huge field of them, a galaxy, a microuniverse. No question about it, they weren't coming from the capsule, they were part of the cosmos. He took out the camera again. He had to photograph them while the light was just right.

"*Friendship 7.*" The Canton Island capcom was coming in. "This is Canton. We also have no indication that your landing-bag might be deployed. Over."

Glenn's first reaction was that this must have something to do with the fireflies. He's telling them about the fireflies and they come in with something about the landing-bag. But who said anything about the landing-bag being deployed?

"Roger," he said. "Did someone report landing-bag could be down? Over."

"Negative," said the capcom. "We had a request to monitor this and to ask you if you heard any flapping, when you had high capsule rates."

"Well," said Glenn, "I think they probably thought these particles I saw might have come from that, but these are . . . there are thousands of these things, and they go out for it looks like miles in each direction from me, and they move by here very slowly. I saw them at the same spot on the first orbit. Over."

And so he thought that explained all the business about the landing-bag.

They gave him the go-ahead for his third and final orbit as he sailed over the United States. He couldn't see a thing for the clouds. He pitched the capsule down sixty degrees, so he could look straight down. All he could see was the cloud deck. It was just like flying at high altitudes in an airplane. He was really no longer in the mood for sightseeing. He was starting to think about the sequence of events that would lead to the retrofiring over the Atlantic after he had been around the world one more time. He had to fight both the thrusters and the gyros now. He kept releasing and resetting the gyros to see if the automatic attitude control would start functioning again. It was all out of whack. He would have to position the capsule by using the horizon as a reference. He was sailing backward over America. The clouds began to break. He began to see the Mississippi delta. It was like looking at the world from the tail-gun perch of the bombers they used in the Second World War. Then Florida started to slide by. Suddenly he realized he could see the whole state. It was laid out just like it is on a map. He had been around the world twice in three hours and eleven minutes and this was the first sense he had had of how high up he was. He was about 550,000 feet up. He could make out the Cape. By the time he could see the Cape he was already over Bermuda.

"This is *Friendship 7*," he said. "I have the Cape in sight down there. It looks real fine from up here."

"Rog, Rog." That was Gus Grissom on Bermuda.

"As you know," said Glenn.

"Yea, verily, sonny," said Grissom.

Oh, it all sounded very fraternal. Glenn was modestly acknowledging that his loyal comrade Grissom was one of the only three Americans ever to see such a sight ... and Grissom was calling him "sonny".

Twenty minutes later he was sailing backward over Africa again and the sun was going down again, for the third time, and the rheostat was dimming and he ... saw *blood*. It was all over one of the windows. He knew it couldn't be blood, and yet it was blood. He had never noticed it before. At this particular angle of the setting rheostat sun he could see it. Blood and dirt, a real mess. The dirt must have come from the firing of the escape tower. And the blood ... *bugs*, perhaps ... The capsule must have smashed into bugs as it rose from the launch pad ... or *birds* ... but he would have heard the thump. It must have been bugs, but bugs didn't have blood. Or the blood red of the sun going down in front of him diffusing ... And then he refused to think about it any more. He just turned the subject off. Another sunset, another orange band streaking across the rim of the horizon, more yellow bands, blue bands, blackness, thunderstorms, lightning making little sparkles under the blanket. It hardly mattered any more. The whole thing of lining the capsule up for retrofire kept building up in his mind. In slightly less than an hour the retro-rockets would go off. The capsule kept slipping its angles, swinging this way and that way, drifting. The gyros didn't seem to mean a thing any more.

And he went sailing backward through the night over the Pacific. When he reached the Canton Island tracking point, he swung the capsule around again so that he could see his last sunrise while riding forward, out the window, with his own eyes. The first two he had watched through the periscope because he was going backward. The fireflies were all over the place as the sun came up. It was like watching the sunrise from inside a storm of the things. He began expounding upon them again, about how they couldn't possibly come from the capsule, because some of them seemed to be miles away. Once again nobody on the ground was interested. They weren't interested on Canton Island, and pretty soon he was in range of the station on Hawaii, and they weren't interested, either. They were all wrapped up in something else. They had a little surprise for him. They backed into it, however. It took him a little while to catch on.

He was now four hours and twenty-one minutes into the flight. In twelve minutes the retro-rockets were supposed to fire, to slow him down for re-entry. It took him another minute and forty-five seconds to go through all the "do you reads" and "how me's" and "overs" and establish contact with the capcom on Hawaii. Then they sprang their surprise.

"*Friendship 7*," said the capcom. "We have been reading an indication on the ground of segment 5–1, which is Landing Bag Deploy. We suspect this is an erroneous signal. However, Cape would like you to check this by putting the landing-bag switch in auto position, and seeing if you get a light. Do you concur with this? Over."

It slowly dawned on him . . . *Have been reading* . . . For how long? . . . Quite a little surprise. And they hadn't told him! They'd held it back! *I am a pilot and they refuse to tell me things they know about the condition of the craft!* The insult was worse than the danger! If the landing-bag had deployed—and there was no way he could look out and see it, not even with the periscope, because it would be directly behind him—if it had deployed, then the heat shield must be loose and might come off during the re-entry. If the heat shield came off, he would burn up inside the capsule like a steak. If he put the landing-bag switch in the automatic control position, then a green light should come on if the bag was deployed. Then he would know. Slowly it dawned! . . . That was why they kept asking him if the switch were in the off position!—they didn't want him to learn the awful truth too quickly! Might as well let him complete his three orbits—then we'll let him find out the bad news!

On top of that, they now wanted him to fool around with the switch. *That's stupid!* It might very well be that the bag had not deployed but there was an electrical malfunction somewhere in the circuit and fooling with the automatic switch might then cause it to deploy. But he stopped short of saying anything. Presumably they had taken all that into account. There was no way he could say it without falling into the dread nervous chatter.

"Okay," said Glenn. "If that's what they recommend, we'll go ahead and try it. Are you ready for it now?"

"Yes, when you're ready."

"Roger."

He reached forward and flipped the switch. Well . . . this was it—

No light. He immediately switched it back to off.

"Negative," he said. "In automatic position did not get a light and I'm back in off position now. Over."

"Roger, that's fine. In this case, we'll go ahead, and the re-entry sequence will be normal."

The retro-rockets would be fired over California, and by the time the retro-rockets brought him down out of his orbit and through the atmosphere, he would be over the Atlantic near Bermuda. That was the plan. Wally Schirra was the capcom in California. Less than a minute before he was supposed to fire the retro-rockets, by pushing a switch, he heard Wally saying, "John, leave your retropack on through your pass over Texas. Do you read?"

"Roger."

But why? The retropack wrapped around the edges of the heat shield and held the retro-rockets. Once the rockets were fired, the retropack was supposed to be jettisoned. They were back to the heat shield again, with no explanation. But he had to concentrate on firing the retro-rockets.

Next to the launch this was the most dangerous part of the flight. If the capsule's angle of attack was too shallow, you might skip off the top of the earth's atmosphere and stay in orbit for days, until long after your oxygen had run out. You wouldn't have any more rockets to slow you down. If the angle were too steep, the heat from the friction of going through the atmosphere would be so intense you would burn up inside the capsule, and a couple of minutes later the whole thing would disintegrate, heat shield or no heat shield. But the main thing was not to think about it in quite those terms. The field of consciousness is very small, said Saint-Exupéry. *What do I do next?* It was the moment of the test pilot at last. Oh, yes! *I've been here before! And I am immune! I don't get into corners I can't get out of!* One thing at a time! He could be a true flight test hero and try to line the capsule up all by himself by using the manual controls with the horizon as his reference—or he could make one more attempt to use the automatic controls. Please, dear God . . . don't let me foul up! What would the Lord answer? (Try the automatic, you ninny.) He released and reset the gyros. He put the controls on automatic. The answer to your prayers, John! Now the dials gibed with what he saw out the window and through the periscope. The automatic controls worked perfectly in pitch and roll. The yaw was still off, so he corrected that with the manual controls. The·capsule kept pivoting to the right and he kept nudging it back. The ALFA trainer! One thing at a time! It was just like the ALFA trainer . . . no sense of forward motion at all . . . As long as he concentrated on the instrument panel and didn't look at the earth sliding by beneath

him, he had no sense at all of going 17,500 miles an hour . . .or
even five miles an hour . . . The humming little kitchen . . . He sat
up in his chair squirting his hand thruster, with his eyes pinned
on the dials . . . Real life, a crucial moment—against the eternal
good beige setting of the simulation. One thing at a time!

Schirra began giving him the countdown for firing the rockets.
"Five, four—"

He nudged it back once more with the yaw thruster.

"—three, two, one, fire."

He pushed the retro-rocket switch with his hand.

The rockets started firing in sequence, the first one, the second
one, the third one. The sound seemed terribly muffled—but in that
very moment, the jolt! Pure gold! One instant, as Schirra counted
down, he felt absolutely motionless. The next . . . *thud thud thud*
. . . the jolt in his back. He felt as if the capsule had been knocked
backward. He felt as if he were sailing back toward Hawaii. All
as it should be! Pure gold! The retro-light was lit up green. It was
all going perfectly. He was merely slowing down. In eleven minutes
he would be entering the earth's atmosphere.

He could hear Schirra saying, "Keep your retropack on until
you pass Texas."

Still no reason given! He couldn't see the pattern yet. There
was only the dim sense that in some fashion they were jerking him
around. But all he said was, "That's affirmative."

"It looked like your attitude held pretty well," said Schirra.
"Did you have to back it up at all?"

"Oh, yes, quite a bit. Yeah, I had a lot of trouble with it."

"Good enough for government work from down here," said
Schirra. That was one of Schirra's favorite lines.

"Do you have a time for going to Jettison Retro?" said Glenn.
This was an indirect way of asking for some explanation for the
mystery of keeping the retropack on.

"Texas will give you that message," said Schirra. "Over."

They weren't going to tell him! Not so much the thought . . .
as the *feeling* . . . of the insult began to build up.

Three minutes later the Texas capcom tracking station came
in: "This is Texas capcom, *Friendship 7*. We are recommending
that you leave the retropackage on through the entire re-entry.
This means that you will have to override the zero-point-oh-five-

g switch, which is expected to occur at 04:43:53. This also means that you will have to manually retract the scope. Do you read?"

That did it.

"This is *Friendship 7*," said Glenn. "What is the reason for this? Do you have any reason? Over."

"Not at this time," said the Texas capcom. "This is the judgment of Cape Flight . . . Cape Flight will give you the reason for this action when you are in view."

"Roger. Roger. *Friendship 7*."

It was really unbelievable. It was beginning to fit—

Twenty-seven seconds later he was over the Cape itself and the Cape capcom, with the voice of Alan Shepard on the radio, was telling him to retract his periscope manually and to get ready for re-entry into the atmosphere.

It was beginning to fit together, he could see the pattern, the whole business of the landing bag and the retropack. This had been going on for a couple of hours now—and they were telling him nothing! Merely giving him the bits and pieces! But if he was going to re-enter with the retropack on, then they wanted the straps in place for some reason. And there was only one possible reason—something was wrong with the heat shield. And this they would not tell him! *Him!*—the pilot! It was quite unbelievable! It was—

He could hear Shepard's voice.

He was winding in the periscope, and he could hear Shepard's voice: "While you're doing that . . . we are not sure whether or not your landing-bag has deployed. We feel it is possible to re-enter with the retropackage on. We see no difficulty at this time in that type of re-entry."

Glenn said, "Roger, understand."

Oh, yes, he understood now! If the landing-bag was deployed, that meant the heat shield was loose. If the heat shield was loose, then it might come off during the re-entry, unless the retropack straps held it in place long enough for the capsule to establish its angle of re-entry. And the straps would soon burn off. If the heat shield came off, then he would fry. If they didn't want him—*the pilot!*—to know all this, then it meant they were afraid he might panic. And if he didn't even *need* to know the whole pattern—just

the pieces, so he could follow orders—*then he wasn't really a pilot!*
The whole sequence of logic clicked through Glenn's mind faster
than he could have put it into words, even if he had dared utter
it all at that moment. He was being treated like a passenger—a
redundant component, a backup engineer, a boiler-room attend-
ant—in an automatic system!—like someone who did not have
that rare and unutterably righteous stuff!—as if the right stuff
itself did not even matter! It was a transgression against all that
was holy—all this in a single limbic flash of righteous indignation
as John Glenn re-entered the earth's atmosphere.

"*Seven*, this is Cape," said Al Shepard. "Over."

"Go ahead, Cape," said Glenn. "You're ground . . . you are
going out."

"We recommend that you . . ."

That was the last he could hear from the ground. He had
entered the atmosphere. He couldn't feel the g-forces yet, but the
friction and the ionization had built up, and the radios were now
useless. The capsule was beginning to buffet and he was fighting
it with the controls. The fuel for the automatic system, the
hydrogen peroxide, was so low he could no longer be sure which
system worked. He was descending backward. The heat shield was
on the outside of the capsule, directly behind his back. If he
glanced out the window he could see only the blackness of the sky.
The periscope was retracted, so he saw nothing on the scope screen.
He heard a *thump* above him, on the outside of the capsule. He
looked up. Through the window he could see a strap. *From the
retropack. The straps broke! And now what!* Next the heat shield!
The black sky out the window began to turn a pale orange. The
strap flat against the window started burning—and then it was
gone. The universe turned a flaming orange. That was the heat
shield beginning to burn up from the tremendous speed of the
re-entry. This was something Shepard and Grissom had not seen.
They had not re-entered the atmosphere at such speed. Nevertheless, Glenn knew it was coming. Five hundred, a thousand times
he had been told how the heat shield would *ablate*, burn off layer
by layer, vaporize, dissipate the heat into the atmosphere, send
off a corona of flames. All he could see now through the window
were the flames. He was inside of a ball of fire. But!—a huge

flaming chunk went by the window, a great chunk of something burning. Then another . . . another . . . The capsule started buffeting . . . The heat shield was breaking up! It was crumbling—flying away in huge flaming chunks . . . He fought to steady the capsule with the hand controller. *Fly-by-wire!* But the rolls and yaws were too fast for him . . . The ALFA trainer gone amok, inside a fireball . . . The heat! . . . It was as if his entire central nervous system were now centered in his back. If the capsule was disintegrating and he was about to burn up, the heat pulse would reach his back first. His backbone would become like a length of red-hot metal. He already knew what the feeling would be like . . . and when . . . *Now!* . . . But it didn't come. There was no tremendous heat and no flaming debris . . . Not the heat shield, after all. The burning chunks had come from what remained of the retropack. First the straps had gone and then the rest of it. The capsule kept rocking, and the g-forces built up. He knew the g-forces by heart. A thousand times he had felt them on the centrifuge. They drove him back into the seat. It was harder and harder to move the hand controller. He kept trying to damp out the rocking motion by firing the yaw thrusters and the roll thrusters, but it was all too fast for him. They didn't seem to do much good, at any rate.

No more red glow . . . he must be out of the fireball . . . seven g's were driving him back into the seat . . . He could hear the Cape Capcom:

". . . How do you read? Over."

That meant he had passed through the ionosphere and was entering the lower atmosphere.

"Loud and clear; how me?"

"Roger, reading you loud and clear. How are you doing?"

"Oh, pretty good."

"Roger. Your impact point is within one mile of the uprange destroyer."

Oh, pretty good. It wasn't Yeager, but it wasn't bad. He was inside of one and a half tons of non-aerodynamic metal. He was a hundred thousand feet up, dropping toward the ocean like an enormous cannonball. The capsule had no aerodynamic qualities whatsoever at this altitude. It was rocking terribly. Out the

window he could see a wild white contrail snaked out against the
blackness of the sky. He was dropping at a thousand feet per
second. The last critical moment of the flight was coming up.
Either the parachute deployed and took hold or it didn't. The
rocking had intensified. The retropack! Part of the retropack must
still be attached and the drag of it is trying to flip the capsule
. . . He couldn't wait any longer. The parachute was supposed to
deploy automatically, but he couldn't wait any longer. Rocking
. . . He reached up to fire the parachute manually—but it fired on
its own, automatically, first the drogue and then the main' parachute. He swung under it in a huge arc. The heat was ferocious,
but the chute held. It snapped him back into the seat. Through
the window the sky was blue. It was the same day all over again.
It was early in the afternoon on a sunny day out in the Atlantic
near Bermuda. Even the landing bag light was green. There was
nothing even wrong with the landing bag. There had been nothing
wrong with the heat shield. There was nothing wrong with his rate
of descent, forty feet per second. He could hear the rescue ship
chattering away over the radio. They were only twenty minutes
away from where he would hit, only six miles. He was once again
lying on his back in the human holster. Out the window the sky
was no longer black. The capsule swayed under the parachute,
and over this way he looked up and saw clouds and over that way
blue sky. He was very, very hot. But he knew the feeling. All those
endless hours in the heat chambers—it wouldn't kill you. He was
coming down into the water only 300 miles from where he had
started. It was the same day, merely five hours later. A balmy
day out in the Atlantic near Bermuda. The sun had moved just
seventy-five degrees in the sky. It was 2:45 in the afternoon.
Nothing to do but get all these wires and hoses disconnected. *He
had done it.* He began to let the thought loose in his mind. He
must be very close to the water. The capsule hit the water. It
drove him down into his seat again, on his back. It was quite a
jolt. It was hot in here. Even with the suit fans still running, the
heat was terrific. Over the radio they kept telling him not to try
to leave the capsule. The rescue ship was almost there. They
weren't going to try the helicopter deal again, except in an
emergency. He wasn't about to attempt a water egress. He wasn't

about to hit the hatch detonator. The Presbyterian Pilot was not about to foul up. His pipeline to the dear Lord could not be clearer. He had done it.

TOM WOLFE,
The Right Stuff

THE ASTRONAUT

Star-sailor, with your eyes on space,
You map an ocean in the sky at night.
I see you stride with scientific grace
Upon the crusted suns of yesterday
As if it were to-morrow, in the place
Of time, the voyager beyond this momentary stay
Whose loaded instruments of light
Shoot rocket-galaxies around the bend of sight.

JAMES KIRKUP,
The Prodigal Son

2. Orbiting the Moon

In July 1969, the American astronauts Neil Armstrong, Buzz
Aldrin and Michael Collins made their historic trip to the moon.

I am everlastingly thankful that I have flown once before, and
that this period of waiting atop a rocket is nothing new. I am just
as tense this time, but the tenseness comes mostly from an
appreciation of the enormity of our undertaking rather than from
the unfamiliarity of the situation. If the two effects, physical
apprehension and the pressure of awesome responsibility, were
added together, they might just be too much for me to handle
without making some ghastly mistake. As it is, I am far from
certain that we will be able to fly the mission as planned. I think
we will escape with our skins, or at least I will escape with mine,
but I wouldn't give better than even odds on a successful landing
and return. There are just too many things that can go wrong. So
far, at least, none have, and the monster beneath us is beaming
its happiness to rooms full of experts. We fiddle with various
switches, checking for circuit continuity, for leaks, and for proper
operation of the controls for swiveling the service module engine.
There is a tiny leak in the apparatus for loading liquid hydrogen
into the Saturn's third stage, but the ground figures out a way to
bypass the problem. As the minutes get short, there really isn't
much for me to do. Fred Haise has run through a check list 417
steps long, checking every switch and control we have, and I have
merely a half dozen minor chores to take care of: I must make
sure that the hydrogen and oxygen supply to the three fuel cells
are locked open, that the tape recorder is working, that the
electrical system is well, and that the batteries are connected in
such a way that they will be available to supplement the fuel
cells, that we turn off unneeded communications circuits just prior
to lift-off . . . all nickel-and-dime stuff. In between switch throws,
I have plenty of time to think, if not daydream. Here I am, a
white male, age thirty-eight, height 5 feet 11 inches, weight 165

pounds, salary $17,000 per annum, resident of a Texas suburb, with black spot on my roses, state of mind unsettled, about to be shot off to the moon. Yes, to the moon.

*   *   *

Inevitably, as the big moment approaches, its arrival is announced by the traditional backward count toward zero. Anesthetists and launch directors share this penchant for scaring people, for increasing the drama surrounding an event which already carries sufficient trauma to command one's entire consciousness. Why don't they just hire a husky-voiced honey to whisper, "Sleep, my sweet" or "It's time to go, baby"? Be that as it may, my adrenalin pump is working fine as the monster springs to life. At nine seconds before lift-off, the five huge first-stage engines leisurely ignite, their thrust level is systematically raised to full power, and the hold-down clamps are released at T-zero. We are off! And do we know it, not just because the world is yelling "Lift-off" in our ears, but because the seats of our pants tell us so! Trust your instruments, not your body, the modern pilot is always told, but this beast is best felt. Shake, rattle, and roll! Noise, yes, lots of it, but mostly motion, as we are thrown left and right against our straps in spasmodic little jerks. It is steering like crazy, like a nervous lady driving a wide car down a narrow alley, and I just hope it knows where it's going, because for the first ten seconds we are perilously close to that umbilical tower. I breathe easier as the ten-second mark passes and the rocket seems to relax a bit also, as both the noise and the motion subside noticeably. All my lights and dials are in good shape, and by stealing a glance to my left, I can tell that the other two thirds of the spacecraft is also behaving itself. All three of us are very quiet—none of us seems to feel any jubilation at having left the earth, only a heightened awareness of what lies ahead. This is true of all phases of space flight: any pilot knows from ready-room fable or bitter experience that the length of the runway behind him is the most useless measurement he can take; it's what's up ahead that matters. We know we cannot dwell on those good things that have already happened, but must keep our minds ever one step ahead, especially now, when we are beginning to pick up speed. There is no sensation of speed, I don't mean that, but from a hundred hours of study simulation, I know what is happening in the real world outside that boost protective cover, even if I can't see it. We have started slowly, at zero velocity relative to the surface of the earth, or at nine hundred miles per hour if one counts the earth's rotational velocity. But as the monster spews out its exhaust gases, Newton's second law tells us we are reacting in the opposite direction. In the first two and a half minutes of flight, four and a half *million* pounds of propellant will have been expended, causing our velocity relative to the earth to jump from zero to nine thousand feet per second, which is how we measure speed. Not miles per hour, or knots, but feet per second, which makes it even more unreal.

*   *   *

Day 4 has a decidedly different feel to it. Instead of nine hours' sleep, I get seven—and fitful ones at that. Despite our concentrated attempt to conserve our energy on the way to the moon, the pressure is overtaking us (or me at least), and I feel that all of us are aware that the honeymoon is over and we are about to lay our little pink bodies on the line. Our first shock comes as we stop our spinning motion and swing ourselves around so as to bring the moon into view. We have not been able to see the moon for nearly a day now, and the change in its appearance is dramatic, spectacular, and electrifying. The moon I have known all my life, that two-dimensional, small yellow disk in the sky, has gone away somewhere to be replaced by the most awesome sphere I have ever seen. To begin with, it is *huge*, completely filling our window. Second, it is three-dimensional. The belly of it bulges out toward us in such a pronounced fashion that I almost feel I can reach out and touch it, while its surface obviously recedes toward the edges. It is between us and the sun, creating the most splendid lighting conditions imaginable. The sun casts a halo around it, shining on its rear surface, and the sunlight which comes cascading around its rim serves mainly to make the moon itself seem mysterious and subtle by comparison, emphasizing the size and texture of its dimly lit and pockmarked surface.

To add to the dramatic effect, we find we can see the stars again. We are in the shadow of the moon now, in darkness for the

first time in three days, and the elusive stars have reappeared as
if called especially for this occasion. The 360-degree disk of the
moon, brilliantly illuminated around its rim by the hidden rays
of the sun, divides itself into two distinct central regions. One is
nearly black, while the other basks in a whitish light reflected
from the surface of the earth. Earthshine, as it's called, is sunlight
which has traveled from the sun to the earth and bounced off it
back to the moon. Earthshine on the moon is considerably brighter
than moonshine on the earth. The vague reddish-yellow of the
sun's corona, the blanched white of earthshine, and the pure black
of the star-studded surrounding sky all combine to cast a bluish
glow over the moon. This cool, magnificent sphere hangs there
ominously, a formidable presence without sound or motion, issuing
us no invitation to invade its domain. Neil sums it up: "It's a
view worth the price of the trip." And somewhat scary too,
although no one says that.

*   *   *

As we ease on around the left side of the moon, I marvel again at
the precision of our path. We have missed hitting the moon by a
paltry three hundred nautical miles, at a distance of nearly a
quarter of a million miles from earth, and don't forget that the
moon is a moving target and that we are racing through the sky
just ahead of its leading edge. When we launched the other day,
the moon was nowhere near where it is now; it was some 40 degrees
of arc, or nearly 200,000 miles behind where it is now, and yet
those big computers in the basement in Houston didn't even
whimper but belched out super-accurate predictions. I hope. As
we pass behind the moon, finally, we have just over eight minutes
to go before the burn. We are super-careful now, checking and
rechecking each step several times. It is very much like the de-
orbit burn of Gemini 10, when John Young and I must have
checked our directions thirty times. If only one digit got slipped
in our computer, the worst possible digit, we could be turned
around backward and be about to blast ourselves into an orbit
around the sun, instead of the moon, thereby becoming a planet
the next generation might discover as the last one has discovered
Pluto. No thanks.

*   *   *

Now it is time for Neil and Buzz to get dressed, and they begin by pulling their lunar underwear out of storage bins. These garments are *liquid*-cooled, with hundreds of thin, flexible plastic tubes sewn into a fishnet fabric. The back pack they will wear on the lunar surface will pump water through these tubes, cooling their bodies much more efficiently than could be done simply by blowing cool oxygen over them. I don't need water-cooled underwear because I don't have any back pack, and because hopefully I won't be working that hard, but I do require a pressure suit, so all three of us struggle into them, helping each other with inaccessible zippers and generally checking the condition of each other's equipment. What would we do if, for example, Neil's zipper broke, or his helmet somehow refused to lock on to his neck ring? He couldn't venture out onto the lunar surface that way, that's for sure, nor could he allow Buzz to, because he would perish as soon as the LM door was opened to the vacuum of space. He couldn't stay in the CM and let Buzz land by himself, because the LM requires simultaneous manipulation by two people. I couldn't take his place because I was not trained to fly the LM. Perhaps he and I could switch suits, but I doubt that he could fit into mine, and mine can't accommodate a back pack. From such fabric are nightmares woven. Fortunately, everything seems to fit together, and I stuff Neil and Buzz into the LM along with an armload of equipment.

Now I have to do the tunnel bit again, closing hatches, installing drogue and probe, and disconnecting the electrical umbilical running into the LM. I am supposed to rig the TV camera to shoot out one of my windows to show the departure of the LM, but I decide I am too busy preparing for undocking to fool with it. I inform Houston, "There will be no television of the undocking. I have all available windows either full of heads or cameras, and I'm busy with other things." Generally one discusses these things with Houston and follows their advice, but this time I'm *telling* them, not asking them, and they must sense this, because they immediately reply, "We concur."

I am on the radio constantly now, running through an elaborate series of joint checks with *Eagle*. In one of them, I use my control system to hold both vehicles steady while they calibrate some of their guidance equipment. I check my progress with Buzz. "I have five minutes and fifteen seconds since we started. Attitude is holding very well." "Roger, Mike. Just hold it a little bit longer." "No sweat, I can hold it all day. Take your sweet time. How's the czar over there? He's so quiet." Neil chimes in, "Just hanging on—and punching." Punching those computer buttons, I guess he means. "All I can say is, beware the revolution," and then, getting no answer, I formally bid them goodbye. "You cats take it easy on the lunar surface; if I hear you huffing and puffing, I'm going to start bitching at you." "O.K., Mike," Buzz answers cheerily, and I throw the switch which releases them. With my nose against the glass of window 2 and the movie camera churning away over in window 4, I watch them go. When they are safely clear of me, I inform Neil, and he begins a slow pirouette in place, allowing me a look at his outlandish machine and its four extended legs. "The *Eagle* has wings!" Buzz exults.

Not long after, and with the lunar module out of sight of the command module, Mike Collins heard Neil Armstrong's exultant cry from the moon's surface; "The Eagle has landed." A quarter of a million miles away the Earth heard it too.

Meanwhile, the command module is purring along in grand shape. I have turned the lights up bright, and the cockpit reflects a cheeriness which I want very much to share. My concerns are exterior ones, having to do with the vicissitudes of my two friends on the moon and their uncertain return path to me, but inside, all is well, as this familiar machine and I circle and watch and wait. I have removed the center couch and stored it underneath the left one, and this gives the place an entirely different aspect. It opens up a central aisle between the main instrument panel and the lower equipment bay, a pathway which allows me to zip from upper hatch window to lower sextant and return. The main reason for removing the couch is to provide adequate access for Neil and Buzz to enter the command module through the side hatch, in the event that the probe and drogue mechanism cannot be cleared from the tunnel. If such is the case, we would have to open the hatch to the vacuum of space, and Neil and Buzz would have to make an extravehicular transfer from the LM, dragging their rock boxes behind them. All three of us would be in bulky pressurized suits, requiring a tremendous amount of space and a wide path into the lower equipment bay. In addition to providing more room, these preparations give me the feeling of being proprietor of a small resort hotel, about to receive the onrush of skiers coming in out of the cold. Everything is prepared for them; it is a happy place, and I couldn't make them more welcome unless I had a fireplace. I know from pre-flight press questions that I will be described as a lonely man ("Not since Adam has any man experienced such loneliness"), and I guess that the TV commentators must be reveling in my solitude and deriving all sorts of phony philosophy from it, but I hope not. Far from feeling lonely or abandoned, I feel very much a part of what is taking place on the lunar surface. I know that I would be a liar or a fool if I said that I have the best of the three Apollo 11 seats, but I can say with truth and equanimity that I am perfectly satisfied with the one I have. This venture has been structured for three men, and I consider my third to be as necessary as either of the other two.

I don't mean to deny a feeling of solitude. It is there, reinforced by the fact that radio contact with the earth abruptly cuts off at the instant I disappear behind the moon. I am alone now, truly alone, and absolutely isolated from any known life. I am it. If a count were taken, the score would be three billion plus two over on the other side of the moon, and one plus God only knows what on this side. I feel this powerfully—not as fear or loneliness—but as awareness, anticipation, satisfaction, confidence, almost exultation. I like the feeling. Outside my window I can see stars—and that is all. Where I know the moon to be, there is simply a black void; the moon's presence is defined solely by the absence of stars. To compare the sensation with something terrestrial, perhaps being alone in a skiff in the middle of the Pacific Ocean on a pitch-black night would most nearly approximate my situation. In a skiff, one would see bright stars-above and black sea below; I see the same stars, minus the twinkling, of course, and absolutely nothing below. In each case, time and distance are extremely important factors. In terms of distance, I am much more remote, but in terms of time, lunar orbit is much closer to civilized conversation than is the mid-Pacific. Although I may be nearly a quarter of a million miles away, I am cut off from human voices for only forty-eight minutes out of each two hours, while the man in the skiff—grazing the very surface of the planet—is not so privileged, or burdened. Of the two quantities, time and distance, time tends to be a much more personal one, so that I feel simultaneously closer to, and farther away from, Houston than I would if I were on some remote spot on earth which would deny me conversation with other humans for months on end.

*   *   *

When the instant of lift-off does arrive, I am like a nervous bride. I have been flying for seventeen years, by myself and with others; I have skimmed the Greenland ice cap in December and the Mexican border in August; I have circled the earth forty-four times aboard Gemini 10. But I have never sweated out any flight like I am sweating out the LM now. My secret terror for the last six months has been leaving them on the moon and returning to earth alone; now I am within minutes of finding out the truth of the matter. If they fail to rise from the surface, or crash back into it, I am not going to commit suicide; I am coming home, forthwith, but I will be a marked man for life and I know it. Almost better not to have the option I enjoy. Hold it! Buzz is counting down: "9—8—7—6—5— . . . abort stage . . . engine arm ascent . . . proceed . . . beautiful . . . thirty-six feet per second up . . ." Off they go: their single engine seems to be doing its thing, the thing earthlings have been insisting it could do for half a dozen years, but it's scary nonetheless. One little hiccup and they are dead men. I hold my breath for the seven minutes it takes them to get into orbit. Their apolune is forty-seven miles and their perilune is ten miles. So far so good. Their lower orbit ensures a satisfactory catch-up rate, and they will be joining me in slightly less than three hours, if all goes well.

'The best sight of my life.' From the command module Michael Collins
photographs Neil Armstrong and Buzz Aldrin returning in the lunar module from
the moon. In the distance, Earth.

All did go well, and when Armstrong and Aldrin rejoined Collins
in the command module, and the lunar module had been jettisoned, Collins ignited the engine to take them out of lunar orbit
and on to a course for home.

Meanwhile, we have two and a half days to sweat out. It took us
three days to get here, but our return trajectory is swifter; even
so, I expect the next two days to be long ones indeed. Right now
we are still tourists, plastered up against the windows as we climb
steeply up from the lunar surface. We approached the moon from
the west in its penumbra, that eerie shadow zone that made it

appear a ghostly globe, with illuminated rim but barely discernible surface. It is just as impressive now, but in a totally different way. We are departing from its eastern side, and it glares brilliantly in the sunlight. We can see it all now, from pole to pole and edge to edge, and we can clearly differentiate between the *maria* and the highlands. Both are cratered, but the seas do seem calm by comparison with the tortured uplands. The *maria* are darker too and seem more neutral gray then the golden hills which surround them. It seems like a cheery place, not the scary one I first saw two days ago, but cheerier yet is the notion that we are leaving it. I have absolutely no desire to come back.

My next concern, of course, is the accuracy of our return-to-earth trajectory. Our own ability to navigate home independent of Houston is very poor when we are close to the moon, so for the time being we are dependent on earth tracking of our position. "How does that tracking look, or is it too early to tell?" "Stand by, Mike . . . looking real good." That's nice. The next call from Houston indicates that Deke Slayton has grabbed the mike away from Charlie Duke. "Congratulations on an outstanding job. You guys have really put on a great show up there. I think it's about time you powered down and got a little rest, however. You've had a mightly long day . . . I look forward to seeing you when you get back here. Don't fraternize with any of those bugs en route except for the *Hornet*." Get some rest? Who cares about rest, although I suppose we must be tired. Neil reports he got only three hours' sleep in the LM last night, and Buzz got four; I suppose I must have gotten five hours in my more comfortable machine. However, we still have a few things to take care of: moon photography, optional, of course; but then the mandatory chores. The platform must be realigned, the spacecraft put into its broadside roll to distribute the sun's heat evenly, lithium hydroxide canisters must be changed, the oxygen-tank heaters need to be turned on for a while, the water supply must be chlorinated . . . when I get to the latter task, I realize how tired I am. I patiently explain to Houston how many chlorine ampules I have left in my storage box and how there are not enough unused ones left to keep using them at the present rate, etc., only to have them point out to me that I have overlooked a second supply cabinet full of them. Dunce! I must have been going flat out for seventeen hours now, but that shouldn't cause me to forget what supplies we have on board. The moon is nearly five thousand miles away as we pack it in for the day. "Goodnight, Charlie. Thank you," says Neil, and Buzz echoes, "Good night, Charlie. Thank you." "Adios," I add. "Adios," says Charlie. "Thanks for a great show, you guys." As long as everybody is congratulating everybody else, I might as well get in the last word. "Thanks again for a great job down there." Lights out.

MICHAEL COLLINS,
Carrying the Fire

WAR

On the Western Front

1. Patrols without action

After the tests were over, four of us were sent up to have a go
at the Fokker—a Morane Biplane, the Parasol, the Nieuport
(another excellent French scout), and the 2c. All of them gave
quite a good account of themselves except the 2c, which, in
performance, was nowhere. Besides, I was flying it, and when
experienced pilots were really on their mettle I was left a long
way behind. Soon all the others came down and landed; but as my
engine was running beautifully, and it was a lovely evening, I
decided to see the sunset from ten thousand feet.

At five thousand over the aerodrome I turned north. The flat
country stretched to the four horizons. To say it looked like a map
was a cliché. There was a resemblance, of course, as between sitter
and portrait; but the real thing had a bewildering amount of extra
detail; a wealth of soft colour, of light and shade, that made it, at
first, difficult to reconcile with its printed counterpart. Main roads,
so importantly marked in red, turned out to be grey, unobtrusive,
and hard to distinguish from other roads. Railways were not clear
black lines, but winding threads, even less well defined than the
roads. Woods were not patches of green, except in high summer;
they were dark browns and blacks, merging, sometimes imperceptibly, into the ploughed fields which surrounded them. Then there
were cloud shadows, darkening patches of landscape and throwing
others into high relief; ground mist, blurring the horizon and
sometimes closing in around you to a few miles, or even a few
hundred yards, an impalpable wall of vapour, mysteriously receding as you advanced. It was not always easy to find your way, or
read your map. You could get lost in the air as easily as in a

forest, and you were just as likely to fly in circles as walk in them on the ground. True, you had a compass to give you a general sense of direction; but compasses in those days, owing to the vibration of the machine, had a maddening habit of spinning like tops. Once lost, there was a tendency to panic. One or two sharp turns to try to pick up a landmark, and you lost all sense of direction. North, south, east, or west might be anywhere. The sharp turns set the compass spinning. Within a minute you grew quite bewildered. There was only one thing to do: keep your head, choose a distant landmark and fly on it, give your compass time to settle, and then try to pick up unmistakable landmarks—lakes, towns, or important railway junctions—and fit them to your map. It was easier high up than low down; but, whatever the height, the pilot had to have a sense of scale. Ten miles on the map looked very different in reality at a thousand or ten thousand feet, so you had to take your height into consideration when locating your position. It needed experience, and it was the lack of this experience that led pilots to do apparently imbecile things like flying machines across the lines and landing them in Germany. The final resort, of course, was to land and ask where you were; but that was a terrible confession of incompetence, except in foul weather— besides, you might be told: Berlin!

But on this particular evening no such danger threatened the novice with his twenty hours of flying. There to the north was the coastline—unmistakable landmark—Boulogne, Calais, Dunkerque. Beneath were the straight French roads, with their avenues of poplars. Calais itself nestled under the right wing-tip, compact and cosy, one tall church spire and ten thousand chimneys, breathing a vague bluish vapour which hung pensive in the sky. Beyond the harbour was the Leave Boat, starting for England: two white furrows and a penn'orth of smoke. An escort of destroyers flanked her; and beyond the steel-grey sea, almost hidden in the evening haze, was the outline of the Dover cliffs, white beyond the water. The Dover cliffs! England! Home!

I turned south towards Boulogne, climbing, always climbing. Already I was two miles above the earth, a tiny lonely speck in the vast rotunda of the evening sky. The sun was sinking solemnly in a black Atlantic cloud-belt. To the east, night crept up: a lofty shade drawn steadily over the warring earth. The earth, so far below! A patchwork of fields, browns and greys, here and there dappled with the green of spring woods, intersecting ribbons of straight roads, minute houses, invisible men ... Men! Standing, walking, talking, fighting there beneath me! I saw them for the first time with detachment, dispassionately: a strange, pitiable, crawling race, to us who strode the sky. Why, God might take the air and come within a mile of earth and never know there were such things as men. Vain the heroic gesture, puny the great thought! Poor little maggoty men!

The upper rim of the circle of fire dipped finally behind the clouds, and a bunch of rays, held as it were in some invisible quiver, shot a beam high into the arc of heaven, where it turned a wraith of cirrus cloud to marvellous gold. The lofty shade had covered the visible earth, and beauty lingered only in the sky. It turned colder ... I remembered suddenly the warmth of the Mess fire and the faces of friends. It would be good to be down again. I turned towards home and throttled down. The engine roar died. The wind sang gently in the wires. A long steady glide carried me inland. Now that the engine was off and the warm air did not blow through the cockpit, I grew chilly and beat my hands on my thighs. It was cold at ten thousand in March. I opened up the engine again to feel its warmth. Slowly the aerodrome rose up through the gauzy swathes of mist spun by the invisible hands of twilight. Above, the cirrus turned copper, faded to pink and mauve, and at last drifted grey and shroudlike in the vast arena of the darkening heaven. I must hurry. It would be night before I was down. Over the sheds at four thousand I went into a vertical bank and rushed earthwards in a tight spiral. At a thousand I pulled out, feeling a bit sick, burst my engine to make sure of the plugs, and then cautiously felt my way in over the hangars and touched with that gentle easy rumble which means a perfect landing, turned, and taxied in.

CECIL A. LEWIS,
Sagittarius Rising

2. Action

After ten hours of this came my first real job—to photograph the enemy second-line trenches. The lines, from the air, had none of the significance they had from the ground, mainly because all contours were non-existent. The local undulations, valleys, ravines, ditches, hillsides, which gave advantage to one side or the other, were flattened out. All you saw was two more or less parallel sets of trenches, clearer in some places than in others according to the colour of the earth thrown up in making them. These faced each other across the barren strip of No-Man's-Land, and behind them started a complicated network of communication trenches, second-line trenches, more communication trenches, and then the third-line trenches. The network was more complex at the important positions along the line; but everywhere it was irregular, following the lie of the ground, opening up to a wide mesh at one place, closing up, compact and formidable, at another. As positions were consolidated more trenches were dug, and later, when I came to know my own section of the line as well as the palm of my hand, I could tell at a glance what fresh digging had been done since my last patrol.

The surveying of the German line was difficult from the ground. You couldn't very well walk about with a theodolite and a chain in full view of the enemy, so the making of maps was largely a matter of aerial photography. In the spring of 1916, with the big offensive on the Somme preparing, the accuracy of these maps was of the greatest importance. So our job that day was to go over the front line at 7,500 feet and fly all along the enemy second-line trenches from Montauban, round the Fricourt salient and up to Boisselle, photographing as we went.

If there was ever an aeroplane unsuited for active service, it was the BE 2c. The pilot sat slightly aft of the main planes and had a fair view above and below, except where the lower main plane obscured the ground forward; but the observer, who sat in front of him, could see practically nothing, for he was wedged under the small centre section, with a plane above, another below, and bracing wires all round. He carried a gun for defence purposes;

but he could not fire it forward, because of the propeller. Backwards, the centre-section struts, wires, and the tail plane cramped his style. In all modern machines the positions are reversed; the pilot sits in front, leaving the observer a good field of fire aft and using his own guns, which can be fired through the propeller, forward. But in 1916 the synchronized gear enabling a machine gun to be fired through the whirling propeller and still miss the blades had not been perfected.

The observer could not operate the camera from his seat because of the plane directly below him, so it was clamped on outside the fuselage, beside the pilot; a big, square, shiny mahogany box with a handle on top to change the plates (yes, plates!). To make an exposure you pulled a ring on the end of a cord. To sight it, you leaned over the side and looked through a ball and crosswire finder. The pilot, then, had to fly the machine with his left hand, get over the spot on the ground he wanted to photograph—not so easy as you might think—put his arm out into the seventy-mile-an-hour wind, and push the camera handle back and forward to change the plates, pulling the string between each operation. Photography in 1916 was somewhat amateurish.

So I set out on that sunny afternoon, with a sergeant-gunner in the front seat, and climbed up towards the lines. As I approached them, I made out the place where we were to start on the ground, comparing it with the map. Two miles the other side of the front line didn't look far on paper; but it seemed a devil of a way when you had to fly vertically over the spot. The sergeant knelt on his seat, placed a drum on the Lewis gun, and faced round over the tail, keeping a wary eye open for Fokkers. But the sky was deserted, the line quiet. Jerry was having a day off. I turned the machine round to start on my steady course above the trenches, when two little puffs of grey smoke appeared a hundred feet below us, on the left. The sergeant pointed and smiled: "Archie!" Then three others appeared closer, at our own height. It was funny the way the balls of smoke appeared magically in the empty air, and were followed a moment later by a little flat report. If they didn't range us any better than that they were not very formidable, I thought, and began to operate the camera handle.

There are times in life when the faculties seem to be keyed up to superhuman tension. You are not necessarily doing anything;

but you are in a state of awareness, of tremendous alertness, ready
to act instantaneously should the need arise. Outwardly, that day,
I was calm, busy keeping the trenches in the camera sight,
manipulating the handle, pulling the string; but inside my heart
was pounding and my nerves straining, waiting for something, I
did not know what, to happen. It was my first job. I was under
fire for the first time. Would Archie get the range? Would the
dreaded Fokker appear? Would the engine give out? It was the
fear of the unforeseen, the inescapable, the imminent hand of
death which might, from moment to moment, be ruthlessly laid
upon me. I realized, not then, but later, why pilots cracked up,
why they lost their nerve and had to go home. Nobody could stand
the strain indefinitely, ultimately it reduced you to a dithering
state, near to imbecility. For always you had to fight it down, you
had to go out and do the job, you could never admit it, never say
frankly, "I am afraid. I can't face it any more." For cowardice,
because, I suppose, it is the most common human emotion, is the
most despised. And you did gain victories over yourself. You won
and won and won again, and always there was another to be won
on the morrow. They sent you home to rest, and you put it in the
background of your mind; but it was not like a bodily fatigue from
which you could completely recover, it was a sort of damage to
the essential tissue of your being. You might have a greater
will-power, greater stamina to fight down your failing; but a
thoroughbred that has been lashed will rear at the sight of the
whip, and never, once you had been through it, could you be quite
the same again.

I went on pulling the string and changing the plates when, out
of the corner of my eye, I saw something black ahead of the
machine. I looked up quickly: there was nothing there. I blinked.
Surely, if my eyes were worth anything, there had been something
. . . Yes! There it was again! This time I focussed. It was a howitzer
shell, one of our own shells, slowing up as it reached the top of its
trajectory, turning slowly over and over, like an ambling porpoise,
and then plunging down to burst. Guns fire shells in a flat
trajectory; howitzers fling them high, like a lobbed tennis ball. It
follows that, if you happen to be at the right height, you catch the
shell just as it hovers at its peak point. If you are quick-sighted
you can then follow its course down to the ground. I watched the

thing fascinated. Damn it, they weren't missing the machine by much, I thought; but I was left little time to consider it, for suddenly there was a sharp tearing sound like a close crack of thunder, and the machine was flung upwards by the force of the explosion of an Archie burst right underneath us. A split second later, and it would have been a direct hit. A long tear appeared in the fabric of the plane where a piece of shrapnel had gone through. There was a momentary smell of acrid smoke. "Ess! Ess!" shouted the sergeant. "They've ranged us!" I flung the machine over and flew west, then turned again, and again, and again . . . The Archie bursts were distant now. We had thrown them off.

"How many more?" shouted the sergeant, with a jerk of his head to the camera box.

"Two."

Flying on a steady course is the surest way to get caught by Archie, and we had been, right enough. If we were quick we might snatch the other two photos and get away before he ranged us again. I turned back over the spot, pulled the string and flew on to make the last exposure, when the sergeant suddenly stiffened in his seat, cocked his gun, and pointed: "Fokker!"

I turned in my seat and saw the thin line of the aeroplane coming down on our tail. He had seen the Archie bursts, no doubt, had a look round to see if we were escorted, and, finding it all clear, was coming down for a sitter.

I got the last photo as he opened fire. The distant chatter of his gun was hardly audible above the engine roar. It didn't seem to be directed at us. He was, I know now, an inexperienced pilot, he should have held his fire. We replied with a chatter that deafened me, the muzzle of the Lewis gun right above my head. The Fokker hesitated, pulled over for a moment, and then turned at us again. The sergeant pulled his trigger. Nothing happened. "Jammed! Jammed!" he shouted. He pulled frantically at the gun, while the stuttering Fokker came up. I put the old 2c right over to turn under him. As I did so, there was a sharp crack, and the little wind-screen a foot in front of my face showed a hole with a spider's web in the glass round it.

It was a Triplex: no splinters; but another foot behind would have put that bullet through my head—which was not Triplex. A narrow shave. Instinctively I stood the machine on its head and

dived for home. At that moment, as if to cap it all, the engine set
up a fearful racket. The whole machine felt as if it would fall to
pieces.

"Switch off! Switch off!" yelled the sergeant. "The engine's
hit."

I obeyed, still diving, turning sharply as I did so to offer a
more difficult target to the Fokker. But, luckily for us, he decided
not to pursue. In those days the Huns did not adventure much
beyond their own side of the lines, and now we were back over
ours.

We saw him zoom away again. He had us at his mercy, had
he known. There was a moment of wonderful relief. We laughed.
It had all happened in much less time than it takes to tell, and
we were still alive, safe!

*   *   *

The zero hour of the Somme offensive drew nearer. The troops,
sent down for a long rest before it, had learnt with us the new
co-operative methods of contact patrol, and had now returned to
the lines, ready for the attack. The guns were all in position, and
most of the squadron spent all their time ranging them. I happened
to be the exception, for I was put on to photography.

The whole section of our front, from Thiepval, down past
Boisselle, round the Fricourt salient, and on to Montauban, was
to be photographed every day, in order that Headquarters might
have accurate information of the effects of the bombardment. This
aimed at destroying all the enemy first- and second-line trenches,
and so making the attack easy for the infantry.

In this it was only partially successful, for the Germans had
constructed concrete redoubts and defences that remained to a
large extent intact, even after the terrific bombardment. Fricourt,
which stood on a sharp rise, was in reality an impregnable concrete
fort, bristling with machine guns. It was only evacuated when the
advance, more successful on either side of it, pinched it off, and
forced those in Fricourt itself to retire.

At leisure we had photographed the line before the bombardment started. But during this last week the weather was poor. On
two days, low clouds and rain prevented us getting any photos at

'Closing Up' by George Horace Davis. A dog-fight over the
Western front.

all. The 3rd and 15th Corps, for whom we were working, got in a
panic. It was essential to know the effect of the shelling. Photos
were to be got at all costs.

We went out in the afternoon. The clouds forced us down to
two thousand feet. A terrific bombardment was in progress. The
enemy lines, as far as we could see, were under a white drifting
cloud of bursting high explosive. The shell-bursts were continuous,
not only on the lines themselves, but on the support trenches and
communications behind.

At two thousand feet we were in the path of the gun trajectories,
and as the shells passed, above or below us, the wind eddies made
by their motion flung the machine up and down, as if in a gale.
Each bump meant that a passing shell had missed the machine
by four or five feet. The gunners had orders not to fire when a
machine was passing their sights, but in the fury of the bombardment much was forgotten—or perhaps the fact that we were not

hit proves the orders were carried out. If so, they ran it pretty fine.

Grimly I kept the machine on its course above the trenches, waiting, tense and numb, for a shell to get us, while Sergeant Hall (who got a D.C.M. and a commission for his work that week) worked the old camera handle, changed the plates, sighted, made his exposures. I envied him having something to do. I could only hold the machine as steady as possible and pray for it to be over. At last, after an hour, I felt a tap on my shoulder. Gratefully I turned for home.

Just above us the heavy cloud-banks looked like the bellies of a school of whales huddled together in the dusk. Beyond, a faintly luminous strip of yellow marked the sunset. Below, the gloomy earth glittered under the continual scintillation of gun fire. Right round the salient down to the Somme, where the mists backed up the ghostly effect, was this sequined veil of greenish flashes, quivering. Thousands of guns were spitting high explosive, and the invisible projectiles were screaming past us on every side. Though they were our own guns, their muzzles were towards us, and suddenly I knew it was at us they were firing. The malevolent fury of the whole bombardment was concentrated on us! Of course it was ridiculous; but for about a minute I was in the grip of nightmare terror. The machine lurched and rolled. It was us they were after! It was us!

In another minute we were through the danger zone; but the vivid memory haunted me back to the aerodrome. Even there we could hear the thud and rumble of the guns, even back in England they were hearing it. For seven nights and days it went on. After dark, we used to come out and watch. Continual summer lightning, flickering and dancing in the eastern sky. Voluminous and austere bursts of thunder rolling by on the night wind. The others used to laugh: "The old Hun's fairly going through it." But I could not forget its blind fury, and pitied the men who for a week lived under that rain. I suppose I was many times nearer death than on that particular evening; but for me it remains, none the less, the most fearful moment of the war.

CECIL A. LEWIS,
Sagittarius Rising

Lieutenant Cecil Lewis of the Royal Flying Corps.

Miss Caroline Ball, of the publishing firm of Peter Davies Ltd., sent Mr. Lewis, who now lives in Cyprus, a request from my researcher Annabel Craig for the above photograph. This was his reply:

'Why do innocent young things like you—or Miss Annabel Craig—who can't even bother to spell SAGITTARIUS properly—imagine that old men should bother to produce photographs for other people's books, just because they happen to want a quote from my book because they are short of words of their own.

I send you, out of the generosity of my heart, a photo taken of me, at the age of 19, just before taking off in the SE5 to lead 56 Sqdn to France, and you had better get Ludovic Kennedy, whoever he is, to write and say thank you.

Faithfully
Cecil Lewis.'

AN IRISH AIRMAN FORESEES HIS DEATH

I know that I shall meet my fate
Somewhere among the clouds above;
Those that I fight I do not hate,
Those that I guard I do not love;
My country is Kiltartan Cross,
My countrymen Kiltartan's poor,
No likely end could bring them loss
Or leave them happier than before.
Nor law, nor duty bade me fight,
Nor public men, nor cheering crowds,
A lonely impulse of delight
Drove to this tumult in the clouds;
I balanced all, brought all to mind,
The years to come seemed waste of breath,
A waste of breath the years behind
In balance with this life, this death.

W. B. YEATS,
Collected Poems

3. The Red Baron

The outstanding German fighter pilot of the First World War
was the legendary Manfred, Baron von Richthofen, nicknamed
the Red Baron after the colour of his aeroplane. Between September 1916 and April 1918, when he was killed in action, he
was credited with having shot down eighty enemy planes. He
was buried by the British will full military honours, a detachment
from the Australian Flying Corps firing a volley over his grave.

We were at the butts trying our machine-guns. On the previous
day we. had received our new aeroplanes, and the next morning
Boelcke was to fly with us. We all were beginners. None of us had
had a success so far. Consequently everything that Boelcke told
us was to us gospel truth. During the last few days he had, as he

The Richthofen brothers, Lothar left and Manfred right,
both wearing Imperial Germany's highest decoration for
gallantry, the Pour le Mérite.

said, shot for breakfast every day one or two Englishmen.

The next morning, the 17th of September, was a gloriously fine day. It was therefore only to be expected that the English would be very active. Before we started Boelcke repeated to us his instructions, and for the first time we flew as a squadron commanded by the great man whom we followed blindly.

We had just arrived at the Front when we recognised a hostile flying squadron that was proceeding in the direction of Cambrai. Boelcke was of course the first to see it, for he saw a great deal more than ordinary mortals. Soon we understood the position, and everyone of us strove to follow Boelcke closely. It was clear to all of us that we should pass our first examination under the eyes of our beloved leader.

We approached slowly the hostile squadron. It could not escape us. We had intercepted it, for we were between the Front and the opponents. If they wished to go back they had to pass us. We counted the hostile machines. They were seven in number. We were only five. All the Englishmen flew large bomb-carrying two-seaters. In a few seconds the dance would begin.

Boelcke had come very near the first English machine, but he did not yet shoot. I followed. Close to me were my comrades. The Englishman nearest to me was travelling in a large machine painted in dark colours. I did not reflect very long, but took my aim and shot. He also fired and so did I, and both of us missed our aim. A struggle began, and the great point for me was to get to the rear of the fellow because I could only shoot forward with my gun. He was differently placed, for his machine-gun was moveable. It could fire in all directions.

Apparently he was no beginner, for he knew exactly that his last hour had arrived at the moment if I got at the back of him. At that time I had not yet the conviction "He must fall" which I have now on such occasions, but, on the contrary, I was curious to see whether he would fall. There is a great difference between the two feelings. When one has shot down one's first, second or third opponent, then one begins to find out how the trick is done.

My Englishman twisted and turned, flying in zig-zags. I did not think for a moment that the hostile squadron contained other Englishmen who conceivably might come to the aid of their comrades. I was animated by a single thought: "The man in front

Germany's leading fighter pilot of the first world war, the
legendary Baron Manfred von Richthofen. Before his death
in action in 1918, he was credited with the destruction of
eighty Allied planes.

of me must come down, whatever happens." At last a favourable
moment arrived. My opponent had apparently lost sight of me.
Instead of twisting and turning he flew straight along. In a fraction
of a second I was at his back with my excellent machine. I gave
a short burst of shots with my machine-gun. I had gone so close
that I was afraid I might dash into the Englishman. Suddenly I
nearly yelled with joy, for the propeller of the enemy machine had
stopped turning. Hurrah! I had shot his engine to pieces; the
enemy was compelled to land, for it was impossible for him to
reach his own lines. The English machine was swinging curiously
to and fro. Probably something had happened to the pilot. The

observer was no longer visible. His machine-gun was apparently deserted. Obviously I had hit the observer, and he had fallen from his seat.

The Englishman landed close to the flying ground of one of our squadrons. I was so excited that I landed also, and my eagerness was so great that I nearly smashed up my machine. The English flying machine and my own stood close together. I rushed to the English machine and saw that a lot of soldiers were running towards my enemy. When I arrived I discovered that my assumption had been correct. I had shot the engine to pieces, and both the pilot and observer were severely wounded. The observer died at once, and the pilot while being transported to the nearest dressing station. I honoured the fallen enemy by placing a stone on his beautiful grave.

MANFRED VON RICHTHOFEN,
The Red Air Fighter

Flight to Arras

Antoine de St.-Exupéry, the French aviator, was a writer of great power and imagination. His most famous book, *Wind, Sun and Stars*, describes his early life as a commercial airline pilot in South America. But, like his hero Conrad, he is sometimes obscure, and I have chosen this simpler excerpt from his last book, *Flight to Arras*. Later in the war de St.-Exupéry disappeared on a flight over the Mediterranean.

"Captain!"
"Yes?"
"Six German fighters on the port bow."
The words rang in my ears like a thunderclap.
You must first . . . You must first . . . Ah! I do want very much to be paid off in time. I do want to have the right to love. I do want to win a glimpse of the being for whom I die.
"Gunner!"
"Sir?"
"D'you hear the lieutenant? Six German fighters. Six, on the port bow."

"I heard the lieutenant, sir."

"Dutertre! Have they seen us?"

"They have, Captain. Banking towards us. Fifteen hundred feet below us."

"Hear that, gunner? Fifteen hundred feet below us. Dutertre! How near are they?"

"Say ten seconds."

"Hear that, gunner? On our tail in a few seconds."

There they are. I see them. Tiny. A swarm of poisonous wasps.

"Gunner! They're crossing broadside. You'll see them in a second. There!"

"Don't see them yet, sir . . . Yes, I do!"

I no longer see them myself.

"They after us?"

"After us, sir."

"Rising fast?"

"Can't say, sir. Don't think so . . . No, sir."

Dutertre spoke. "What do you say, Captain?"

"What do you expect me to say?"

Nobody said anything. There was nothing to say. We were in God's hands. If I banked, I should narrow the space between us. Luckily, we were flying straight into the sun. At high altitude you cannot go up fifteen hundred feet higher without giving a couple of miles to your game. It was possible therefore that they might lose us entirely in the sun by the time they had reached our altitude and recovered their speed.

"Still after us, gunner?"

"Still after us, sir."

"We gaining on them?"

"Well, sir. No . . . Perhaps."

It was God's business—and the sun's.

Fighters do not fight, they murder. Still, it might turn into a fight, and I made ready for it. I pressed with both feet as hard as I could, trying to free the frozen rudder. A wave of something strange went over me. But my eyes were still on the Germans, and I bore with all my weight down upon the rigid bar.

Once again I discovered that I was in fact much less upset in this moment of action—if "action" was the word for this vain expectancy—than I had been while dressing. A kind of anger was going through me. A beneficent anger. God knows, no ecstasy of sacrifice. Rather an urge to bite hard into something.

"Gunner! Are we losing them?"

"We are losing them, sir."

Good job.

"Dutertre! Dutertre!"

"Captain?"

"I . . . nothing."

"Anything the matter?"

"Nothing. I thought . . . Nothing."

I decided not to mention it. No good worrying them. If I went into a dive they would know it soon enough. They would know that I had gone into a dive.

It was not natural that I should be running with sweat in a temperature sixty degrees below zero. Not natural. I knew perfectly well what was happening. Gently, very gently, I was fainting.

I could see the instrument panel. Now I couldn't. My hands were losing their grip on the wheel. I hadn't even the strength to speak. I was letting myself go. So pleasant, letting oneself go . . .

Then I squeezed the rubber rube. A gust of air blew into my nose and brought me life. The oxygen supply was not out of order! Then it must be . . . Of course! How stupid I had been! It was the rudder. I had exerted myself like a man trying to pick up a grand piano. Flying thirty-three thousand feet in the air, I had struggled like a professional wrestler. The oxygen was being doled out to me. It was my business to use it up economically. I was paying for my orgy.

I began to inhale in swift repeated gasps. My heart beat faster and faster. It was like a faint tinkle. What good would it do to speak of it? If I went into a dive, they would know soon enough. Now I could see my instrument panel. . . . No, that wasn't true. I couldn't see it. Sitting there in my sweat, I was sad.

Life came back as gently as it had flowed out of me.

"Dutertre!"

"Captain?"

I should have liked to tell him what had happened.

"I . . . I thought . . . No."

I gave it up. Words consume oxygen too fast. Already I was

out of breath. I was very weak. A convalescent.
      "You were about to say something, Captain?"
      "No . . . nothing."
      "Quite sure, Captain? You puzzle me."
      I puzzle him. But I am alive.
      "We are alive."
      "Well, yes. For the time being."
      For the time being. There was still Arras.

ANTOINE DE ST.-EXUPÉRY,
Flight to Arras
(trans. Lewis Galantiere)

'First Air Post' by Terence Cuneo. The first successful scheduled airmail service
was started by the Royal Engineers Postal Services on 1 March 1919, taking mail
to the British occupation forces in the Rhineland in converted bombers.

Death in the morning (1)

Richard Hillary was a young, handsome British fighter pilot
whose book *The Last Enemy* became a minor classic of the last
war. In it he describes how, after being shot down with terrible
burns, he was taken to Sir Archibald Macindoe's plastic-surgery
hospital at East Grinstead, and in the course of many painful
operations had grafted on to him a new face. He survived to fly
again, but later in the war disappeared on a night flight in
Scotland.

The voice of the controller came unhurried over the loud-speaker,
telling us to take off, and in a few seconds we were running for our
machines. I climbed into the cockpit of my plane and felt an
empty sensation of suspense in the pit of my stomach. For one
second time seemed to stand still and I stared blankly in front of
me. I knew that that morning I was to kill for the first time. That
I might be killed or in any way injured did not occur to me. Later,
when we were losing pilots regularly, I did consider it in an
abstract way when on the ground; but once in the air, never. I
knew it could not happen to me. I suppose every pilot knows that,
knows it cannot happen to him; even when he is taking off for the
last time, when he will not return, he knows that he cannot be
killed. I wondered idly what he was like, this man I would kill.
Was he young, was he fat, would he die with the Fuehrer's name
on his lips, or would he die alone, in that last moment conscious
of himself as a man? I would never know. Then I was being
strapped in, my mind automatically checking the controls, and
we were off.

We ran into them at 18,000 feet, twenty yellow-nosed Messerschmitt 109's, about 500 feet above us. Our Squadron strength
was eight, and as they came down on us we went into line astern
and turned head on to them. Brian Carbury, who was leading the
Section, dropped the nose of his machine, and I could almost feel
the leading Nazi pilot push forward on his stick to bring his guns
to bear. At the same moment Brian hauled hard back on his own
control stick and led us over them in a steep climbing turn to the
left. In two vital seconds they lost their advantage. I saw Brian

Richard Hillary. By E. H. Kennington.

let go a burst of fire at the leading plane, saw the pilot put his machine into a half roll, and knew that he was mine. Automatically, I kicked the rudder to the left to get him at right angles, turned the gun-button to "Fire", and let go in a four-second burst with full deflection. He came right through my sights and I saw the tracer from all eight guns thud home. For a second he seemed to hang motionless; then a jet of red flame shot upwards and he spun out of sight.

For the next few minutes I was too busy looking after myself to think of anything, but when, after a short while, they turned and made off over the Channel, and we were ordered to our base, my mind began to work again.

It had happened.

My first emotion was one of satisfaction, satisfaction at a job adequately done, at the final logical conclusion of months of specialized training. And then I had a feeling of the essential rightness of all. He was dead and I was alive; it could so easily have been the other way round; and that would somehow have been right too. I realized in that moment just how lucky a fighter pilot is. He has none of the personalized emotions of the soldier, handed a rifle and bayonet and told to charge. He does not even have to share the dangerous emotions of the bomber pilot who night after night must experience that childhood longing for smashing things. The fighter pilot's emotions are those of the duellist—cool, precise, impersonal. He is privileged to kill well. For if one must either kill or be killed, as now one must, it should, I feel, be done with dignity. Death should be given the setting it deserves; it should never be a pettiness; and for the fighter pilot it never can be.

RICHARD HILLARY,
The Last Enemy

'Take-off' by Dame Laura Knight. A Stirling Mk. iii
bomber about to set off on a raid over Germany.

LOSSES

It was not dying: everybody died.
It was not dying: we had died before
In the routine crashes—and our fields
Called up the papers, wrote home to our folks,
And the rates rose, all because of us.
We died on the wrong page of the almanac,
Scattered on mountains fifty miles away;
Diving on haystacks, fighting with a friend,
We blazed up on the lines we never saw.
We died like aunts or pets or foreigners.
(When we left high school nothing else had died
For us to figure we had died like.)

In our new planes, with our new crews, we bombed
The ranges by the desert or the shore,
Fired at towed targets, waited for our scores—
And turned into replacements and woke up
One morning, over England, operational.
It wasn't different: but if we died
It was not an accident but a mistake
(But an easy one for anyone to make).
We read our mail and counted up our missions—
In bombers named for girls, we burned
The cities we had learned about in school—
Till our lives wore out; our bodies lay among
The people we had killed and never seen.
When we lasted long enough they gave us medals;
When we died they said, "Our casualties were low."

They said, "Here are the maps;" we burned the cities.

It was not dying—no, not ever dying;
But the night I died I dreamed that I was dead,
And the cities said to me: "Why are you dying?
We are satisfied, if you are; but why did I die?"

RANDALL JARRELL,
The Complete Poems

Death in the morning (2)

Group Captain Peter Townsend is best known for his ill-fated
courtship of Princess Margaret, when he was serving as an
equerry to her father, King George VI. During the war he was
an outstanding fighter pilot, winning the D.S.O. and D.F.C., and
being credited with 11 enemy kills.

The crew of the Heinkel I spotted that morning never saw us until
the bullets began tearing into their bomber. Only then did red
tracer come spurting from their rear guns, but, in the first foolish
rapture of combat, I believed myself, like Achilles, invulnerable.
The Heinkel scraped over the cliffs at Whitby and crash-landed
in the snow behind the town—the first German bomber down on
English soil since World War I.

I felt elated as I watched the enemy bomber crash. Then the
full implication struck me. Someone heard me murmur, as I
climbed out of the cockpit, "Poor devils, I don't think they're all
dead." Two of them were. Remorse, rather than curiosity, impelled
me to visit the survivors in hospital. One of them, Karl Missy, the
rear gunner, had tried to kill me; he was prevented when the
bullets from my guns sawed through his leg and felled him. Despite
the harm I had done him, he clasped my hand, but, in his steady
brown eyes, was the reproachful look of a wounded animal.

Victory in the air called for champagne in the mess—a horribly
uncivilised way of behaving, really, when you have just killed
someone. But an enemy bomber down was proof of our prowess,
and that was a legitimate pretext for celebration. For the enemy
crew, whom we had shot to pieces, we gave no thought. Young,
like us, they had existed, but existed no longer. Deep down we
knew, but dared not admit, that we had little hope of existing
much longer ourselves. So, meanwhile, we made merry.

A few days later, I killed four more men. "Did you really have
to kill them?" asked my 12 year-old Pierre when, many years
later, I told him of that morning. I never had the slightest wish
to kill anybody, least of all young people like myself, with the
same passion for flying. It was not them but their bomber, invading
our sky, that filled my sights after I had stalked it, with all my

cunning, four miles up in a deserted sky. There I did it to death in cold blood. Only later did I picture the crew, with one more mission accomplished, chatting on the intercom, perhaps munching a sandwich or drinking *ersatz* coffee, as they headed for home and safety, where their comrades and their loved ones waited. How could I escape a feeling of remorse when it was I who put an end to all that, I who struck them down? I, the shy one, ever unsure of myself, afraid of death and darkness, who shunned a fight, of whom it had always been said, "Needs encouragement". Now I needed none. A terrible change had come over me.

The squadron moved north, to Wick, to defend the naval base of Scapa Flow. There, at the extreme tip of Scotland, we stood guard throughout the long northern days and, during the bitter cold of the night, slept briefly, fitfully, under rough blankets and newspapers. Not that the hard lying was a bad thing—it made it easier to go out, face the weather and the enemy and, if need be, die.

Outside the crude comfort of our wooden huts, the storm raged, dragging our aircraft from their pickets, burying them in snow, lashing the sea, more menacing than ever, and sending it battering against the coast or racing, churned into whirlpools, through the Pentland Firth. One morning, Tiger Folkes, patrolling with me, low above the tumultuous waters, disappeared.

The Luftwaffe men faced the double hazard of our fighters and the sea. We sat, strapped into our cockpits, waiting to sally forth against them. With the approach of the enemy, the radio jamming grew louder and louder, and the tension became so unbearable that it sometimes drove us from our cockpits to vomit. When at last the code word SCRAMBLE unleashed us, we surged forward, throttle wide open, tails up like baying hounds. Only a kill could satisfy our lust for the chase. But the scent, thanks to imperfect radar coverage, was sometimes false.

One night, after searching vainly, high among the A.A. bursts over Scapa, and low, where bombs and unspent shells were plopping into the Pentland Firth, the controller called me in to land. I switched off my radio and continued to search. Then, high up in the glow of the departed day, a speck materialised. With my radio still mute, I began to stalk, silently, stealthily, my eyes glued on

Group Captain Peter Townsend DSO, DFC.

the speck in the sky. But when I closed in on my prey, he resisted desperately.

In aerial combat, you usually only hear the enemy's fire if you stop a close one. But there in the darkness, far out to sea, Heinkel and Hurricane were fighting a terrible gun battle at point blank range, so that when I came in for the *coup de grâce* I could actually hear the Heinkel's guns, in their last dying fury, firing just above my head. I was now seized with an irresistible desire to destroy. Down went the bomber into the sea, and with it four more dead men. I all but died with them, as I realised when, next morning, I examined my Hurricane. It was riddled with bullets.

That fight made me think. The killing game was increasing in pace, and this time I had barely escaped death. It was a sobering thought. But a more awful one was that I myself had become an implacable agent of death. Next day, when a small horde of us pounced on another Heinkel, I did not bother to fire—the machine was already foundering. I flew in close beside it. The young pilot and his companions regarded me helplessly as their flying tumbril bore them on, down to the sea. I would have given anything to save them; instead, I found myself escorting them to their grave. A few minutes later they were swallowed up by the sea.

PETER TOWNSEND,
Time and Chance

Hess flies in

On 10th May 1941, Rudolf Hess, Germany's Deputy Fuehrer and Hitler's right-hand man, made his celebrated flight to Britain—the beginning of more than forty years of continuous imprisonment. He describes the flight in a letter to his wife, Ilse.

To Frau Ilse Hess

The North Sea was illuminated by an evening light of unearthly loveliness, such as is found in the far north. It was utterly lonely. But how magnificent! A multitude of small clouds far below me looked like pieces of ice floating on the sea, clear as crystal; the whole scene was tinged with red. Then the sky was swept clean—alas, much too clean! There was not a trace of the "dense carpet of clouds at about five hundred metres", predicted in the weather report, and where I had thought to take shelter in case of need. For a moment I even thought of turning back. But a night landing with *this* machine, I reflected—that will never do. Even if I saved myself, the Messerschmitt would suffer serious damage, possibly beyond repair. Then, indeed, the cat would be out of the bag; nothing could be kept secret. The whole business would be reported in the highest quarters and then all would be over—for ever.

So I told myself to "Stick it out, no matter what happens!"

Then I had a stroke of luck. A veil of mist hung over England. Its surface shone so much in the evening light that nothing down there could be seen from above. I took shelter, of course, at once, flying with the throttle full out and coming slap down from a height of two thousand metres towards the coast at a truly terrific speed. The action of that moment saved me then. There was a Spitfire in pursuit which I outdistanced before I was aware of its presence. I could not look behind; I was too enclosed in my cabin and too dazzled by the reflections. Had I not been tempted to dive for cover, but remained in the clear air at the pace I had been going he could easily have shot me down.

As it was, I crossed the East Coast a little below Holy Island at about ten o'clock and after sunset, flying low over a little town whose inhabitants must have been terrified, so low did I roar past, barely higher than the houses, at some 750 km. per hour with my two thousand h.p. engines at full throttle and the exhaust echoing through the sleepy streets. At this level the visibility was surprisingly good. I could see several miles, but must have been invisible to my pursuer. I took good care not to rise too high, but flew on at not more than sixteen feet from the ground—even less at times—skimming over trees, men, beasts and houses; what English airmen call "hedge-hopping". It seems to have impressed them a good deal, according to the Duke of Hamilton and judging by the honour done me in a critique in an English flying journal!

I enjoyed every minute of it! At home, this sort of flying was forbidden, although I did occasionally do a bit of it—but not so drastically as on this flight over enemy territory.

"Father" Bauer[1] always said that what I really liked was to fly through barn doors, and it was in this spirit I aimed at the Cheviot, now looming out of the misty evening. This was my guiding point, as previously determined, and keeping within a few yards of the ground I literally climbed up the slope. Never before had I ascended a mountain so rapidly. With a slight alteration of course to the right, I slid down on the other side. On I went over level ground, skimming merrily over house tops and trees, and waving greetings to men working in the fields. The variometer told me I was ascending, until suddenly I was over my next point of orientation—a little dam in a narrow range of hills with Broad Dav the highest summit. Here my course bent to the left.

I had no need to bother with a map; all the details of the course, compass points, distances, etc. were already stored in my memory. After my flight from Harlaching, they may have found a sketch which I had for pinning on my bedroom wall where I could study it during the many sleepless nights, by the light of the reading lamp—the disappearance of which was, quite rightly, debited to my account by my dear wife. In the end I could have flown the whole route while asleep.

In case these sketches should, by some mistake, have been seen

[1]Hans Bauer, Hitler's chief pilot.

prematurely by my much too intelligent wife, who might become altogether too curious about the mysterious X and Y which then played a part in our lives, I had taken the precaution of simply writing *Ostsee* in place of *Nordsee*. That her womanly gift of putting two and two together during the long months of my silent preparations had inclined her to think that I intended to fly on the *southern* course—towards old Marshal Pétain, as she later wrote me in Nuremberg—was a thing I could not then guess. For so many years she had been educated almost to my own level of taciturnity!

At about ten forty p.m. I found myself over Dungavel, the country seat of the Duke of Hamilton, my quite unconscious future host, or so I hoped. Yet, to avoid all possibility of error, I flew on to the coast, a matter of a few minutes. The smooth sea lay beneath me, as calm as a mirror, lit by the rising moon. Just off the mainland, a towering rock, five hundred metres high, rose out of the water, magnificently illuminated, a pale reddish colour. All looked so peaceful and beautiful. What a contrast to the hazardous and exciting experience then just about to come —immediately before my *first* parachute jump! Never shall I forget this picture.

I flew a few kilometres along the coast until I reached a small place on a spit of land with what might have been a mole, as on my map. Satisfied that I was on the spot, I turned east again and was able to pick out the railway and a small lake which was shown on the map with a road by it and south of the residence at Dungavel. I made a curve, ready to land by parachute after rising to a safe height of some 2,000 metres. Then I switched off the engines, turned the propeller indicator to null to check rotation regardless of the following wind, so that I could drop without being churned into mincemeat—such a superfluous precaution! For I found out afterwards that it would be easier to squeeze through a solid wall than to press forward against that prodigious air pressure. The first engine did not dream of stopping but, being ignited by the red-hot cylinders, went on spinning and humming merrily and took no notice of the fact that the ignition was off and that its conduct was against the rules!

However, the motor did come to its senses finally, senses which nevertheless soon sealed its fate.

Now I fastened everything up and opened the cabin roof, with the notion of climbing out—not without some scepticism and with much curiosity but all the same in excellent spirits. It was out of the question! The air pressure was something that cannot be imagined, even when the machine was going so slowly; and it pressed me up against the back partition as if I were screwed to it. In spite of all the care I had taken to find out about *everything* from my good friends at Messerschmitts, there was just *one* thing I had overlooked. I had never asked about how to jump; I thought it was too simple!

When I think back to that time, I find it astonishing that I never once thought of using the landing gear to slow down the machine. With no motors running, I had sunk lower and lower. Then I suddenly remembered that Greim[2] had once mentioned that one had to turn the machine over on its back and allow oneself to fall out! I then began to turn the machine over but, although I had done all sorts of acrobatics in the air, this was the one thing I had never done with this 'plane. And yet even that was lucky, because I instinctively pulled the joystick as if for a semi-loop instead of setting it for horizontal flight. Coming right over, the centrifugal force held me inside. But, with my head hanging down, had I slid out even a very little, the pressure of air would have broken my neck and spine. But the centrifugal force is immense with such a machine; it made the blood drain from my head and I began to "see stars". I was just able to think, "I am only just above the ground and flying straight down. Soon the crash must come! Is this the end?"

Then everything went black and I passed out. There I sat hurling earthwards, upside down, with no power of control. A desperate, indeed, hopeless situation! The next moment I had recovered consciousness, with full clarity of mind, and found myself staring at the speed gauge: the pointer stood at zero. I flung myself away and at the same moment the machine dropped like a stone.

I pulled at the parachute; the strands held me up, and I hovered in the air; an indescribably glorious and victorious experience all things considered. While unconscious, I had done what

[2] General Ritter von Greim.

I *should* have done, had I been conscious. I had brought the plane out of its semi-looping curve to finish almost perpendicular on its tail. The power of the swing spent, the machine stood motionless, immediately before plunging. Momentarily it had thrown me into a position for the blood to flow back into my head.

A second later would have meant death—Kismet!

So there I was, swaying about in the air, the mist barely illuminated by a full moon which sent no more than a thin reddish light through the night. The sudden checking of speed when I reached the ground was sufficient, after my previous experience, to send the blood again from my brain into my legs, so that I stumbled forward and once more all was as black as night; in short, I had my second "black-out". This time I recovered consciousness very slowly. Had it happened this way when I was in the machine, it would have proved fatal. Everything around me was swimming; I finally awoke, my expression, I dare say, resembling that of Adam when, having been formed from earth, he saw the world for the first time. For at first I had not the remotest idea of what had happened to me or where I was. Only gradually did it become clear to me that I had reached my goal—or rather a new beginning. Alas, more of a *beginning* than I dreamed!

I came down not far from the door of a farmhouse standing alone, and out of the door came a man who asked me if I was British or German and, as I could not walk easily, helped me very nicely into the house and placed me by the fire with a cup of tea. In jumping, I had hurt my ankle, probably knocked it somehow against the parachute gear.

What happened next was much less encouraging; a civil official appeared at the head of a troop of soldiers—a man who had quite evidently, judging by the smell, been celebrating Saturday with good Scottish spirits, probably having taken an extra shot when he heard that a German parachutist had come down. At any rate he staggered about in a cloud of alcoholic vapour, marching me off and prodding me all the while in the back with a large revolver, his finger never leaving the trigger. As I listened to his incessant belching and stumbling, I felt there must have been the finger of God intervening between his shaking hand and the impending shot. A little later the leader of the military asked me to enter a house, but the alcoholic official protested energetically against this and prevented my entry, poking his revolver, this time, into my stomach. I certainly did not move a muscle at this delightful little game with Fate but urged the two to unite in deciding what to do. Finally we did enter the house, where a really nice little Tommy made all well once more by offering me a bottle of milk which he had no doubt brought for himself. After five hours flying and two "black-outs", I expect I looked as if I needed it—as indeed I *did*, for on top of the somewhat exciting adventures of the last few hours I now knew that I was under arrest. Little did I know for how long!

RUDOLF HESS,
Prisoner of Peace

Wavell flies out

In June 1941, the Commander-in-Chief Middle East, General Sir Archibald Wavell, was ordered by Winston Churchill to change posts with the Commander-in-Chief India, General Sir Claude Auchinleck. Bernard Fergusson, one of Wavell's A.D.C's flew out with him.

The party in the aircraft, which was flown by an excellent character called Burberry who was to drop supplies on me in Burma a year later, consisted of Wavell, myself, and Sandy Reid-Scott of the 11th Hussars, who had been in my house at Eton some years after me, and had lost an eye in one of the desert battles. There was also a rather lugubrious Group-Captain from Air Headquarters, India. Egypt fell away from beneath us as we took off and flew westward, towards and across the Suez Canal. I watched Wavell from my seat on the starboard side, as he looked down at Sinai with his good left eye from a port-side window. It isn't for me to reconstruct what he was thinking about; but surely he must have remembered the great days of Allenby, (on whose staff he had been), the battles of Gaza and Beersheba, and his own brief taste of victory against odds which might have overwhelmed him.

We landed at Lydda to re-fuel; and here again was a little

cluster of officers to say goodbye. Among them was the burly figure of Brigadier Joe Kingstone, formerly of The Queen's Bays, who, until he was very gently checked, made some insubordinate remarks about Wavell's supersession. We flew on, over the familiar cities of Jerusalem and Jericho and Amman, with Wavell still looking out of the window. He was showing no emotion, of any sort or kind, beyond a mild interest in the view.

When we got to the featureless country beyond Amman, he screwed himself round and said, across the aisle of the aircraft, "Have you got anything for me to read?"

I was reading it myself, but I offered him Flecker's *Hassan*. He screwed up his eye as he looked at the title; and then, without opening the book, turned to me and quoted in full the following lines from it—Ishak's song:

> Thy dawn, O Master of the world, thy dawn;
> The hour the lilies open on the lawn,
> The hour the grey wings pass beyond the mountains,
> The hour of silence when we hear the fountains,
> The hour that dreams are brighter and winds colder,
> The hour that young love wakes on a white shoulder,
> O Master of the world, the Persian Dawn.
>
> That hour, O Master, shall be bright for thee:
> Thy merchants chase the morning down the sea,
> The braves who fight thy war unsheathe the sabre,
> The slaves who work thy mines are lashed to labour,
> For thee the waggons of the world are drawn—
> The ebony of night, the red of dawn!

He read it all the way to Habbaniyah; and I never got it back.

BERNARD FERGUSSON,
Wavell, Portrait of a Soldier

Across the Atlantic

Prime Minister to Lord Privy Seal
12 Jan 42

As I shall soon be silent for a while, though I trust not for ever, pray cable to-night any outstanding points which require decision here before I leave.

On the 14th I took leave of the President. He seemed concerned about the dangers of the voyage. Our presence in Washington had been for many days public to the world, and the charts showed more than twenty U-boats on our homeward courses. We flew in beautiful weather from Norfolk to Bermuda, where the *Duke of York*, with escorting destroyers, awaited us inside the coral reefs. I travelled in an enormous Boeing flying-boat, which made a most favourable impression upon me. During the three hours' trip I made friends with the chief pilot, Captain Kelly Rogers, who seemed a man of high quality and experience. I took the controls for a bit, to feel this ponderous machine of thirty or more tons in the air. I got more and more attached to the flying-boat. Presently I asked the captain, "What about flying from Bermuda to England? Can she carry enough petrol?" Under his stolid exterior he became visibly excited. "Of course we can do it. The present weather forecast would give a forty miles an hour wind behind us. We could do it in twenty hours." I asked how far it was, and he said, "About three thousand five hundred miles." At this I became thoughtful.

However, when we landed I opened the matter to Portal and Pound. Formidable events were happening in Malaya; we ought all to be back at the earliest moment. The Chief of the Air Staff said at once that he thought the risk wholly unjustifiable, and he could not take the responsibility for it. The First Sea Lord supported his colleague. There was the *Duke of York*, with her destroyers, all ready for us, offering comfort and a certainty. I said, "What about the U-boats you have been pointing out to me?" The Admiral made a disdainful gesture about them, which showed his real opinion of such a menace to a properly escorted and fast

Winston Churchill at the controls of the Boeing 314 flying boat which he
describes in this letter

battleship. It occurred to me that both these officers thought my
plan was to fly myself and leave them to come back in the *Duke
of York*, so I said, "Of course there would be room for all of us."
They both visibly changed countenance at this. After a considerable pause Portal said that the matter might be looked into, and
that he would discuss it at length with the captain of the flying-
boat and go into weather prospects with the meteorological authorities. I left it at that.

Two hours later they both returned, and Portal said that he thought it might be done. The aircraft could certainly accomplish the task under reasonable conditions; the weather outlook was exceptionally favourable on account of the strong following wind. No doubt it was very important to get home quickly. Pound said he had formed a very high opinion of the aircraft skipper, who certainly had unrivalled experience. Of course there was a risk, but on the other hand there were the U-boats to consider. So we settled to go unless the weather deteriorated. The starting time was 2 p.m. the next day. It was thought necessary to reduce our baggage to a few boxes of vital papers. Dill was to remain behind in Washington as my personal military representative with the President. Our party would consist only of myself, the two Chiefs of Staff, and Max Beaverbrook, Charles Wilson, and Hollis. All the rest would go by the *Duke of York*.

That afternoon I addressed the Bermuda Assembly, which is the oldest Parliamentary institution in the Western Hemisphere. I pleaded with them to give their assent and all their aid to the establishment of the United States naval and air bases in the island, about which they were in some distress. The life of the whole Empire was at stake. The smooth working of our alliance with the United States made final victory certain, however long the journey might be. They did not demur. The Governor, Lord Knolleys, gave a banquet that night to the island notables and their fleeting guests. We were all in high spirits. Only Tommy, my Flag Commander, as I called him, was in terror that there would be no room for him. He explained how deeply wounded he was at the idea of going home by sea. I reminded him of his devotion to the naval service, and of the pleasures to a hardy sailor of a life on the ocean wave. I dwelt upon the undeniable hazards from the U-boats. He was quite inconsolable. However, he had a plan. He had persuaded one of the stewards of the flying-boat to let him take his place; he would do the washing up himself. But what, I asked, would the captain say? Tommy thought that if at the last moment the captain were confronted with the arrangement he would make no objection. He had ascertained that he weighed less than the steward. I shrugged my shoulders, and on this we went to bed in the small hours of the morning.

I woke up unconscionably early with the conviction that I

should certainly not go to sleep again. I must confess that I felt rather frightened. I thought of the ocean spaces, and that we should never be within a thousand miles of land until we approached the British Isles. I thought perhaps I had done a rash thing, that there were too many eggs in one basket. I had always regarded an Atlantic flight with awe. But the die was cast. Still, I must admit that if at breakfast, or even before luncheon, they had come to me to report that the weather had changed and we must go by sea I should have easily reconciled myself to a voyage in the splendid ship which had come all this way to fetch us.

Divine sunlight lapped the island, and the favourable weather prospects were confirmed. At noon we reached the flying-boat by launch. We were delayed for an hour on the quay because a picket-boat which had gone to the *Duke of York* for items of baggage had taken longer than expected. Tommy stood disconsolate. The captain had brushed his project aside in a way that captains have. The steward was a trained member of the crew; he could not take one single person more; every tank was filled to the brim with petrol. It would be quite a task getting off the water even as it was. So we taxied out to the far end of the harbour, leaving Tommy lamenting as bitterly as Lord Ullin in the poem,* but for different reasons. Never before and never afterwards were we separated in these excursions.

It was, as the captain had predicted, quite a job to get off the water. Indeed, I thought that we should hardly clear the low hills which closed the harbour. There was really no danger; we were in sure hands. The flying-boat lifted ponderously a quarter of a mile from the reef, and we had several hundred feet of height to spare. There is no doubt about the comfort of these great flying-boats. I had a good broad bed in the bridal suite at the stern with large windows on either side. It was quite a long walk, thirty or forty feet, downhill through the various compartments to the saloon and dining-room, where nothing was lacking in food or drink. The motion was smooth, the vibration not unpleasant, and we passed an agreeable afternoon and had a merry dinner. These boats have two storeys, and one walks up a regular staircase to the control room. Darkness had fallen, and all the reports were good. We were

* Thomas Campbell's *Lord Ullin's Daughter*.

now flying through dense mist at about seven thousand feet. One could see the leading edge of the wings, with their great flaming exhausts pouring back over the wing surfaces. In these machines at this time a large rubber tube which expanded and contracted at intervals was used to prevent icing. The captain explained to me how it worked, and we saw from time to time the ice splintering off as it expanded. I went to bed and slept soundly for several hours.

*   *   *

I woke just before the dawn, and went forward to the controls. The daylight grew. Beneath us was an almost unbroken floor of clouds.

After sitting for an hour or so in the co-pilot's seat I sensed a feeling of anxiety around me. We were supposed to be approaching England from the south-west and we ought already to have passed the Scilly Islands, but they had not been seen through any of the gaps in the cloud floor. As we had flown for more than ten hours through mist and had had only one sight of a star in that time, we might well be slightly off our course. Wireless communication was of course limited by the normal war-time rules. It was evident from the discussions which were going on that we did not know where we were. Presently Portal, who had been studying the position, had a word with the captain, and then said to me, "We are going to turn north at once." This was done, and after another half-hour in and out of the clouds we sighted England, and soon arrived over Plymouth, where, avoiding the balloons, which were all shining, we landed comfortably.

As I left the aircraft the captain remarked, "I never felt so much relieved in my life as when I landed you safely in the harbour." I did not appreciate the significance of his remark at the moment. Later on I learnt that if we had held on our course for another five or six minutes before turning northwards we should have been over the German batteries in Brest. We had slanted too much to the southward during the night. Moreover, the decisive correction which had been made brought us in, not from the south-west, but from just east of south—that is to say, from the enemy's direction rather than from that from which we were expected. This had the result, as I was told some weeks later, that we were reported as a hostile bomber coming in from Brest, and six Hurricanes from Fighter Command were ordered out to shoot us down. However, they failed in their mission.

To President Roosevelt I cabled, "We got here with a good hop from Bermuda and a thirty-mile wind."

WINSTON S. CHURCHILL,
The Second World War

From *Catch 22*

By the time of the mission to Bologna, Yossarian was brave enough not to go around over the target even once, and when he found himself aloft finally in the nose of Kid Sampson's plane, he pressed in the button of his throat mike and asked,

"Well? What's wrong with the plane?"

Kid Sampson let out a shriek. "Is something wrong with the plane? What's the matter?"

Kid Sampson's cry turned Yossarian to ice. "Is something the matter?" he yelled in horror. "Are we bailing out?"

"I don't know!" Kid Sampson shot back in anguish, wailing excitedly. "Someone said we're bailing out! Who is this, anyway? Who is this?"

"This is Yossarian in the nose! Yossarian in the nose. I heard you say there was something the matter. Didn't you say there was something the matter?"

"I thought you said there was something wrong. Everything seems okay. Everything is all right."

Yossarian's heart sank. Something was terribly wrong if everything was all right and they had no excuse for turning back. He hesitated gravely.

"I can't hear you," he said.

"I said everything is all right."

The sun was blinding white on the porcelain-blue water below and on the flashing edges of the other airplanes. Yossarian took hold of the colored wires leading into the jackbox of the intercom system and tore them loose.

"I still can't hear you," he said.

He heard nothing. Slowly he collected his map case and his three flak suits and crawled back to the main compartment. Nately, sitting stiffly in the co-pilot's seat, spied him through the corner of his eye as he stepped up on the flight deck behind Kid Sampson. He smiled at Yossarian wanly, looking frail and exceptionally young and bashful in the bulky dungeon of his earphones, hat, throat mike, flak suit and parachute. Yossarian bent close to Kid Sampson's ear.

"I still can't hear you," he shouted above the even drone of the engines.

Kid Sampson glanced back at him with surprise. Kid Sampson had an angular, comical face with arched eyebrows and a scrawny blond mustache.

"What?" he called out over his shoulder.

"I still can't hear you," Yossarian repeated.

"You'll have to talk louder," Kid Sampson said, "I still can't hear you."

"I said I still can't hear you!" Yossarian yelled.

"I can't help it," Kid Sampson yelled back at him. "I'm shouting as loud as I can."

"I couldn't hear you over my intercom," Yossarian bellowed in mounting helplessness. "You'll have to turn back."

"For an intercom?" asked Kid Sampson incredulously.

"Turn back," said Yossarian, "before I break your head."

Kid Sampson looked for moral support toward Nately, who stared away from him pointedly. Yossarian outranked them both. Kid Sampson resisted doubtfully for another moment and then capitulated eagerly with a triumphant whoop.

"That's just fine with me," he announced gladly, and blew out a shrill series of whistles up into his mustache. "Yes sirree, that's just fine with old Kid Sampson." He whistled again and shouted over the intercom, "Now hear this, my little chickadees. This is

Admiral Kid Sampson talking. This is Admiral Kid Sampson squawking, the pride of the Queen's marines. Yessiree. We're turning back, boys, by crackee, *we're turning back!*"

Nately ripped off his hat and earphones in one jubilant sweep and began rocking back and forth happily like a handsome child in a high chair. Sergeant Knight came plummeting down from the top gun turret and began pounding them all on the back with delirious enthusiasm. Kid Sampson turned the plane away from the formation in a wide, graceful arc and headed toward the airfield. When Yossarian plugged his headset into one of the auxiliary jackboxes, the two gunners in the rear section of the plane were both singing "La Cucaracha".

Back at the field, the party fizzled out abruptly. An uneasy silence replaced it, and Yossarian was sober and self-conscious as he climbed down from the plane and took his place in the jeep that was already waiting for them. None of the men spoke at all on the drive back through the heavy, mesmerizing quiet blanketing mountains, sea and forests. The feeling of desolation persisted when they turned off the road at the squadron. Yossarian got out of the car last. After a minute, Yossarian and a gentle warm wind were the only things stirring in the haunting tranquillity that hung like a drug over the vacated tents. The squadron stood insensate, bereft of everything human but Doc Daneka, who roosted dolorously like a shivering turkey buzzard beside the closed door of the medical tent, his stuffed nose jabbing away in thirsting futility at the hazy sunlight streaming down around him. Yossarian knew Doc Daneeka would not go swimming with him. Doc Daneeka would never go swimming again; a person could swoon or suffer a mild coronary occlusion in an inch or two of water and drown to death, be carried out to sea by an undertow, or made vulnerable to poliomyelitis or meningococcus infection through chilling or over-exertion. The threat of Bologna to others had instilled in Doc Daneeka an even more poignant solicitude for his own safety. At night now, he heard burglars.

Through the lavender gloom clouding the entrance of the operations tent, Yossarian glimpsed Chief White Halfoat, diligently embezzling whiskey rations, forging the signatures of non-drinkers and pouring off the alcohol with which he was poisoning himself into separate bottles rapidly in order to steal as much as he could before Captain Black roused himself with recollection and came hurrying over indolently to steal the rest himself.

The jeep started up again softly. Kid Sampson, Nately and the others wandered apart in a noiseless eddy of motion and were sucked away into the cloying yellow stillness. The jeep vanished with a cough. Yossarian was alone in a ponderous, primeval lull in which everything green looked black and everything else was imbued with the color of pus. The breeze rustled leaves in a dry and diaphanous distance. He was restless, scared and sleepy. The sockets of his eyes felt grimy with exhaustion. Wearily he moved inside the parachute tent with its long table of smoothed wood, a nagging bitch of a doubt burrowing painlessly inside a conscience that felt perfectly clear. He left his flak suit and parachute there and crossed back past the water wagon to the intelligence tent to return his map case to Captain Black, who sat drowsing in his chair with his skinny long legs up on his desk and inquired with indifferent curiosity why Yossarian's plane had turned back. Yossarian ignored him. He set the map down on the counter and walked out.

JOSEPH HELLER,
Catch 22

Alkemade touches down

Nicholas Alkemade, son of a Dutch father and English mother, was born in North Walsham, Norfolk. He joined the RAF in 1940 at eighteen and served in Air-Sea Rescue launches until, "wanting more excitement", he transferred to Bomber Command as a rear-gunner.

At 21,000 feet the rear turret of a Lancaster bomber is a cold and lonely place, separated from the rest of the crew by two sets of doors and 12 yards of fuselage. It's a cramped space, little more than a shell for the body of the gunner, clad in his bulky flying clothes. There is not even room for him to wear a parachute—only the harness; his chute pack is stowed in the main fuselage, a few feet inside the second door, and separate from the other crew members' packs.

In an emergency the gunner has to leave his turret, get his chute pack, book it on to the harness, then bale out, hoping that the trailing radio aerial will not cut him in two. Being a "Tail-End Charlie" was rated by the RAF a "hazardous occupation".

As our Lancaster neared Berlin on the night of March 24th–25th, 1944, we could see the long fingers of searchlight beams probing the sky. Closing in, we spotted the sparkling red and green markers laid down for us by our Pathfinders ahead. Plane after plane made its bombing run, and fireworks erupted below us: golden incendiary fires, brilliant white and red explosions and the orange flashes of ack-ack guns. Then . . .

Bombs away! Our own 4,000-pound "cookie" and three tons of incendiaries hurtled downwards. Through weaving searchlight beams we turned for home, keeping a sharp watch for Jerry night fighters. I could see them at work in the distance. A flash of white light would burst into a great red-and-orange ball of fire, to arc across the sky towards the black earth below. Some poor "Lanc" had got it, and some of my chums would not return to base.

We were somewhere over the Ruhr when suddenly a series of shuddering crashes raked our aircraft from nose to tail, then two terrific thunderclaps as two cannon shells exploded on my turret ring mounting. The plexiglass blister shattered and vanished—one large fragment slicing into my right leg.

Luckily my turret had been facing astern. I quickly depressed my guns and stared out. Not more than 50 yards from me was the shadowy outline of a Junkers 88 fighter, his leading edge a line of brilliant white flashes as he blazed away at our wounded ship. I aimed point-blank and squeezed the trigger of my four banked 303 Brownings. They fired simultaneously and the Junkers was transfixed by four streams of fiery tracers. He peeled off, his port engine trailing flame. I did not watch to see his fate; I was too concerned about my own.

Flaming fuel from our tanks was streaking past me. On the intercom I started to report to the captain that the tail was on fire, but he cut me short with, "I can't hold her for long, lads. You'll have to jump. Bale out! Bale out!"

Flicking the turret doors behind me open with my elbows, I turned and opened the fuselage door beyond—and stared for a horrified instant into a giant cauldron. Flame and smoke swept towards me. I recoiled, choking and blinded, into my turret. But I *had to get my chute!* I opened the doors again and lunged for the pack.

Too late! The case had been burnt off and the tightly-packed silk was springing out, fold after fold, and vanishing in puffs of flame.

In the turret I took stock. Here I was, only 21 years old, and this was the end of the road. Already oil from the turret's hydraulic system was on fire and flames seared my face and hands. At any moment the doomed aircraft might explode.

Should I endure this roasting hell or should I jump? If I was to die, better a quick, painless end by diving into the ground . . . Quickly I hand-rotated my turret abeam, flipped the doors open and, in an agony of despair, somersaulted backwards into the night.

Oh, the blessed relief of being away from that shrivelling heat! Gratefully I felt the cold air against my face. I had no sensation of falling. It was more like being at rest on an airy cloud. Looking down I saw the stars beneath my feet.

"Must be falling head first," I thought.

If this was dying it was nothing to be afraid of. I only regretted that I should go without saying good-bye to my friends. I would never again see Pearl, my sweetheart back home in Loughborough. And I'd been due to go on leave the following Sunday.

Then—nothing. I must have blacked out.

In slow stages my senses returned. First there was an awareness of light above me which gradually became a patch of starlit sky. The light was framed in an irregular opening that finally materialized as a hole in thickly interlaced boughs of fir trees. I seemed to be lying in a deep mound of underbrush heavily blanketed with snow.

It was bitterly cold. My head throbbed and there was terrible pain in my back. I felt all over my body. I found I could move my legs. I was all in one piece. In a sudden up-welling of unworthiness and delight, the very first thought to flash into my conscious mind was a heartfelt prayer of thanksgiving, of humble praise and utter wonderment. On the floor of the little patch of fir forest, into which I had hurtled parachuteless from a hell three and two-fifths miles above it, this was not blasphemy. "Jesus Christ," I said. "I'm alive!"

I tried to sit up—but it hurt too much. Craning my neck I could see that my flying boots were gone and my clothes scorched and tattered. I began to be afraid of freezing to death. In the pocket of my tunic I found the flat tin, badly bent, in which I kept my cigarettes and my lighter. The cigarettes were unharmed; I lit up. My watch, I found, was still ticking. The luminous hands showed 3.20; it had been close to midnight when our aircraft was hit.

Attached to my collar was the whistle for use in case of ditching at sea to keep crew members in contact with one another.

"Here is one man who is happy to become a prisoner of war," I said to myself. From time to time I blew the whistle. It seemed hours later I heard a far-off "Hulloo!"

I kept whistling and the answering shouts grew closer. At last I could see flashlights approaching. Then some men and boys were standing over me. After relieving me of my cigarettes they growled, " 'raus! Heraus!" ("Get up!") When they saw I couldn't they put a tarpaulin under me and dragged me across a frozen pasture to a cottage. There an old lady with a gnarled but kindly face gave me the finest egg nog I ever tasted.

As I lay on the floor I heard a car pull up outside. Two men in plain clothes clumped into the room. They looked me over carefully. Then, quite indifferent to my pain, they yanked me to my feet and bundled me out to their car. We seemed to hit all the bumps on our way to a hospital.

I was a long time in the operating room. Only later did I learn the sum of my injuries: burnt legs, twisted right knee, a deep splinter wound in my thigh, strained back, slight concussion and a deep scalp wound; first-, second- and third-degree burns on face and hands. Most of this damage I had sustained before jumping.

Finally, cleaned up and with most of the plexiglass fragments picked out of me, I was installed in a clean bed—but not to sleep! In came a tall, pompous character in a *Wehrmacht* uniform, thin as a hatchet in the face and wearing rimless glasses. Through an interpreter, a young convalescent soldier, he asked me the usual, probing questions: What targets did you attack? Where is your base? How many aircraft are there at your base? . . . and many others. I stated my name, rank and number. To the other questions I could only reply, "I am not allowed to answer."

Then they began asking about my parachute. "Where did you hide it? Did you bury it?" (Spies dropping into enemy territory commonly concealed their parachutes; airmen falling out of sky battles did not.)

"Parachute?" I said. "I didn't use one!"

I thought Hatchet-Face would burst with rage. He let out a stream of oaths, then turned on his heel and stalked out. For three days the questioning was repeated. Finally I was left alone.

After three weeks, when my wounds were fairly healed, I was whisked off to Dulag Luft near Frankfurt and put into solitary confinement. The time gave me opportunity to think out how I might convince my interrogators that my incredible story was true.

So I was ready when a week later a young *Luftwaffe* lieutenant led me into the office of the *Kommandant* of Dulag Luft. On the *Kommandant's* desk I was amused to see a packet of English cigarettes and a bar of chocolate.

"We have to congratulate you, I understand, Sergeant," the *Kommandant* said drily, in excellent English. "Would you tell me all about your remarkable escape yourself, please? I have only a garbled account from the *Herr Leutnant*. I gather you claim to have jumped from a blazing bomber at a height of 6,000 metres without a parachute—a very tall story, Sergeant, *nicht wahr?*"

He could prove the story if he cared to, I told him. Hadn't a wrecked Lancaster fallen in the area on the night of March 24th–25th? If so, that would be the plane I had jumped from. The burnt remnants of my parachute pack could be found just forward of the rear fuselage door. Also, he could examine my parachute harness—to see for himself that *it had never been used*.

The *Kommandant* listened to me in silence. "A really remarkable story," he said—"and I hear many!"

He fired some rapid German at the lieutenant, who saluted and left.

The *Kommandant* handed me a cigarette and we chatted pleasantly for the next quarter of an hour. Then the lieutenant, waving my parachute harness, burst into the office with three other officers, all shouting excitedly in German.

The lieutenant flung the harness on to the desk, pointed to the snap-hooks that were still in their clips and the lift webs still fastened down on the chest straps. The *Kommandant* soberly took in these facts, then leant back in his chair and studied each of us thoughtfully in turn. I'll never forget his next words; he spoke in English:

"Gentleman! A miracle—no less!"

He rose, came round his desk and offered me his hand. I took it. "Congratulations, my boy, on being alive! What a story to tell your grandchildren!"

Then I was assailed with slaps on the back, handshaking and vociferous good wishes. The *Kommandant* dismissed me with, "Tomorrow, I promise, your comrades will be told about how you became a POW."

In the *Kommandant's* office next morning I saw that the *Luftwaffe* authorities had been busy. On his desk lay some pieces of scorched metal, including the D-handle of a parachute ripcord and a piece of wire that would be the ripcord itself.

"The remains of your parachute pack," the *Kommandant* explained. "We found it where you said it would be. To us it is the final proof."

The wrecked Lancaster lay about 20 kilometres from where I had landed, I was told. Four crew members had been burnt to death and had been buried in a military cemetery near Meschede with full military honours. From their names and numbers I realized that only "Ginger" Cleary, our navigator, Geoff Burwell, the radio operator, and myself were left. (They had been blown clear in the final explosion, I learnt later.)

A German flying-officer and two NCO's marched me into the compound, where some 200 captured Allied flyers were assembled. I was directed to stand on a bench. Then the *Luftwaffe* officer recounted my story to the incredulous airmen.

There was pandemonium. Nationalities were forgotten. I was mobbed by French, German, British and Yank, shaking my hand, shouting questions, forcing upon me gifts of a cigarette or a square of chocolate. Then I was presented with a paper, signed by the senior British officer at the demonstration, who had taken down the German authentication in writing and had it witnessed by the two senior British NCO's. It is only a faded scrap of paper but it will always be the proudest thing I own:

> *Dulag Luft*
> "*It has been investigated and corroborated by the German authorities that the claim made by Sgt. Alkemade, 1431537 RAF, is true in all respects, namely, that he made a descent from 18,000 feet without a parachute and made a safe landing without injury, his parachute having been on fire in the aircraft. He landed in deep snow among fir trees.*
> *Corroboration witnessed by*
> *F/Lt. H. J. Moore*
> *Senior British Officer*
> *F/Sgt. R. R. Lamb 1339582*
> *F/Sgt. T. A. Jones 411*
> *Senior British NCO's*
> *Date: 25/4/44*

After liberation came in May 1945, RAF Intelligence checked the records at Dulag Luft, found the reports of my strange adventure to be true and included them in the official records of the Royal Air Force.

Today Pearl and I are living happily in Loughborough, where I am a buyer in a department store. (Geoff Burwell was best man at our weddding.) I have taken the first important steps towards following the *Kommandant's* advice—to tell my story to my grandchildren. I'll have to wait, though, till little Valerie and Nicholas provide me with grandchildren to hear it.

In the meantime, I can only wonder why such a marvellous thing should have happened to a man as ordinary as myself.

NICHOLAS ALKEMADE,
from Readers' Digest